AFRICAN PHILOSOPHY

An Introduction, Third Edition

Edited by

Richard A. Wright
University of Toledo

=1984=

UNIVERSITY
PRESS OF
AMERICA

LANHAM • NEW YORK • LONDON

Copyright © 1984 by

University Press of America,™ Inc.

4720 Boston Way
Lanham, MD 20706

3 Henrietta Street
London WC2E 8LU England

University Press of America published the First Edition of this work in 1977,
and the Second Edition in 1979.

Library of Congress Cataloging in
Publication Data

African Philosophy

    Bibliography: p.
    Includes index.
      1. Philosophy, African--Addresses,
essays, lectures.
I. Wright, Richard A., 1943-
B5305.A37   1984   199'.6   83-25937
ISBN 0-8191-3784-7 (alk. paper)
ISBN 0-8191-3785-5 (pbk. alk. paper)

All University Press of America books are produced on acid-free
paper which exceeds the minimum standards set by the National
Historical Publications and Records Commission.

To Mother and Dad

ACKNOWLEDGMENTS

In a project of this sort, encompassing several years work, several editions, and assistance from people around the world, one runs up many debts of gratitude. Among the most important is my debt to the students of Talladega College who, through their questions and persistent interest, caused me to begin looking for source material on African Philosophy. Once the task was begun, the Research Liason Committee of the African Studies Association, the African Studies Association of the United Kingdom, and the Rev. F. B. Welburn, University of Bristol, were instrumental in helping me contact scholars and secure source materials. Brian Winters assisted with preparation of the bibliography, helped with indexing the second edition bibliography, and served ably as official translator for correspondence. Brian Lockrey and Kathy Skurzewski rendered invaluable assistance in computerization of the bibliography; and David Pankratz and Diana Goldfarb did an excellent job as my editorial assistants for the final stages of manuscript preparation, David for the first edition, Diana for the second. I particularly want to thank Leonore Johnson, Marie Warrington, and my wife Pat for their efforts in typing manuscript for the first and second editions; they did a splendid job often under very trying circumstances. Finally, I am particularly indebted to Kathy Skurzewski who prepared and processed the camera copy for the third edition.

TABLE OF CONTENTS

PREFACE TO THIRD EDITION

When I was first asked by the publisher to do a third edition of this book, I was initially reluctant because I was not convinced that I would be able to produce a book which would really *be* a new edition. I was also not convinced that the book indeed had enough merit to warrant other than its quiet demise. Letters from people who had used the book, as well as analysis of the many reviews which have been done on the first and second editions, convinced me, however, that people did find the book useful, although open to improvement in a number of areas. A new edition thus did seem to be possible, the problem being to develop that edition.

The first important feature of the new edition is the inclusion of three new papers. The new lead paper by P.O. Bodunrin is intended to help set the tone of the text more clearly, and to raise issues for which the remaining papers are either examples or intended solutions. The two other new papers, by R. Onwuanibe and K. Gyekye, are specifically intended to broaden the book's development of the metaphysics of personhood, because I see the concept of personhood as one of the most central in African thought. With some rearranging of the remaining papers, the thrust of the book should now be clearer: early chapters deal with the nature and problematic of African Philosophy; attention is next turned to historical and sociological/anthropological discussions; and, finally, to analyses of particular concepts, e.g., 'personhood', and philosophical contexts, e.g., political philosophy.

The second feature of the new edition is the extensive revision of the bibliography, both in content and indexing. A number of items included in the first two editions were, upon reexamination, found not to meet the criteria for inclusion, and were dropped. At the same time, over 120 new items have been added, thus expanding both the breadth and depth of the bibliography. The index for the bibliography has also been extensively modified, with the addition of new primary and secondary references. As as result, the index is quite specific, having fewer general references, e.g., 'metaphysics', but many more detailed references, e.g., 'Metaphysics in Akan Ritual'. These changes should make the bibliography more helpful and the content of the listed works more accessible.

As with prior editions, my aim here is to further cross-cultural understanding. Peace comes only through understanding the ideas of others; if we never attempt that understanding, peace will never be possible. I submit this new edition as my small contribution to the increasingly necessary pursuit of peace.

R.W.
Toledo, Ohio
1984

PREFACE TO SECOND EDITION

My purpose in producing the first edition of this text was two-fold: first, to bring to public view an important though neglected area of philosophical study; and, second, to stir debate on the issues raised in that area of studies. On the basis of these goals being accomplished, it was hoped that African philosophical thought would achieve more currency in overall philosophical considerations, since it is clear that Western philosophers have a great deal to learn from their African colleagues.

From all appearances, the two primary goals have been at least modestly achieved; only time will tell how influential African thought will become, but, regardless, the work must continue and our areas of concern must be constantly expanded and deepened. To this end, Professor Menkiti's paper is an important addition to the original text, since it broadens our base of understanding and brings an additional dimension to our studies. Moreover, the expanded bibliography, now fully indexed, should aid in continuing the studies begun with this volume, while the new text index will make specific material more readily accessible.

Because communication is important, I would be pleased to hear from others with an interest in African philosophy; also, suggestions for improvement of the text and additions to the bibliography are also most welcome. If African philosophy is to achieve its rightful place in intellectual history those with an interest must work together and help bring it to its proper light. If this volume contributes something to that effort, then I shall consider it of value. I hope that you find it so.

PREFACE TO FIRST EDITION

      Although the African people have existed perhaps longer than any other on earth, it has only been within the past few decades that scholars have taken other than a patronizing or economic interest in Africa. Even then, whatever studies resulted, a clear overtone of bias and prejudice could usually be found; as a result of latent attitudes, African thinkers were given credit for only those ideas somehow "learned" from their Western "benefactors," or else their ideas were viewed as primitive, childlike, and inconsequential. Unfortunately, today's level of "enlightment" has done little to change this deplorable situation. It is true that the amount and level of African studies has increased dramatically in the past few years, but the tendency is still to "study" the African and his lifestyle, to treat the African as an object of research, not as a person, with ideas, feelings and values. It is only with reluctance that non-Africans give up their mistaken, stereotyped views of Africa and Africans; most think of Africa as in the Tarzan movies, one big jungle filled with all sorts of harmful creatures; most conceive of Africans as "savages" living in grass huts, left behind by all that is valuable in the world. Even scholars of importance, whose work is widely read, perpetuate some of these views, as evidenced by C. Levi-Strauss's book *The Savage Mind* or V. Brelsford's article "The Philosophy of the Savage."

      When serious studies are undertaken, most of the scholars involved are sociologists, anthropologists, and historians. Moreover, that which captures our pragmatic attention also captures our scholastic attention; thus, the social and political crises which hold our attention in African affairs seems to dominate, and influence the direction of, our African studies. As a consequence, political, sociological and anthropological treatises appear with increasing regularity. Not surprisingly, since the writers are not philosophers, the majority of these contributions either overlook or underrate the fact that philosophy of some sort is substratum to the thoughts, thus the actions of all men. In this way, an important piece in the puzzle of understanding African affairs is missing, as Professor Axelsen so nicely points out in her paper in this book. Until philosophers begin to show the intrinsic value of African thought, until that thought is examined and understood, this missing piece will not be supplied and the non-African world will continue to be at odds with the African world.

Unfortunately, it is not just proper scholarly studies which are lacking; lacking also are proper attitudes. Because of latent prejudices and misconceptions, most non-Africans find it difficult to consider the possibility that Africans could have anything to contribute to philosophical understanding. To make matters even worse, non-African scholars often refuse to even consider African thought as potentially philosophical. Perhaps these thinkers are so enamoured with the Western philosophical tradition that their intellectual worlds would be crushed if it were ever discovered that philosophy did not spring into existence in 600 B. C. when Thales first encountered the drainage ditch. Perhaps these thinkers feel that if it can be shown that Africans think philosophical thoughts their own will become worthless. Perhaps they are simply afraid to consider alternatives to their well rehearsed views and counterviews. Or, perhaps they foresee that African philosophy may require the equivalent of a change in intellectual perception, a change they might not care to make.

Whatever the reasons, we can no longer allow such persons and their views to dominate honest attempts to understand African thought. Our work may require something akin to the Copernican revolution; if that is necessary, so be it. We must cease acting as if the traditional Western corpus of Philosophical literature, with its traditional sets of questions and traditional answers to those questions, is the last word in philosophical thinking. We must begin to look for alternatives to the traditional views, not so that those views may be necessarily displaced, but so that we may come to a wider, fuller understanding of man *qua* man. We must be willing to look at all views, no matter how diverse, and learn what we may from them; even if we learn that a certain view is worthless, we have learned something important. We need to see the opening of new perspectives as an exciting event, rather than a threat. We need to continue to follow Plato's suggestion, in the Theateatus (168A)

xiv

and engage in philosophical dialogue, no matter where that takes us, no matter what we have to explore to do so, because, in the end, only that will allow us to "escape from [our] former [ignorant] selves and become different men." Philosophy is not the perquisite of one people or national state, but is a human understanding in which people have been engaged for thousands of years. We can no longer ignore the thought of the African people because we judge ahead of time that nothing philosophical is to be found there; we must, instead, work to understand what *is* found there and, in so doing, broaden our own perspectives on the human enterprise.

The aim of the book is thus to present, substantively, significant writing on African Philosophy, in a form which will be useful both in the classroom and in the library of those interested in Africa. While all of the contributors are scholars, with extensive academic skill and diverse indepth academic training, the works included are not intended for elitist academicians. Furthermore, even though the writers have strong philosophical backgrounds, the book is not intended as an advanced analysis of an established realm of philosophical literature. Ideally, any interested reader, without regard to background and training, should be able to work his way through these papers and come away enlightened, as well as excited by the intellectual possibilities unearthed in their pages. At the least, one should come away holding new respect for the philosophical thought of the African people.

Ultimately, a work of this sort comes down to a dialogue between author and reader. It is my sincere hope that the dialogue involved in this particular book will help initiate continued studies of African philosophical thought, with the result that African philosophy will take its rightful place in the history of man's intellectual advancement, as an important, crucial factor in our ever-present quest for knowledge and understanding of our fellow men and the world in which we all must live.

Richard A. Wright

THE QUESTION OF AFRICAN PHILOSOPHY[1]

P. O. Bodunrin

Philosophy in Africa has for more than a decade now been dominated by the discussion of one compound question, namely, is there an African philosophy, and if there is, what is it? The first part of the question has generally been unhesitatingly answered in the affirmative. Dispute has been primarily over the second part of the question as various specimens of African philosophy presented do not seem to pass muster. Those of us who refuse to accept certain specimens as philosophy have generally been rather illogically said also to deny an affirmative answer to the first part of the question. In a paper presented at the International Symposium in Memory of Dr. William Amo,[2] the Ghanaian philosopher who taught in German universities in the early part of the eighteenth century, Professor Odera Oruka identified four trends, perhaps more appropriately approaches, in current African philosophy. The four trends identified by Oruka are as follows:

1. *Ethno-philosophy.* This is the term Paulin Houn-tondji used to refer to the works of those anthropologists, sociologists, ethnographers and philosophers who present the collective world views of African peoples, their myths and folk-lores and folk-wisdom, as philosophy.[3] What ethno-philosophers try to do is "to describe a world outlook or thought system of a particular African community or the whole of Africa". As opposed to seeing philosophy as a body of logically argued thoughts of individuals,

1

ethno-philosophers see African philosophy as communal thought and give its emotional appeal as one of its unique features. Representative authors in this category are Tempels, Senghor, Mbiti and Kagame.[4] Oruka says that this is strictly speaking not philosophy, but philosophy only in a "debased" sense of the word.

2. *Philosophie sagacity.* This trend implicitly rejects a holistic approach to African philosophy. Rather than seek African philosophy by the study of general world outlooks, customs, folk-lores, etc., the attempt is made to identify men in the society who are reputed for their wisdom. The aim is to show that "literacy is not a necessary condition for philosophical reflection and exposition", and that in Africa there are "critical independent thinkers who guide their thought and judgments by the power of reason and inborn insight rather than by the authority of the communal consensus",[5] and that there are in Africa men uninfluenced by outside sources who are capable of critical and dialectical inquiry. In Marcel Griaule's *Conversations with Ogotemmeli: An Introduction to Dogan Religious Ideas,* published for the International African Institute by the Oxford University Press (1965), Ogotemmeli displays a great philosophic sagacity in his exposition of the secret doctrines of his group. How much is Ogotemmeli's own philosophy and how much belongs to his secret group may not be known.

3. *Nationalist-ideological philosophy.* This is represented by the works of politicians like Kwame Nkrumah, Julius Nyerere and Leopold Senghor.[6] It is an attempt to evolve a new and, if possible, unique political theory based on traditional African socialism and familyhood. It is argued that a true and meaningful freedom must be accompanied by a true mental liberation and a return, whenever possible and desirable, to genuine and authentic traditional African humanism.

4. *Professional philosophy.* This is the work of many trained philosophers. Many of them reject the assumptions of ethno-philosophy and take a universalist view of philosophy. Philosophy, many of them argue, must have the same meaning in all cultures although the subjects that receive priority, and perhaps the method of dealing with them, may be dictated by cultural biases and the existential situation in the society within which the philosophers operate. According to this school, African philosophy is the philosophy done by African philosophers whether it be in the area of logic, metaphysics, ethics or history of philosophy. It is desirable that the works be set in some African context, but it is not necessary that they be so. Thus,

2

if African philosophers were to engage in debates on Plato's epistemology, or on theoretical identities, their works would qualify as African philosophy. It is the view of this school that debate among African philosophers is only just beginning and that the tradition of philosophy in the strict sense of the word is just now being established. According to this school, criticism and argument are essential characteristics of anything which is to pass as philosophy. Hence mere descriptive accounts of African thought systems or the thought systems of any other society would not pass as philosophy. Oruka identifies four African philosophers---Kwasi Wiredu, Paulin Hountondji, himself and myself--whose works reflect this position.[7] I agree with Oruka that the four of us broadly belong to the same "school." We have met more frequently perhaps than any other group in Africa and have exchanged and discussed our published and unpublished works to the extent that I am afraid I may be doing just what Ayer did in *Language, Truth and Logic,* expounding, explaining and defending the views of a school. Nevertheless, some subtle differences, as is to be expected, remain among us. In this paper, I shall not repeat in detail our usual arguments for rejecting the works of others as not being philosophical.

Recent discussions and further reflections on the matter have convinced me that the different positions as to the nature of African philosophy held by various contemporary Africans reflect different understandings of the meanings of philosophy itself. I now think that our not wholly terminological dispute as to what is and what is not to count as African philosophy cannot be settled without answering some important questions. Some of these questions are: What exactly are African philosophers trying to do, namely, what challenges are they trying to meet? What is the proper answer to these challenges? In other words, what would constitute an appropriate answer to the problems African philosophers are trying to solve? What is the difference between a piece of philosophical discourse and discourse in some other discipline? What is it for a given idea or philosophy to be correctly definable as African philosophy? I shall attempt in this paper to answer these and related questions.

Philosophy begins in wonder. The universe itself provided men with the first source of wonder. There are the stars, the oceans, the phenomena of birth, life, death, growth and decay. Men wondered about the fate of the dead. About the living, they wondered about the purpose of life, about what is the proper way to behave. They wonder about whether there is a guiding force behind all these things, etc. All human societies have answers to these questions. The life of a society is organized according to what are accepted as the answers to these fundamental questions. These answers may in fact be grounded in error and ignorance but they are usually not questioned. Rarely do men turn around to criticize themselves without some (usually external) impetus, rarely do men feel the necessity to provide justifications for their beliefs without some challenge.

In Africa, the challenge to the traditional world view and belief systems came chiefly from contact with Western Europeans. For although there must have been some contact through trade and other means between the different peoples of sub-Saharan Africa from time immemorial, yet because of the similarity of their environment and hence the similarity of the problems the universe posed for them, the world views of these peoples, their customs and social organizations were not sufficiently dissimilar to provide significant challenges to one another. The similarity which social anthropologists have found among several African cultures is not surprising for, given identical problems, it is to be expected that some solutions would be similar since human options are not infinite. But things changed upon contact with the West. Large parts of Africa were colonized, evangelization began and writing was introduced. Two different world views came face to face.[8] The four trends identified by Oruka are different attempts to meet the challenges created by the new situation. What are those challenges?

1. Partly out of a desire to understand the Africans better in order to make their governance or conversion to Christianity easier, or, simply out of curiousity in the presence of new and to the Europeans, strange ways of life, European ethnographers began to study the Africans. Their findings were unanimous in concluding that not only were the Africans radically different from Europeans in the hue of their skin, but that they were also radically different in their mode of life and in their capacity for rational thinking. They emphasized the irrational and non-logical nature of African thought. Many of the early anthropologists and ethnographers being clergymen, their interest was in the religious and spiritistic thoughts of the African. The usual verdict was that the African mentality was primitive, irrational, and illogical. With the growth of education among Africans it began to be realized that an unworthy picture of Africans was being presented and that a misinformed and false interpretation was being given to African thought and way of life. A new interpretation which would do the black man proud was called for.[9] This is what the authors described by Oruka as practitioners of ethno-philosophy are trying to do.

4

2.   The second challenge came with the rise of African, or shall we say, black nationalism.   There was struggle for political independence.   It was felt that political independence must be accompanied with a total mental liberation, and if possible a total severance of all intellectual ties with the colonial masters.   By this time Africans had acquired western modes of life in many ways -- we wore Western type of dress, spoke English or French, etc.   The political system was modelled after the Westminster pattern or after that of some other European parliament.   The traditional method of government was displaced in most places. This was not without tension.   It is easier and less damaging to a people's self-pride to adopt a foreign language, a foreign mode of dress and culinary habits than it is to adopt and internalize foreign ways of social organization.   The Westminster model was failing in several places.   We began to think of the traditional social order and to seek salvation in the pristine values of our ancestors.   Nationalist-ideological philosophy is a response to this challenge.

3.   A third challenge arises from man's natural urge to look for comparisons everywhere.   The way we understand the world is by putting things into categories.   If you come across a strange object somewhere you think of what it is like, you compare it with other things of the same sort you have seen elsewhere.   Africans who study the intellectual history of other peoples naturally want to know the intellectual history of their own people.   They are naturally curious to find out whether there are African opposite numbers to the philosophers they have studied, say, in Western intellectual history, or least whether there are equivalent concepts to the ones they have come across in Western philosophy, and if so how the concepts are related or different in their logical behaviour from those of Western philosophy.   This point has become immensely important because of the honorific way in which philosophy has come to be seen.   Philosophy has become a value-laden expression such that for a people not to have philosophy is for them to be considered intellectually inferior to others who have.   No one laments the lack of African physics.   African mathematicians have, as far as I know, not been asked to produce African mathematics.   No one has asked that our increasing number of express-ways be built the African way.   Yet philosophers in Africa are asked, if not directly, yet in a subtle way, to produce an autochthonous African species of their discipline.[10]   It is natural for the nationalist non-philosopher colleague on a university curriculum committee to wonder why a philosophy department in an African university is not offering courses in African philosophy while there are courses on British

5

philosophy, American philosophy, European philosophy, etc.   He
would simply argue that if these other peoples have philosophies,
the African too must have a philosophy.   Unacquainted with what
is taught in these other courses and fully acquainted with the
many rich "philosophical" and witty sayings and religious practices of his own people, the nationalist cannot understand why
African philosophers do not teach African philosophy.   To fail to
teach African philosophy is almost tantamount to crime and an
unpatriotic omission.   What seems to be unclear to many is the
sense in which a philosophy or an idea is described as the
philosophy or idea of a people.   What does an expression like
"British philosophy" really mean?   I shall address myself to this
question towards the end of this paper.

Philosophers might try to face the challenges by introducing ethno-philosophy or teaching the political ideologies of
African politicians as philosophy.   They may also adopt the
method of the social anthropologists and engage in field work:
have a tape recorder in hand and visit, and conduct interviews
with, people who are reputed to be wise men in the society,
hoping that they will discover African philosophy that way.

4.   Added to the foregoing, there is a rather recent
and growing challenge arising from the scarcity of resources in
Africa.   Philosophy, and indeed the whole of the education
sector, has to compete with other social needs in the allocation of
scarce resources.   Roads must be built, hospitals equipped and
agriculture developed.   In these circumstances, that a philosopher
like any one else may be required to show the relevance of his
discipline is understandable.   The emergence of African this and
African that is a familiar phenomenon in the African academic
scene.   It is as if anything becomes relevant once you stick on it
the prefix 'African'.   It might even be argued that if historians
and students of literature have succeeded in creating African
history and African literature, we too ought to create African
philosophy.   It is against these challenges that we must now
examine the different approaches mentioned earlier.   We shall
consider them in a rather different order, treating nationalist-ideological and philosophic sagacity first, and ethno-philosophy
last.   Ethno-philosophy is the one which stands in the sharpest
opposition to the position we wish to urge, and it is in consideration of it that our own conception of philosophy will become
clearer.   We can give the other positions a fair day fairly
quickly.

I sympathize with the efforts of our African political
thinkers.   It would be great indeed if we could evolve a new

6

political system, a new socio-political order which is different from those found elsewhere and based on an autochthonous African philosophy. That indeed is a worthwhile aspiration which one must not give up without trial. But I am disturbed at certain presuppositions of attempts so far made. To begin with, I think that the past the political philosophers seek to recapture cannot be recaptured. Nkrumah seems to realize this in his *Consciencism*. That is why he advocated a new African socialism that would take into account the existential situation of Africa. Contact with the West through colonization and Christianity and the spread of Islam have had far-reaching effects on African traditional life. Any reconstruction of our social order must take these into account. Yet Nkrumah and Nyerere both think that the traditional way of life must be their *point de depart*. But the traditional African society was not as complex as the modern African societies. The crisis of conscience which we have in the modern African society was not there. In the sphere of morality there was a fairly general agreement as to what was right and what was expected of one. In a predominantly non-money economy where people lived and worked all their lives in the same locale and among the same close relatives African communalism was workable. Africa is becoming rapidly urbanized. The population of a typical big city neighbourhood today is heterogeneous. People come from different places, have different backgrounds, do not necessarily have blood ties and are less concerned with the affairs of one another than people used to be. The security of the traditional setting is disappearing. African traditional communalism worked because of the feelings of familyhood that sustained it. This was not a feeling of familyhood of the human race, but a feeling of closeness among those who could claim a common ancestry.[11] I do not know how to check continued urbanization with its attendant problems. We may advocate the organization of our cities into manageable units and encourage the sense of belonging among people however diverse their origins, as Wiredu suggested.[12] Still, it should be realized that this would have to be based on new premises, not on the old ones.

Political thinkers are also guilty of romanticizing the African past. Certainly not everything about our past was glorious. Anyone who has watched *Roots* (even if he has not read the book), and however melodramatic the movie version might have been, does not need to be told that.[13] The interminable land disputes between communities, sometimes within the same village, show that the communalism we talk about was between members of very closed groups. A way of life which made it possible for our ancestors to be subjugated by a handful of Europeans cannot be described as totally glorious. Any reconstruction of our past

7

must examine features of our thought system and our society that made this possible.[14] African humanism must not be a backward-looking humanism. There is no country whose traditional ideology could cope with the demands of the modern world. Despite claims to the contrary, the works of Nkrumah, Senghor and Nyerere are not entirely divorced from foreign influence. Indeed they have studied philosophy in Western schools and the influence of this training is noticeable in their idioms. However, they do not claim to be merely describing for us the African traditional philosophy, nor do they claim that their work represents the collective view of the traditional African. What they are doing is trying to *base* a philosophy of *their own* on the traditional African past. The fact that they may have given an inaccurate picture of the past is beside the point. Divorced from their nationalistic-ideological bias and with a more critical approach, their work may be significant contributions to political theory, and it is hair splitting trying to make a distinction between political theory and political philoso-phy. What is needed in these works is more rigour and more systematization.

There appear to be two ways of approaching the inves-tigation of philosophic sagacity. One is the procedure currently being used by Dr. Barry Hallen, an American philosopher at the University of Ife. He is investigating the Yoruba concept of a person. Certain persons who are reputed for their knowledge of Yoruba thought and religion are identified. The philosopher, tape-recorder in hand, visits them and attempts to get into a real dialogue with them on the Yoruba concept of a person. The answers obtained are as diverse in their details as the persons interviewed, but contain essential similarities. These essential similarities or common features are then written up by the trained philosopher to get the Yoruba concept of a person. He may do follow-up visits to have his account checked. In the dialogue the philosopher is expected to try not to impose pre-established conceptual categories on his African colleague. Perhaps during the dialogue both parties would point out the inconsistencies[15] in each other's position, leading to abandonment of, or amendments to, positions. I see nothing in principle unphilosophical in this approach and would not object to it. One might wish to point out that this is not how we approach our study of Western philoso-phy. This would not be a valid objection. Philosophers still visit one another for philosophical discussions although confer-ences, seminars and the pages of learned journals are now the principal forums for philosophic exchanges. In a predominantly illiterate culture it is not obvious that the method described above is an unphilosophical way of approaching our subject, if one had the interest in probing folk thought. Another is the method of

Dr. Oruka and his colleagues at the University of Nairobi, Kenya. It consists in recording the philosophy of an individual Kenyan (they hope to find many more such Kenyans) uninfluenced by modern education. It is not pretended that they are recording the common thought of the Kenyan Luo tribe. The purpose seems to be to find out the critical thinking of some native Kenyans, and thereby establish that there are native Africans capable of doing rigorous philosophy.

But a number of questions must be asked. First, whose philosophy does the philosopher produce as a result of such research? What does he succeed in doing *vis-a-vis* the challenges earlier discussed? I suggest that what the philosopher is doing here is helping people to give birth to philosophical ideas already in them. The product of the joint enquiry of the traditional sage and the trained philosopher is a new phenomenon. Both the traditional sage and the trained philosopher inevitably enter the dialogue with certain presuppositions. What they come out with is a new creation out of their reflections on the beliefs previously held by them. But, and this is the important point to remember, the philosopher and the sage are "doing their own thing." They are doing African philosophy only because the participants are Africans *or* are working in Africa, *and* are interested in a philosophical problem (howbeit universal) from an African point of view. As will be argued later, if they were merely interested in how and what Africans think about persons their work would not be philosophically interesting, not any more interesting than the works of ethnographers. Second, this "going out quite literally into the market place ... something we are told philosophers used to do before they became encapsulated in our academic institutions",[16] is not to be understood as being the same as what Socrates and his contemporaries did in the Athenian *agora.* Metaphors can be misleading. Socrates' interlocutors, if Plato's dialogues have any verisimilitude, are his intellectual peers. Among them were etymologists like Euthyphro (*Cratylus* 396d) after whom Plato named the *Euthyphro,* renowned orators like Gorgias (*Symposium* 198c), mathematicians like Theaetetus, etc. The Athenian *agora* was not a mere market place in our sense of the word; it was the speakers' corner, the conference centre and the seminar auditorium of the Athenian free and leisure class citizenry. Socrates did not leave us any written work but he was not an illiterate. There is indeed evidence that Socrates and a large section of the Athenian free adult male citizenry was not illiterate.[17] It is reasonable to assume that those who met in the *agora* for intellectual discussions were well-educated persons thoroughly familiar with the written and oral traditions of their people. Their search was not for the Athenian conception of

9

justice, piety or what have you. In fact, Socrates insisted almost *ad nauseam* on the necessity of distinguishing between popular conceptions of notions like justice and piety and the real meaning of these concepts--what the thing is in itself. It was in this process of searching for the real meaning of concepts (mostly ethical concepts, at first) as opposed to popular beliefs about them that Greek philosophy was born. It was a criticism of traditional cultural beliefs.

Philosophy is a conscious creation. One cannot be said to have a philosophy in the strict sense of the word until one has consciously reflected on one's beliefs. It is unlikely that such conscious reflection did not take place in traditional Africa; it is however left to research to show to what extent it has. That it has cannot be denied *a priori*. However, this social-anthropologist's method of field enquiry seems to me to be an implicit admission that an African philosophical tradition is yet in the making. The philosopher and the sage are helping this creative work. Those interested in philosophic sagacity would succeed and have succeeded in showing that ability to philosophize is not necessarily tied to literacy and that there exist among Africans men and women capable of engaging in serious philosophical discourse. Still, it does not seem to me that this last point is what those who do not see the definite establishment of African philosophy in the results of such researches are denying; none but the extremely naive person could deny all the members of a whole race philosophic abilities. What some seem to be denying is the existence of a tradition of organized critical reflections such as the philosopher and the sage are trying to help create. For it is one thing to show that there are men capable of philosophical dialogue in Africa and another to show that there are African philosophers in the sense of those who have engaged in organized systematic reflections on the thoughts, beliefs and practices of their people. Even if writing cannot be a precondition for philosophy, nevertheless, the role of writing in the creation of a philosophical tradition cannot be underrated. More will be said about this later.

Let us now come to ethno-philosophy. The sources are African folk-lore, tales, myths, proverbs, religious beliefs and practices, and African culture at large. In respect of these it is necessary to make clear what we are denying. We are not denying that they are worthy of the philosopher's attention. We are not denying the existence of respectable and in many ways complex, and in some sense rational and logical conceptual analysis in Africa. In one sense a system of beliefs is rational if, once you understand the system, individual beliefs within it make

10

sense; in other words, if one could see why members of the society within the system would hold such beliefs as they do in fact hold. And a belief system is logical if, once you identify the premises or assumptions upon which the system is based, individual beliefs would follow from them and can be deduced from them alone. Such a system may also even be coherent. That there are rational (in the sense described above), logical and respectable conceptual systems among African and other peoples once thought by Europeans to be mentally primitive is no longer the point at issue. As far back (far back?) as 1962 at the First International Congress of Africanists in Accra, Ghana, a well-known anthropologist, Jean-Paul Lebeuf, had asserted (howbeit with some exaggeration) the existence in Africa of perfectly balanced metaphysical systems in which all the phenomena of the sensible world are bound together in harmony, adding that "it cannot be said too often that the recording of these ontologies has rendered accessible a form of thinking which is as unimpeachable in ' its logic as Cartesianism, although quite separate from it."[18] The works of Professor Evans-Pritchard and more recent studies of Professor Robin Horton have gone a long way to confirm this. But not every rational, coherent and complicated conceptual system is philosophy. Science and mathematics are eminently rational, logical and, to a large extent, consistent conceptual systems, but they are not philosophical systems. I think that many ethno-philosophers mistakenly believe that all rational, logical and complicated conceptual systems are philosophical systems. I believe that they are wrong in this.

The usual criticisms against ethno-philosophers[19] have taken the following forms. (1) That some of the things they say about African culture are false; such as when one shows that Mbiti's claim that Africans have no conception of the future beyond the immediate future to be false by drawing attention to various modes of reference to the distant future in African language and social life,[20] or that Senghor is wrong for claiming that "Negro African reasoning is intuitive by participation" by showing the unemotional rationality of some African thinking (as in Robin Horton's works). This method by itself does not show that the works so criticized are unphilosophical works. A philosophical work does not cease to be philosophical merely because it contains false claims. (2) Since we hold that philosophy is properly studied, according to us, through the examination of the thoughts of individuals, another argument we have used against ethno-philosophers is that the collective thought of peoples upon which they concentrate is not genuine philosophy. Although any attempt to give an account of the collective thoughts of a whole people lends itself to a usual objection against holistic

11

explanations of social phenomena (namely, that they must posit the existence of group minds), this objection is, in and of itself, not sufficient to dismiss such attempts as non-philosophical. Philosophers like anyone else may err. At any rate, it is not clear why the thought of groups, if there is such a thing, cannot be a proper subject for philosophical study. To argue that it cannot[21] is to beg the question, for it is to assume that the question of what methods and materials belong to philosophy has been settled in advance.[22] This history of philosophy is replete with discussions of different sorts of things and various approaches to the subject. One cannot dismiss the discussion of anything and the use of any method as unphilosophical without argument. To opt for one method is to take a philosophical stance. There is no *a priori* reason why proverbs, myths of gods and angels, social practices, etc., could not be proper subjects for philosophical enquiry.

Ethno-philosophers and ourselves and indeed all who engage in cognitive endeavors have a common object (not objective) of enquiry. What we all wish to know more about is this universe of ours; its content, the events and activities which take place within it. About these things several questions may be asked to which different answers are expected. The kind of answers expected depends both on the kind of questions posed *and* on the method of enquiry. Different disciplines approach the study of the world in different ways and seek understanding at different levels and with different goals. Thus, the discovery of the most fundamental laws governing the behaviour of matter is the goal of physics; the discovery of the general laws governing the functioning of the human mind is the goal of psychology. Disciplines are not in water-tight compartments, and areas of interest overlap. And what in one generation belongs to one discipline may in another generation belong to another discipline. Scholars in each discipline generally adopt the methods accepted by their age, and deal with the sorts of questions that are of concern to their age, and work within the background of the basic assumptions of their disciplines--at least until these assumptions "boil-over". Wright may be right that there is no one method which is *the method* of philosophy today.[23] Still, in whatever tradition of philosophy one is working and whatever method one is applying, some assumptions seem to be generally agreed on today. Thus, when one is putting forward a philosophical thesis for our acceptance, we expect him to state his case clearly, to state the issues at stake as clearly as possible so that we know what we are being invited to accept. We expect him to argue for his cases--show us why we must accept his case. He may do this by showing the weaknesses of rival

12

theories, if any, or by showing how his theory solves the prob-
lem(s) that has (have) always worried us, or how it enlarges our
understanding of something else we already knew. In arguing for
his thesis and in showing how the thesis makes a difference he is
carrying out a synthesis the result of which may be a new view
of the world. If this new view conflicts with other views he must
attempt to justify which of them he thinks we ought to opt for.
We expect him to let us have a say; let us, that is, ask and raise
questions about his thesis. In other words we do not expect him
to be so dogmatic as to think that his position is the final word
on that with which it deals. We expect him to be prepared to
change his view, and are ourselves prepared to change ours,
according to evidence. We do not expect him to have a theological dogmatism about his position. We expect these things even of
the speculative metaphysician and the existentialist. Philosophers
do not always succeed in doing and being all these things. It is
only required that they try to. A mere description of the empirical world cannot satisfy these conditions. The pity is that
ethno-philosophers usually fall in love so much with the thought
system they seek to expound that they become dogmatic in the
veneration of the culture to which the thought system belongs.
They hardly see why others may refuse totally to share their
esteem for the system they describe. They do not raise philosophical issues about the system (because for them no problems
arise once we "understand" the system); therefore they do not
attempt to give a philosophical justification of the belief system or
of issues that arise in it. It is for these reasons that we find
their works philosophically unsatisfactory; it is not because we
consider the material on which they have worked unworthy of the
philosopher's attention, or their work unscholarly. It must be
pointed out, however, that an otherwise competent professional
philosopher may manifest an unexpressed reverence for traditional
culture by simply leaving us with an analysis of philosophical
concepts and saying nothing about his analysis--as if to say he
has found a new and impeccable conceptual system.

The African philosopher cannot *deliberately* ignore the
study of the traditional belief system of his people. Philosophical
problems arise out of real life situations. In Africa, more than in
many other parts of the modern world, traditional culture and
beliefs still exercise a great influence on the thinking and actions
of men. At a time when many people in the West believe that
philosophy has become impoverished and needs redirection, a
philosophical study of traditional societies may be the answer.
The point, however, is that the philosopher's approach to this
study must be one of criticism, by which one does not mean
"negative appraisal, but rational, impartial and articulate

appraisal whether positive or negative. To be 'critical' of received ideas is accordingly not the same thing as rejecting them: it consists rather in seriously asking oneself whether the ideas in question should be reformed, modified or conserved, and in applying one's entire intellectual and imaginative intelligence to the search for an answer."[24] What seems to me clear is that the philosopher cannot embark on a study of African traditional thought wholesale. He would have to proceed piece-meal. He may have to begin by an examination of philosophical issues and concepts that have loomed largely in the history of world philosophy, and he must not be charged for being unoriginal or being irrelevant as an African philosopher simply because he is discussing in the African context issues that have also received attention elsewhere. If a problem is philosophical it must have a universal relevance to all men. Philosophical systems are built up by systematic examination of specific features of the world and out of the relationships that are perceived to obtain between them. Some contemporary African philosophers have begun the piecemeal study of philosophical concepts embedded in African traditional thought. I shall discuss two recent attempts.

In "Notes on the Concept of Cause and Chance in Yoruba Traditional Thought",[25] by a comparison of several quotations from Yoruba proverbs, the playwright Ogunde, the Ifa corpus, Hume, Horton, etc., and obviously doing the same thing which Henri Frankfort has done with Greek pre-scientific pre-philosophic speculative thought,[26] and reaching exactly the same conclusions, Professor Sodipo successfully established the following theses. (1) That the Yorubas do distinguish between chance and cause. (2) That scientific causal explanations (usually done in terms of impersonal entities) cannot explain certain unique features of some occurrences. Thus while the wetness of the road, the ineffectiveness of the brakes and driver carelessness, etc., may explain why accidents generally happen, they cannot explain why it has happened to a particular person, in a particular place and at exactly the time it happened. (3) That where human personal interests are at stake, as when a coin is tossed to decide who is to reign, the Yorubas believe that in such a case luck is not due to chance but to the action of the gods or some other personal agent. (4) The reason for this is that the preoccupation of explanation in Yoruba traditional thought is *religious;* because it is *religious* it must satisfy "emotional and aesthetic needs" and because of this its explanations *must be given* in terms of persons or entities that are like persons in significant respects. For it is explanations like these that can reveal the motives that lay behind particular happenings; they alone answer the *emotional* question why the thing happened *here,*

14

now and *to me* in particular.[27]

I think that we must admit that this account has enabled us to see that the Yoruba conception of cause and chance fits very well into the Yoruba traditional system of beliefs, especially our religious belief system. It also shows that there are reasons, and understandable reasons for that matter, why the traditional Yorubas explain significant occurrences in personal idioms. Professor Sodipo points out that for the Yorubas, the gods take over where the scientists would have a recourse to chance. He also points out that the Yorubas are not unaware of the technical notion of chance. What Professor Sodipo has done is to put these concepts (cause and chance) in this specific category of events (events that are significant for human beings) in context. He has "put himself in the place of men living [in the traditional Yoruba culture] to understand the principle and pattern of their intentions".[28] But something is required beyond the analysis provided by Sodipo.

Since we have now, through Sodipo's analysis, come to see that there is a difference between the traditional Yoruba account of cause and effect and the scientific account, the important question is: which is the truer account? Which are we to prefer? The only answer one can deduce from Sodipo is; it all depends on what you want. If you want emotional or aesthetic satisfaction you ought to prefer the Yoruba traditional account. If you want some other thing then ---. If two accounts are so radically different one must be nearer truth than the other, and one of the aims of philosophy is to enable us to decide which. Surely that which is emotionally and aesthetically satisfying does not for that reason alone compel our acceptance. This feature alone cannot confer truth on a proposition.

In a more important sense of "rational", showing why a people hold a particular belief is not sufficient to show that the belief is rational. Given any human social practice one can always find a reason for it. In the case in point here, an explanation of an event in terms of the motives of a person or a god is rational only if evidence is given for the existence of the person or god, or sufficient reasons given why their existence must be assumed *and* arguments adduced as to why the person or god should be supposed to be implicated in the particular event. Surely, to show that a belief arises from emotional needs, if this is in fact true, can hardly be construed as having shown it to be rational. In all this one notices a reluctance to evaluate lest it be understood as condemning a particular culture. This same reluctance to pass evaluative judgments is evident in Hallen's

15

discussion of the concept of destiny in the Yoruba thought system.[29]

Hallen argues that the Yorubas reject the Western radical dichotomy between the rational and emotional parts of the human personality and that this fundamentally affects the structure of their beliefs and conceptual systems generally. According to Hallen there are three elements in the human personality: the individual spirit *(emi)* which continues to live after death but without its earthly body *(ara)* and destiny *(ori)*. Like the souls in Plato's *Republic* (Book X, 617d-621b) the *emi* can go through a number of reincarnations. Before each reincarnation, the *emi* has to choose a new destiny *(ori)* which "encompasses every event of significance that will take place during his lifetime, including time and manner of both birth and death ... The *emi* is the conscious deciding self; what it decides is determined by the *ori,* a part of the self that is not part of self-consciousness".[30] The *ori* must be seen as somehow external to and other than the self. Hallen argues that the *ori* must not be compared to the Freudian notion of an unconscious because this would introduce the personality dichotomy into a conceptual system where it does not occur. The *ori* has both reason and desires of his own. Here is the interesting passage from Hallen:

> A Yoruba will say that once a destiny is "fixed" by *Olorun* it cannot be changed. It must take place. Nevertheless on other occasions the same person will say that it is possible to "miss" the destiny one has been apportioned, in the sense of becoming confused and lost during one's lifetime and doing things for which one is not at all suited. Or an external force can interfere with one's destiny. Neither of these is entirely consistent with the belief that once a destiny is fixed, it is unalterable and must take place. Or with the fact that people will flatter and praise their destiny in hopes of improving it. Or with the aforementioned possibility that a person might be blamed for not making the most of the destiny allotted to him.[31]

Hallen rightly points out that the inconsistency implied in the Yoruba conception of destiny *(ori)* must not be seen as evidence of primitive mentality. Human beings everywhere sometimes hold

16

(usually unconsciously) inconsistent beliefs. However, Hallen argues that the inconsistency in this case is merely apparent and becomes a problem only if we judge the Yorubas conceptual system in terms of the Western hypotheticodeductive paradigm:

> Rather the various beliefs that may be called upon when an explanation or prediction is required should be compared to the various moveable partitions that are ranged along the wings of a stage and may be swung into position depending upon the demands of the next scene. Each partition corresponds to a certain belief. There are other belief panels in the wings that would be inconsistent with it if they were brought into play simultaneously. But this does not happen (except in very exceptional circumstances) because when a certain kind of problem occupies stage centre the same partition is always moved out to serve as its explanatory background.[32]

Again what we see here as in Sodipo's account of the Yoruba concept of cause and chance is a good account of why the Yorubas do not find it odd to live with inconsistent beliefs. Hallan's account can hardly be construed as showing that the Yorubas hold consistent views on destiny as expressed in their concept of *ori;* rather his account explains why the Yorubas do not *see* any inconsistencies in their belief system. But this does not remove the inconsistency. It is better to recognize here the existence of genuine perennial philosophical problems--the problems of determinism and freedom, the self and consciousness--to which philosophers have not yet found a solution, than to portray the Africans as radically different from the rest of mankind in their conceptual system and in being immune to the laws of logic. In an attempt to establish the uniqueness of the African both Sodipo and Hallen have refused to cite parallel beliefs from elsewhere lest perhaps they be accused of importing alien models into their study or appear to be doing nothing new. Our culture may be dear to us, but truth must be dearer.

The discussion is already getting too long, but there are still two more points to be considered. One is the call that we produce an African philosophy even if there is yet none, as if philosophers could put up a command performance. We are told that if historians and students of literature could create the

17

P. O. BODUNRIN

African species of their disciplines, African philosophers can do
the same. Those who argue this way miss the essential differences between philosophy and these other disciplines. Peoples
and nations *necessarily* have a history as long as their existence
spans space and time and as long as they engage in human social
activities. Unless they are simply stupid, those who are reported
to have said that Africans had no history can only mean that they
do not know of any significant events (by what standards significance is to be determined is another matter) that took place in
African history. Our historians have proved them wrong by a
close study of our oral traditions coupled with archaeological and
other material evidence. African writers are doing for African
literature what Aeschylus, Sophocles and Euripides did for Greek
literature. They took popular myths, well-known celebrations,
and popular customs, and gave them a literary twist. It is in
doing this that they are helping to create African literature.
However, it seems to me that what one may properly compare with
philosophy is historical and literary criticism. These are, in
Africa, as far as I know, a product of the modern age. The
influence of writing in all these cannot be under-estimated. Writing helps us to pin down ideas and to crystallize them in our
minds. It makes the ideas of one day available for later use. It
is by its means that the thoughts of one age are made available to
succeeding generations with the least distortion. We do not
always, as it were, have to begin again. How much of the present discussion would I carry in my memory ten years from now?
How much of it, if I were to rely on oral transmission, would
remain undistorted for the future? Surely, writing is not a
prerequisite for philosophy but I doubt whether philosophy can
progress adequately without writing. Had others not written
down the sayings of Socrates, the pre-Socratics and Buddha, we
would today not regard them as philosophers, for their thoughts
would have been lost in the mythological world of proverbs and
pithy sayings.

The remaining point is this: what does an expression
like "British Philosophy" mean?[33] It does not mean the philosophy
of the average Englishman, nor a philosophy generally known
among the British people. The average Briton is not aware of
much of *Principia Mathematica* or of the contents of the *Tractatus.*
British philosophy is not a monolithic tradition. At this point in
time empiricism and logical analysis seem to be the predominating
features of that tradition but by no means can all present philosophers in the British tradition be described as empiricists or
analysts. Towards the close of the last century, the dominant
figure was Bradley, a Hegelian idealist. British philosophy is not
a body of thoughts that had its origins in the British Isles.

18

Greek thought (itself informed by early Egyptian thought), continental idealism, and scientific philosophy (the philosophy of the Vienna Circle) have all had influences on British thought. Some of the most influential figures in British philosophy have not even been British by birth--e.g. Wittgenstein and Popper. Similarly, Alfred North Whitehead was born in England and began his philosophical career in England, but his later philosophical work belongs to the history of American philosophy. The thoughts of the ancient Greeks belong to the history of Western philosophy but the ancient Greeks and ancient Britons were mutually ignorant of each other. Caesar described the Britons as barbarians when he first went there. The point I am trying to make is that the philosophy of a country or region of the world is not definable in terms of the thought-content of the tradition nor in terms of the national origins of the thinkers. As Wiredu puts it, "for a set of ideas to be a genuine possession of a people, they need not have originated them, they need only appropriate them, make use of them, develop them, if the spirit so moves them, and thrive on them. The intellectual history of mankind is a series of mutual borrowings and adaptations among races, nations, tribes, and even smaller sub-groups."[34] And "the work of a philosopher is part of a given tradition if and only if it is either produced within the context of that tradition or taken up and used in it."[35] If these points are realized the philosopher should be allowed the intellectual liberties allowed his colleagues in other disciplines. He may be asked to apply his training to the study of his culture and this would be an understandable request, but it would have to be understood that his reaction will be guided by his own philosophical interests.

The view of philosophy advocated here is not narrow. It enables us to study African traditional thought, but it cautions that it be done properly. Philosophy as a discipline does, and must, have autonomy. The view that anything can pass for philosophy will hurt the development of philosophy in Africa. Not everyone is a philosopher. Philosophy requires training. Why must we lament a late start in philosophy? No one laments our late start in mathematics. I think that we must disabuse ourselves of the evaluative and honorific undertones that philosophy has come to have and regard it just as one discipline among others. That certainly is the way professional philosophers see their subject. It is just another of man's cognitive activities, not especially superior to others. A department of philosophy in a university is one among many other academic departments in the university, but in order that the foundations of the discipline be well laid it is necessary that the boundaries of it be clearly delimited. We are probably all capable of doing philosophy, but

19

we are not all philosophers, just as we are not all historians. We must advocate rigour. Whether we like it or not we will have science and technology. We have to acquire the thought habits needed to cope with life in a technological age. It is now time to begin self-criticism in Africa. Philosophers cannot afford to expend all their energies on the often unproductive and self-stultifying we-versus-you scholarship. We as Africans must talk to one another. We are likely to have a more honest and frank debate that way. If Marx is right that the important thing is to change the world, then it seems to me that our choice is obvious. No doubt many things are worth preserving in our traditional culture--especially in the moral sphere--but we stand in danger of losing these if we do not take pains to separate these from those aspects that are undesirable. This we can do only by the method of philosophical criticism.[36]

FOOTNOTES

1.   This paper was first published in *Philosophy,* and is reprinted here with the permission of the author, editor, and Cambridge University Press, the publisher.

2.   H. O. Oruka, "Four Trends in Current African Philosophy", presented at the *William Amo Symposium* in Accra, 24-29 July 1978.

3.   Paulin Hountondji, "Le Mythe de la Philosophie Spontanee", in *Cahiers Philosophiques Africains,* No. 1 (Lubumbashi, 1972). Although Oruka had Hountondji in mind, it must be realized that Hountondji was not the first to use this expression. Kwame Nkrumah had written a thesis on "Ethno-philosophy" in his student days in America.

4.   (i) Placid Tempels, *Bantu Philosophy* (Paris: Presence Africaine, 1959); (ii) Leopold S. Senghor, *On African Socialism,* trans. with introduction by Mercer Cook (New York: Frederic A. Praeger, 1964); (iii) J. S. Mbiti, *African Religions and Philosophies* (New York: Doubleday, 1970); (iv) *La Philosophie Bantu--Rwandaise de l'Etre* (Brussels: Academie des Sciences Coloniales, 1956).

5.   This is from an unpublished version of the paper referred to in footnote 2 above.

6.   Kwame Nkrumah, *Consciencism: Philosophy and Ideology* (New York: Monthly Review Press, 1970) and J. K. Nyerere, *Ujamaa: Essays in Socialism* (OUP 1968).

7.   See the revised version of Oruka's paper referred to in note 4, footnote 15.

8.   Just as the contact of the Greeks with the Egyptians, and that of Medieval Europe with Arabic thought had influences on the thoughts of those peoples.

9.   Jean-Paul Lebeuf called attention to this in 1962. See

"The Philosopher's Interest in African Thought: A Synopsis," *Second Order: An African Journal of Philosophy* 1. No. 1 (1972), 43.

10. Some of my colleagues critized the syllabus I drew up for the Philosophy Department, University of Ibadan, in 1974 as being not sufficiently African and too Western.

11. This is in disagreement with Professor Ntumba's universalist interpretation of African familyhood, and Nyerere's own claim in his *Ujamaa.* See note 6 above.

12. Kwasi Wiredu, "Philosophy and Our Culture", *Proceedings of the Ghana Academy of Arts and Sciences* (forthcoming).

13. Alex Haley, *Roots* (New York: Doubleday, 1976).

14. Kwasi Wiredu, loc. cit.

15. *Inconsistencies?* This point will be discussed later.

16. Barry Hallen, "A Philosopher's Approach to Traditional Culture", *Theoria to Theory* 9, No. 4 (1975), 259-272.

17. In defending himself against the charge of atheism brought against him by Meletus, Socrates said that the views attributed to him were in fact those of Anaxagoras whom he would not plagiarize. Anaxagoras' book, Socrates adds, was readily available at a cheap price at every corner store. Of the Athenian jury Socrates asks Meletus, "Have you so poor an opinion of these gentlemen, and do you assume them to be so illiterate as not to know that the writings of Anaxagoras of Clazomenae are full of theories like these?" (Plato, *Apology,* 26d).

18. Quoted by W. A. Hart, loc. cit., note 9 above.

19. I do not use this term with any pejorative connotations.

20. E. g., J. A. Ayoade's "Time in Yoruba Thought," *African Philosophy: An Introduction,* Richard A. Wright (ed.) University Press of America, 1977), 83-106. [p. 93 of this edition. ed.]

21. I argued this way in my "Problems and Prescriptions for an Action Philosophy in Africa", *Proceedings of the Inter-African Council of Philosophy,* Proceedings of the

1975 Accra Conference.

22. See R. Wright's arguments in his book cited in note 19 above, pp. 21-24. [p. 43-53 of this edition. ed.]

23. Ibid., 23-25.

24. H. S. Staniland, "What is Philosophy?" *Second Order: An African Journal of Philosophy,* 7, (1978).

25. *Second Order,* 2 No. 2 (1973) 12-20.

26. Henri Frankfort, *Before Philosophy* (Penguin, 1951).

27. Sodipo, op. cit., 18.

28. W. A. Hart, op. cit. 47, quoting from Evans-Pritchard.

29. Barry Hallen, loc. cit., note 16 above, pp. 265-270.

30. Ibid., 266.

31. Ibid., 268.

32. Ibid., 270.

33. In the line of argument that follows I am greatly indebted to Professor Kwasi Wiredu's "What is African Philosophy?", presented at the *William Amo International Symposium* referred to earlier.

34. Ibid., 7.

35. Ibid., 11-12.

36. An earlier version of this paper was read to the Philosophy Department, University of Notre Dame, Notre Dame, USA, and before the Ibadan Philosophical Society. My thanks are due to the audiences in these two places. My thanks are also due to Professor Kwasi Wiredu of the Department of Philosophy, University of Ghana, Legon, for his useful criticism of a later draft.

DO WE HAVE
AN AFRICAN PHILOSOPHY?[1]

Henri Maurier

Mildred M. McDevitt, Translator

The answer must surely be: No! Not Yet! Certainly we have ground breakers:[2] P. Tempels with *Bantu Philosophy;* A. Kagame with *The Bantu-Rwandaise Philosophy of Being;* Vincent Mulago with *An African Vision of Christianity.* Many articles and dissertations exist which, however, are very hard to come by.[3] We have some recent studies which endeavor to penetrate the intelligible universe of certain cultures: *Meat and Seed, Dogon Mythology,* Presence Africaine, 1969; R. Jaulin, *Death among the Sara,* Plon 1967; B. Holas, *The Bete Image of the World,* PLIF, 1968. The excellent *Notes on African Religions* increases the possible avenues of approach.[4] Yet despite all these studies, we must admit that we still have not really gotten hold of an African philosophy or even the necessary first steps toward an African philosophy. The real enterprise has not yet gotten off the ground.

Why? Because, the necessary conditions for, first, a philosophy, and then, for an African philosophy have not yet been met.

25

HENRI MAURIER

The Conditions for Genuine Philosophy

          Philosophy, like mathematics and the physical sciences, is a discipline with a distinctive set of universally agreed upon ground rules.[5] Without opening up endless discussions, every one would agree that philosophy as a discipline is reflective, rational, and systematic. Now it so happens that the research pursued in Africa up till now--at least that part that we are acquainted with--does not satisfactorily meet these requirements.

          The reflective character is doubtless the one met most often. The studies already mentioned are reflections and not bare facts or descriptions of beliefs. The reflective character of this type of work is already evident in the sayings of the Ogotemmeli published (with commentary by Griaule) in *Water Sayings*, Chene, ed., Paris 1948; this appears again in the texts of Frederic Bouabre Bruly with commentary by B. Holas in *The Bete Image of the World*. Certainly, the level of philosophical sophistication in these reflections can be more or less profound; let us grant, however, that the reflective character is at least making its appearance. But let us go on... .

          Philosophy aims to be *(se veut)* a rational discipline. In philosophy, reflection becomes reason. This means that philosophy works over and elaborates concepts extracted from the ore of myth and magic, or at least tries to do so. If one adopts this point of view, then it must be admitted that the majority of the studies here cited do not satisfy this condition. In *The Bete Image of the World,* mentioned above, a rational elaboration of concepts is non-existent; what is given is a mythological picture. The same may be said of the works concerning Dogon. In the area of Bantu study, the exigencies of rationality are more seri- ously felt, for instance, in the criticism of the idea of the 'being-force', criticism which makes little headway, since the doctrine continues to be invoked without any hesitation.[6] Now, in our opinion this 'force' is a mythological notion and in no wise rational. I shall not attempt here to prove my opinion, such is not my purpose in writing this article. Doubtless the objection will be made, "But the Bantu say that in their view being is conceived of as a force." I answer that even if Bantu common sense accepts and operates with this concept, it does by no means follow that philosophical reasoning should accept it purely and simply. Bantu philosophy is not philosophy because it takes one notion or another from the level of ordinary language, sayings, or common beliefs. *All philosophy should be a thorough and rational critique of concepts in general use.* Recall

26

discussions of the notions of being, of one, of motion, of time, space and matter, of becoming in Greek philosophy. The same comment might be made here, in reference to the Bantu, that C. Levi-Strauss makes regarding the HAU, a theory developed by the New Zelanders to explain gift-giving and exchange: [7]

> The native theory is in a much more direct relation with native reality than would be a theory elaborated on the basis of our categories and problems. Therefore, at the time when Mauss was writing, attacking an ethnographic problem which from the viewpoint of its New Zealand or Melanesian theory, rather than with occidental notions like animism, was a great step forward. But, native or western, *a theory is never more than a theory.* The HAU is a product of native thought... [now natives] when they reason about themselves--which happens not infrequently--behave as ethnographers, or more accurately as sociologists; that is to say like colleagues with whom one might hold a discussion.

Therefore there is room to discuss, to point out subjective illusions, mythical mirages, and to separate out view points that are genuinely rational. That in no wise means that a part of Bantu life or thought will be minimized or passed over; no, but it will be treated according to a reasoning that aims to be critical and conscious of its internal exigencies.

Other instances could be given of this lack of critical sense. Here we shall limit ourselves to the reflections of D. Zahan in *Dialectic of the Word among the Bambara,* Mouton, 1963. The author explains the customs of the *griots,* the influence of their flattering or insulting words on individuals. In doing so, he utilizes and perpetuates the Bambara theory of the NYAMA, a sort of vital force:

> In order to evoke the Nyama we have seen that there must be either insulting terms or else words which serve to glorify the living being, showing it forth in a favorable light, enlarging its value in its own eyes, or in those of others.... What does the *griot* do when singing the

27

> praise of an individual? He "enlarges"
> that person, he "blows him up" (i.e.
> magnifies) him, placing him in danger of
> bursting." Moved by the instinct of
> self-preservation, the individual in ques-
> tion intends to give the *griot* presents, to
> put a limit to this "dilation" and prevent
> "splitting apart." A *griot* does not stop
> saying compliments until he has received
> the gift. (p. 134)

These explanations certainly present a strange pneumatology!
The first task should have been to demythologize the theory of
NYAMA itself, instead of weighing it down with these dubious
spiritual elements. I think therefore, that an African philosophy
will not be accomplished until an effort has been made toward
rational criticism.[8]

Philosophy should also be critical in the Kantian sense
of the term; philosophy should question itself about the proper
value of its rational procedure and on the epistemological or
gnostic validity of its results. In fact, note must be taken of the
fact that the African philosopher finds himself in a situation
which is certainly not unique, but which is different from that of
western philosophers who are working within a long vein of philosophical thinking. The African philosopher is a ground breaker;
he plunges straight into African life as seen in its myths, its
beliefs, its rites, and in its everyday language. He uses the
studies of sociologists and ethnographers; but how accurately
defined are his own procedures? Interpretation of myths and
rites poses a difficult problem of hermeneutics; how shall the
African philosopher show that his interpretation is valid?[9] That is
the problem that I fail to see even considered in current studies.
Admittedly, Tempels has a chapter on "The Wisdom and the
Criteriology of the Bantus":[10] but what it amounts to is a statement that the Bantu firmly believe in their system, which they
deem obvious "on the basis of internal and external evidence";
however, Tempels never questions the validity of the elaboration
[of that evidence].

Finally, philosophy has to be systematic. What has to
be done is to organize into a coherent whole the profound things
Africa has to tell us of man, life, the world, God, etc. There is
no thought of finding fault with the present state of African
philosophy for not having achieved this! It is an immense task
and we have only just begun! At the same time, it would be a
mistake to expect that one fine morning this synthesis would

burst forth from a mass of heterogeneous considerations. A synthesis is not constructed as an after-thought; it is already present and operative in the first basic intuition. At this point one must be careful not to fall into what might be called a "proliferating" of philosophical notions taken out of the highly exact context where they have been elaborated. I read in *Voices of Volta*[11] a reflection of this sort. The author is speaking of the belief, common in Africa, which holds that a baby is used for the "reincarnation" or "return" of an ancestor of a deceased elder brother. Hence the names given the child: *Baalebia* (father come back), *Lewaya* (returned), *Lebende* (having come back). The author draws the following conclusion: "while taking account of other viewpoints that it would require too much time to analyze here, but to which we shall return, it would not be difficult to show that among the Mossis, Being is affirmed as originally One." We will certainly wait to hear the promised explanation, but, for the time being, this notion of "the One" seems about as plausible as a Martian commando attack!

This criticism is severe. Is it justified? Can one, under the pretext of practicing African philosophy, say anything one wants? Whatever it may be?

An African might reproach perhaps saying, "But you want to impose upon us your western concept of philosophy. We want an African philosophy, fully African not only in its authors and its subject, but also in its method."

We are [all] aware of this criticism. It is currently in vogue to criticize Cartesianism, its preoccupation with clear distinct ideas, its requirements for proof, etc., and then claim the right to a non-Western way, a way "truly our own," to work out a philosophy which is purely African. And if the Occidental procedure identifies itself with the rational and the scientific, then so much the worse for the rational and the scientific.

I consider this protest exaggerated. It springs, I believe, from a misunderstanding. It is not the demand to be rational, or critical, or scientific which keeps us from being truly African; on the contrary, that is what is pushing us to be really so, freed from fruitless self-satisfaction. We simply have to find the best way to go about it. At least, let us try here to suggest something.

But first let us reply again to the foregoing objection by an *ad hominem* argument. President Senghor opposes the "eye-reason" (*raison-oeil*) of the white European to the

29

"embrace-reason" (raison-entreinte) of the African; he says that reason is hellenic and emotion black; that "classical European reason is analytical through use, [while] black-African reason [is] intuitive through participation." It could be concluded that African philosophical style exists sui generis, more affective than rational, more participative than objective. But if things are to adhere exclusively to such a picture, we advise modern Africa to multiply its traditional instructional centers instead of opening classes and chairs of philosophy in its lycees and universities.

So let us try to find out what it is that can make African philosophy truly African. We will show at the same time, and in passing, why, in our view, the present efforts do not accomplish this task.

We find in the little book of J. B. Metz, Christian Anthropocentric Outlook (Mama, 1968) an interesting method which, so it seems to us, may give a useful [procedural] clue. For a precise interpretation of the philosophy of Saint Thomas, Metz's aim is to make clear what conceptual framework (forme de pensee) suits the reading of this theologian. But what is a "conceptual framework"? A philosophical statement, whatever it may be, cannot be understood in isolation, by simply examining what is said; it derives its meaning as well from other statements which balance it, support it, elaborate upon it, give it its "shadings," Each theme is linked to a whole set of themes which reciprocally hold together and influence one another. However, presupposed by these statements and these themes is a conceptual perspective, perceived scarcely or not at all in and of itself: the basic opinions, the prejudices, the things that go without saying, which are never in themselves subjected to criticism, which most of the time are not even conscious. This perspective, this all pervading atmosphere which serves to nourish thought is what we mean by a "conceptual framework."[12] A framework is thus opposed to subject matter, that is, to the variety of philosophical notions, themes, and statements which it supports. The conceptual framework actually constitutes a fundamental idea which pervades all other intellectual activities; it gives thought its internal consistency, its wholeness, its originality, in such a way that to understand a thought is to grasp hold of it by that unspoken principle which unifies and illuminates it.[13] [Once this principle is "established"] J. B. Metz shows that Saint Thomas is to be interpreted not in a cosmo but in an anthropocentric conceptual framework.

Let us apply this method to the subject which concerns us here. We may conclude that our African philosophy will become truly African when this philosophy is finally thought through in a conceptual framework properly African, adapted to African realities. For were we to impose upon these realities a foreign framework, we would be placing on them an iron collar, we would torture them in a Procrustean bed, we would not be able to readily connect reality with the particular savor it has [when viewed through African eyes], we would be posing all sorts of false problems and giving them pseudosolutions.

Such is the problem of the One referred to just above. We definitely do not think that African thought applies itself to this type of problem. Indeed, an accomplished connoisseur of things African, L. V. Thomas, believes that Africa takes a special pleasure in multiplicity.

Take an example of greater importance, *Bantu Philosophy* by P. Tempels. In what conceptual framework is Bantu reality worked out? It is not derogatory to say of this pioneer that he was not a professional philosopher, but rather, above all, a missionary. We easily recognize that his philosophical perspective is Aristotelian, indeed scholastic; or, to be even more precise, it is the ecclesiastical scholasticism which so long flourished in our seminaries and appeased our intellectual appetite from its meager stores. We have no trouble in recognizing this *"philosophia perennis"* in the organization of the chapters: ontology, wisdom, criteriology, psychology, ethics. Let us look at a specific case. Tempels admits that the Muntu, man, is the center of Bantu thought: "the Bantus see in man THE living force; the force of the being who possesses life in its truest, most complete, most elevated form..." (p. 66) But in the theory which Tempels develops, man is by no means at the center of things; it is only a particular case in a theory of being, the object of a psychology which comes after an ontology and a discussion of the conception of the world. If, then, Bantu man is looked at through a conceptual framework that is cosmocentric and not, accurately speaking, anthropocentric, one risks losing hold of what is essential.

V. Mulago, in *An African Vision of Christianity*, quotes Father P. Colle's "The Bashi notion of the Disincarnate Soul," p. 150:

> We may affirm with the author quoted above that the Bashi, The Banyarwanda and the Barundi, are not only spiritualist philosophers, since they recognize in man a spirit distinct from matter, a

31

> suprasensible spirit which is free,
> responsible, and immortal, but, further,
> spiritualists of a rigorous sort since they
> implicity presuppose in living beings, in
> man above all, the existence of matter
> and form. For at bottom the *muzimu* for
> them is none other than the form which
> animated what has now become a corpse.

The *muzimu* for them is none other than--in scholastic
language--"the substantial form of the body." Here we have a
full confession! Scholasticism has colonized a new territory! But
have we really grasped the Bantu world-view in as much as it
concerns the makeup of the person? There is clearly room for
doubt. The author adds in fact this short sentence--apparently
of little significance and which he abandons without further
commentary: "It takes the name of *muzimu* only after separation
from the body." How is that? Why should the putative substantial form change its name before and after death if we are dealing
here with the same reality? There is something here which
remains unexplained. It is certain that the methodological viewpoint (*problematique*) of Aristotle, based as it is on the substantialist and cosmocentric philosophical viewpoint, is the appropriate
tool for the rational reconstruction of African concepts? The
detail of the changing of the name is in itself significant, as
important *a priori,* for a true African philosophy, as the "spiritu-
alist" belief in the separation of body and soul. We can read in
Meeting the African Religions (Rome-Anchora, secretariate for
non-Christians, 1969), p. 29:

> Basil Davidson has reproduced these
> observations by a group of Ugandans
> which were reported at the second inter-
> national Congress of Africanists (Dakar,
> 1967). What interests us is our attitude
> toward life, culture, and our heritage.
> In choosing NTU we have seen it as the
> representation of a philosophy which
> extends throughout all Africa. The
> majority of the ideas reflecting the Afri-
> can art of living are found in the NTU
> philosophy.[14]

This is a legitimate declaration of faith. But what is the content
of this NTUism? We are told

> In the Bantu languages, the root NTU

signifies Being, primal being, for the
supreme Being is not NTU, and that sets
it off in its complete transcendance. It
transcends the category NTU. NTU is a
term expressing an idea, an intuition of
the real, and the structural base of a
considerable series of linguistic root-
forms. In effect by the interplay of
determinatives under the guise of
attached particles, NTU, primal being
comprises four large categories: 1)
MUNTU - being with intelligence (in the
plural BANTU); 2) KINTU - being without intelligence, things (animals, vegeta-
bles, minerals) are classed in this second
category (plural BL NTU); 3) KU NTU a
way of being (quantity, quality, relation,
action, passion, situation); 4) HA NTU -
localization in space and time.

Let us not criticize the little brochure for being satisfied with
that; its aim is quite other than the development of an African
philosophy. But since this analysis is frequently reproduced, we
may ask ourselves if it enables us to really grasp what is essential to NTUism. I greatly fear that we'll be satisfied with a dim
copy of the Aristotelian categories, for it so happens that these
Bantu categories are structured in a completely different way
from those of the Stagyrite.[15] And if we content ourselves with
the analyses of this great man, it won't be a Bantu philosophy
that we will construct but rather an Aristotelian one on a Bantu
basis. NTUism will have been digested by Aristotle. And the
one who does the digesting is the one who profits thereby.

The studies on *"The God of our Fathers,"*[16] are
certainly useful and important. But once again do they give us a
genuine African philosophy? One gets the impression that the
model applied to the Bantu conception of the attributes of God is
the same as that of the Christian theodicy of our religion textbooks. Who tells us that this model does not overlook other realities? Or who assures us that in organizing the material[17] in this
or that way, African reality is not being destroyed or that these
"materials" could be seen in a different light? It is a question of
finding the conceptual loci about which the attributes of the
Bantu conception really cluster. As it is, the attributes, as
given by our theodicy, are not truly comprehensible until they
are put back into the framework of the account of salvation.
They take on a different meaning seen in the framework of an

33

abstract occidental philosophy, or if situated in the dogmatic framework of human intelligence naturally capable of knowing God. But is it possible that, by means of these "conceptual frameworks", of these foreign "intentions," specific to certain ways of formulating problems, to discover African philosophical reality, properly so called?

Let us be fair. The use of foreign [intellectual] tools is not necessarily harmful. They are a kind of "testing agent"; they allow and guide research. They are like those scientific hypotheses which experimentation shows to be false [yet] which have the negative advantage of clearing the ground. But they also risk confusing trails and forming bad mental habits. Let us instead look for a conceptual framework better suited to Africa.

First, we shall eliminate certain frameworks which seen unsuitable. For instance, a cosmocentric framework like Stoicism. There is no doubt that an African copy could be made of Stoicism; the cosmos is very important in African thought, and it would be easy to find African counterparts of *apatheia* and *atarazie*. We eliminate this cosmocentric viewpoint, which takes as the fundamental type of being being-as-thing, or being-over-there; for to us it seems evident that African thought is eminently anthropocentric. [18]

Neither do we think that the objectivist framework, which opposes subject and object and considers the object independent of the subject, to be suitable for the study of African reality. Things, the cosmos, the realities of this world, supernatural beings are too much mingled with human realities for them to be looked upon from an *objectivist* and *substantialist* viewpoint. [19] Here instead we shall speak of a framework which is relational or participative (but the term participation connotes so many philosophical positions from Plato and Plotinus to Levy-Bruhl that it is heavily laden with western points of view).

If man is the center of the African philosophical perspective, it is assuredly not in the style of Descartes and his cogito. [20] Put differently, African philosophy would go astray if it took up a solipsistic or individualistic option. [21] For it is sufficiently obvious that "for the Bantus man never appears as an isolated individual, as an independent substance." [22] [Likewise] "the Munti is a man who exists in a community and for the community." [23] Let us again make use of the term 'relational' to characterize the conceptual framework of African philosophy.

34

Western philosophy is polarized by the problem of knowledge, the problem of universals, the problem of immediate awareness, the problem of empiricism, the problem of philosophical critique, and, recently, the question of phenomenology. We do not believe that this sort of problem seriously exercises African thinking. The problem of living, of life, is far more important than the problem of knowledge. We say then that the conceptual framework most suitable here is not the gnosiological but the "vitalist."

Right into the heart of African anthropocentrism we can bring this additional clarification: we are not of the opinion that the African subject is drowned in a crushing collectivism, as we too often hear. We can speak of an African subjectivism, but in a very different sense from that of western subjectivism. The latter, having evolved in an individualist and objectivist perspective, looks upon the subject as self-sufficient, autonomous, a consciousness, a free agent, a strong personality, competitive, who should assert himself, master himself in and by the independence he is assumed to have. African subjectivism will have a quite different flavor because it will be developed in a relational setting; the subject will affirm himself (strengthen his personality) not by isolating himself but by cultivating contacts with others, constantly exchanging with others.

One might agree to designate this properly African conceptual framework by two words: I - WITH; the "I" marking the anthropocentric aspect both subjectivist and vitalist, and the word "WITH" marking the relational, the communitarian attitude essentially and existentially characterizing the "I."

The conceptual framework having been thus focused upon,[24] clarified and made conscious, African realities can be approached with an eye freed from Western options. What African thought can contribute to universal culture is more clearly seen; instead of being polarized by such notions as the individual, knowing, and awareness, African thought *is* polarized by the vital relationship that everyone necessarily maintains with others and with the world. One might even ask ironically, how is it that the West for so many centuries has centered its thought on the isolated individual? How could it be that it only recently discovered the presence of others and of being-in-the-world?[25] The awakening to a properly African conceptual framework will enable us to escape the "imperialism" of western thought, as the politician might say. We will be better able to locate our concrete problems. The West has used an individualistic and objectivist framework, and that has given it a civilization where the

35

individual is powerful; where liberty is a good that is absolute, where there is room for the play of free enterprise, where scientific and technological progress covers the world with its achievements. In Africa things are quite otherwise, since African civilization is characterized above all by solidarity, communitarianism, traditionalism, "participation." The West is trying now to get away from its individualism (source of so many precious values but also of so many abuses). But the communitarianism it is covering is post-individualist, it is not relinquishing anything of whatever good it has acquired by its former individualism; people, subjects, must continue to be more and more themselves by participating. "Union personalizes," "True union does not confound identity, it differentiates it," said Teilhard de Chardin. The present movement in Africa is quite different. One may say that Africa bites deeper and deeper into individualism; but this is a post-communitarian individualism which intends to retain the best of what its communitarianism has produced. Must we think that Africa, after centuries of solidarity, is to pass through an individualistic stage before reaching a new communitarian synthesis? Must we not take care to keep in mind that modern development was accomplished in the West by means of a conceptual framework far removed from that of Africa? Should the latter imitate the western framework, or should Africa work out an entirely new type of development in harmony with its own distinct spirit?[26] Here we see what is at stake. Once again philosophy flows into life and politics.

It flows out also into theology. African theology will of necessity depend upon a genuinely African conceptual framework. But doesn't Christianity carry along with it its own conceptual framework? And is that framework compatible with the African framework? We see how the problems link together.[27]

However that may be, for the present, the essential seems to be this: that there be a multiplicity of African studies in this field and that they be attentive to the conceptual framework they use; let us bring to the surface the incontestable characteristics of a conceptual framework which is really African; and let the habit be formed of considering African problems against *this* background, while retaining an awareness of other conceptual frameworks at work in the wide world. Then there will be a methodology and a problem area which are truly African. In such a case we expect that African philosophy will have nothing to lose but everything to gain. It will be perfectly philosophical because it will be wholly rational and critically grounded; and it will be truly African, unfolding its own special wealth for the greater good of culture everywhere.

FOOTNOTES

1. This paper first appeared, in French, in the *Revue du Clerge Africain* (now *Telema*), is translated and used here by permission of the author and the editor of *Telema*.

2. Complete references to all cited works are found in the bibliography at the end of this volume. (ed.)

3. The disadvantages should be noted in passing, namely that the majority of East-African publications are not known in the West (and doubtless vice-versa); that many interesting studies remain hidden away in the archives of a university or a bishopric, and either cannot be found or are difficult to consult. Certain recent tests have prohibitive prices; for example *Clearings in the Metaphysics of Africa*, the J. C. Bahoken, Presence africaine editions, Paris, 1967, 124 pages, cost in Paris, in August, 1969, 48.10 French francs. Even editions aiming at the diffusion of African culture are not readily available. In Ouagadougou it is seldom and with difficulty that the Presence africaine editions can be found.

4. One more comment, with no intention of reproach: West Africa is practically absent from these publications. Once again the problem of communication and of reciprocal interest on the continent.

5. Let us consider at least the philosophy born and developed in the West since the Greeks; leave aside for the moment the Hindu or Chinese philosophies, not that they are negligible, but because up till the present Africa seems to tend toward assimilating and applying the intellectual disciplines of western origin.

6. Hountandji [1969] is a good example of exactly this sort of criticism. For the doctrine being criticized, see Tempels *Bantu Philosophy*, P. 39 ff. (ed.)

7. See "Introduction to the Work of M. Mauss," in *Sociology*

and Anthropology PUF 1960, p. XXXIX-XL. The italics in the quote are mine.

8. The paper by L. Keita, above in this volume, attempts to do this. (ed.)

9. The problem raised here is twofold. On the one hand, it is a question of the accuracy, or validity of a particular analysis, e.g. that of Tempels in his *Bantu Philosophy.* There is considerable literature on this aspect of the problem. On the other hand, there is the metaphilosophical question of how <u>any</u> interpretation or understanding of a <u>different</u> conceptual system is to be certified as valid, *vis a vis* their essential differences. In western philosophy questions of this nature have been raised by W. V. Quine, with his notion of the indeterminacy of translation; the ensuing discussions, centered on Quine's work, have dealt extensively with this problem of interpretation; however, this discussion has not filtered significantly into African philosophy. It is thus the contention here that Africans should concern themselves with this issue, if for no other reason than to solidify their criticisms. (ed.)

10. Cf. *Bantu Philosophy,* Chapter II (ed.)

11. Quarterly review for the Volta Association for African Culture, No. 5, April - June, 1969, Ouagadougou BP 563; article by A. Wininga, "Language and Nation," p. 35.

12. Compare this with the *Present Position of Catholics in England,* Chapter VI, "First Principles," by Cardinal Newman, 1858 (tr.)

13. Compare the discussion here with the Kantian treatment of categories and their role in experience. (ed.)

14. For a good, basic discussion of the notion of NTU from the non-African viewpoint (i.e. the point being criticized here) see Jahn [1958] (ed.)

15. A reference to Aristotle stemming from his birthplace. (ed.)

16. Third Kinshasa week, July 1969. R.C.A., May-July 1967.

17. With the meaning of electro-magnetic field, gravitational field.

18.   Frequent affirmation with authors. For example: E. Mujynga, "Evil and the Ultimate Basis of Morality," in *Publications of African Religions,* no. 5, 1969, p. 76.

19.   One quotation from amongst others: "The dynamology of the ntu is felt around them; beings interact with one another through "being" influences which establish the increase of diminution of the beings. This is true above all of the ntu who have had a common source of life or of vital means, of the ntu who are in contact through some of their belongings." V. Mulago, loc. cit. p. 154.

20.   See the paper by B. Oguah, above in this volume, for an argument concluding exactly the opposite of this point. (ed.)

21.   It is most surprising to read these reflections of Maurice Got: "Impenetrable to his fellow man, 'for no one can put his arm inside his companion even though they share the same bed' defined, he too, by the increase of internal strength, by an intimate relation of action and feeling, the "Munti" reminds us of the monad of Leibniz. Windowless on the outside, he is placed in his life-rank in universal and organic reality." Note on black spirituality in *Aspects of our Culture,* Fayard, Paris, 1958, p. 78. There you have ntuism annexed by Leibniz! That is evidence of the dis-services coming from the spreading influence of ideas from another world and which we mentioned already.

22.   Tempels, *Bantu Philosophy,* p. 73.

23.   Mulago, *African Vision,* p. 113.

24.   In a short article like this there can be a question only of suggestions. I am proving nothing, I am suggesting. Besides, this conceptual framework would have to be put into practice in order to see its value; its speculative and practical worth is what will judge it.

25.   Think of recent works -- compared with the life (or age) of western philosophy -- of Martin Buber, *Life as Dialogue,* translation by Aubier, 1959; and Maurice Nedoncelle, *Reciprocity of Consciousness,* Aubier, 1942.

26.   An interesting instance of the telescoping of perspectives is furnished by J-Y Calvez, "Future-oriented Outlook on Society," in *Tradition and Modernism in Black Africa,*

Bouake International Congress, le Seuil, Paris, 1965, p. 293. The author analyzes the conjecture of tradition and modernism in western perspectives; the passing from individualism to an ever increasing communitarian interdependence, to man becoming a person only through recognizing others. The audience immediately accepts this viewpoint without realizing that in Africa the direction (literally "movement") to be taken is quite different.

27. Those who have a special interest in African Theology would do well to think over chapters III and IV of the book by J. B. Metz, already mentioned.

INVESTIGATING AFRICAN
PHILOSOPHY

Richard A. Wright

Introduction

There have been a number of recent studies dealing
with the nature of African philosophy; in particular, there seems
to be considerable concern as to whether or not African philosophy somehow "exists."[1] At first glance the question "Do we have
an African philosophy?" has every sign of innocence; unfortunately, its appearance is deceptive, on two counts. First, the
grammar of the question is similar to questions such as "Do we
have a box of cornflakes?" or "Do we have a final exam in this
course?", questions which we answer by looking. As a result,
we may be misled into thinking that 'African philosophy' is something the existence of which is an empirical matter. That is, if,
in trying to answer the question, we take ourselves to be locating
some object called "African philosophy" we are being misled by
the grammar of the question. What we *are* attempting to locate is
a means for determining whether or not a specific body of African
thought is properly classified as philosophy. Only in this sense
is the question even appropriate; however, as we shall show
below, dealing with the question in *this* sense necessitates assuming the answers to a number of important, prior questions.
Thus, secondly, the question is deceptive because it appears to
require only a simple 'yes' or 'no' answer. As such, it may lull

41

us into simplistic analyses wherein we arrive at our answer but in so doing overlook a number of important considerations.

Our task in this paper will be to try to set out some of these underlying considerations in the hope that both deceptive aspects of the question "Do we have an African Philosophy?" may be better avoided. Unfortunately we cannot undertake an in depth study here, for the requisite studies are far from easy, and they would encompass the work of more than one book, let alone a short paper. To begin, the establishment or verification of a new era for study poses three specific problems: (1) a proper description of the area; (2) adequate delineation of the data to be studied; and (3) establishment of an appropriate methodology for the study of that data, thus the area. W. A. Hart argues that, in addition, two important questions must be answered if there is to be a profitable study of African thought by philosophers: (a) "What is the philosopher that he should be interested in African thought?" and (b) "Is traditional African thought really of a nature to be of interest to the philosopher?"[2]

I agree with Hart, that, until his questions are answered, especially the first, our approach to African thought within the philosophical perspective must be quite careful. However, it is important to acknowledge that there are at least two other significant questions involved in answering those raised by Hart: (c) "What is the nature of philosophy?" and (d) "What constitutes acceptable material for philosophical studies?" For we cannot know what the philosopher is if we do not know what philosophy is, and we cannot know whether traditional African thought is of interest to the philosopher until we know whether it is the sort of thing which is relevant to philosophical consideration.

In order to show the importance of these points to an over-all consideration of African philosophy we shall examine two major papers, H. Maurier's "Do We Have An African Philosophy?" and P. Hountondji's "Comments On Contemporary African Philosophy."[3] Specifically, we will try to show how the writers assume answers to questions (c) and (d) above and how those assumed answers affect their approach to the question "Do we have an African philosophy?" We cannot hope to clearly establish once and for all the validity of any specific claims regarding the nature of African philosophy; however, we should be able to establish a framework within which work in this area may be better analyzed and understood. By seeing how others handle the general issues we will become better equipped to handle the problems ourselves.

Presuppositions

In a new survey Jean-Paul Lebeuf claims that

> [Recent studies have shown] the
> existence [in African thought] of
> perfectly balanced metaphysical systems in
> which all the phenomena of the sensible
> world are bound together in harmony. . . .
> It cannot be said too often that the
> recording of these ontologies has
> rendered accessible a form of thinking
> which is as impeachable in its logic as
> Cartesianism, although quite separate
> from it.[4]

This claim, and others like it (or contradicting it) have raised an important issue: is there an African philosophy and, if so, what is it and how are we to understand it? Lebeuf's claim is important because it directly links African philosophy to Western philosophy through Rene Descartes. As such it is interesting and insightful; moreover, it would not be at all startling were it not for the fact that Henry Maurier was arguing, at nearly the same time, that there is not African philosophy, at least "not yet." How do we deal with this apparent contradiction? How can Maurier and Lebeuf arrive at such seemingly diverse conclusions?

Maurier's position, as presented in "Do We Have An African Philosophy?", is lucid and carefully argued: to do philosophy is to do conceptual analysis; African thinkers do not do conceptual analysis, therefore, African thinkers do not do philosophy. The answer to the question "Do we have an African Philosophy?" is thus seen to hinge on two specific claims; (1) Doing philosophy is doing conceptual analysis, and (2) No African thinkers do conceptual analysis. Moreover, on his view, only a change in (2) will allow a different answer to the question; there can be no African philosophy until African thinkers engage in conceptual analysis. However this further point presupposes the correctness of the claim that philosophy is conceptual analysis.

Since Maurier's assertion rests on two claims, *both* of them must be true if the argument is to be of any value.[5] Given the fact that there are over 40 different countries in Africa, each with a number of different language groups (Ghana, for example, has 95 distinct language groups), Maurier would indeed be hard pressed to support his claim that *no* African does philosophy. But the claim regarding the nature of philosophy is clearly more important to the argument. Maurier thus has a lot of work to do in demonstrating the accuracy of his claim that conceptual analysis is solely constitutive of philosophy. For the question "What is philosophy?" is very broad; moreover, it is fundamental because of the widespread disagreement among philosophers as to its answer.[6] Almost every philosopher has a view as to what constitutes philosophy; and this view is decisive in determination of whether African philosophy exists. That is, as in Maurier's case, one's conception of philosophy will influence what one accepts as philosophical, both in the broad sense and in the sense of 'philosophical materials'. Since there is no widespread opinion on the answer to this question, and since work at its answer is ongoing,[7] it seems presumptuous, at best, to rule out the possibility of African philosophy on this basis.

Paulin Hountondji likewise relies heavily on a view of the nature of philosophy when he argues that a "text" (which we shall see below is not easily described) is "African philosophy" if, and only if, (i) the author is African, and (ii) the author describes his own work as philosophic.[8] If either of these criteria remain unmet, then the materials in question may not properly be called "African philosophy."

Aside from the fact that this is an extremely narrow definition, and apart from the questions which may be raised regarding the scope of its terms (is 'African' to include Egyptian?), Hountondji's claim entails two significant problematic assertations: (1) there are no general, objective, or universal characteristics of or criteria for what may be called philosophy; and (2) philosophy is somehow nationalistically, or at least geographically based (depending on how one construes 'African'). Perhaps these assertions are simply an effort to bring attention to the fact that Africa may require unique considerations and that Africans hold unique philosophical views. Yet the assertions do need very careful evaluation, simply because they encompass definitive elements which are far from readily accepted in analyses of the nature of philosophy.

The assertion that there are no general, objective, or universal characteristics of or criteria for what may be called "philosophy" if correct, surely disposes of Maurier's claim. There *is* African philosophy if at least one African claims that he is doing philosophy.

Unfortunately, this move does not really get us anywhere because we must ask, at some point, how an individual determines whether what he is doing is philosophical. If the answer involves some criteria or other, we are back to Maurier's line of argument. However, if the answer is that we only have subjective ideas, feelings perhaps, and no formal criteria, then we destroy the distinction between reasonable and unreasonable discourse because the same thing could count as philosophy at one time but not at another. In this sense then, the question "Do we have an African philosophy?" becomes trivial and uninteresting; moreover, African philosophy could not exist as a subject area, since a subject area by definition, involves consensus and relativism disallows consensus. Thus Hountondji's criterion if applied to its logical conclusion, is self defeating and must be rejected.

Before moving on to the second assertion it is worth noting that, apart from the difference of absolute vs. relative criterion, the disagreement between Maurier and Hountondji also involves the problem of whether method or content is to be a factor in determining correct application of the label 'philosophy'. Maurier's argument entails the assumption that the substance of philosophical inquiry, at least regarding one topic or another, is less important than *how* one goes about that inquiry. Thus for Maurier, methodological considerations are the final arbiter. On the other hand, Hountondji's argument presupposes that content or substance of inquiry is crucial, while method of inquiry is irrelevant, to determining whether some inquiry is philosophical. The problem with both approaches is that you must establish ahead of time what is an allowable matter for study. But to establish ahead of time restrictions which preclude the open consideration of the full gamut of topics traditionally the concern of philosophers seems contrary to the spirit of philosophical inquiry. For this reason, establishment of restrictions requires far more argument and support than either writer has given.

The second of Hountondji's assertions, that philosophy is somehow nationalistically, or geographically based, is also problematic. Briefly put, to suggest that philosophy may be nationalistically based (or geographically based) seems to entail the possibility that *all* academic disciplines may be nationalistically or geographically based. Thus, on analogy, African physics should be that physics practiced by an African and recognized by himself as physics. This, however, is absurd. Could Hountondji be arguing this position, none the less?

45

The answer must be "No," primarily because philosophy is unlike physics in a number of important ways. In particular, there is a body of knowledge which we call 'physics', a 'universal physics' if you will. As such the African physicist is not practicing 'African physics', whatever that might be, but is instead applying physics to an African situation. Philosophy, on the other hand, has no such claims, Hountondji seems to argue. There is no body of knowledge which is philosophy and within which all philosophers work and to which all philosophers subscribe. Accordingly, there *is* nothing which the African may apply to his situation, as in the physics analogy. Instead, he must formulate and apply his philosophy as he proceeds; since he is African, the result is necessarily African philosophy.

Clearly this argument rests on the first assertions, that there is no objective basis for determining what is philosophical. If there were, then there would be a body of knowledge, called "philosophy," to be learned and applied. There is also a new element here, what J. E. Wiredu calls the "universalist," and the "nationalist" approaches to philosophy. [9] Wiredu points out that some philosophers (among whom I would count Hountondji) hold that, since philosophical concerns are personal, and since a person's needs, surroundings, education, etc., differ from country to country, there can be little value in studying or working with the philosophical views of another country. Instead, the argument goes, each should stay in his own area of concern, steep himself in the philosophical views and traditions of his own nation, and let it go at that.

Responding to his argument, Wiredu reminds his readers of a distinction worth noting here:

> ...[There is] a certain fluctuation in the connotation of the word "philosophy"...a shift back and forth from the broad sense of the word in which philosophy is, so to speak, a guide to the living of life, to the narrower concept of philosophy as a theoretical discipline full, (in the ideal), of minute and elaborate argumentation. [10]

Accordingly, we need to be certain, at all times, of the sense of 'philosophy' in our discussion. For, as Wiredu notes, there are legitimate nationalistic concerns in the first, "living of life" sense of philosophy, but *not* in the second. Again, quoting Wiredu,

> For instance, the truth value of a
> proposition to the effect that God is
> Three in One...should be arguable on
> grounds other than who propounded it,
> provided that responsible definitions are
> available for the crucial terms.[11]

Moreover, Wiredu concludes,

> Unless all issues of philosophy are
> called *issues* only by courtesy, some phil-
> osophical positions must be nearer the
> truth than others, independently of the
> place of enunciation.[12]

Thus, if we are dealing with theoretical issues, then philosophers are, in some sense, working on a universal, non-relative level at which nationalistic concerns are irrelevant. However, when working at the level where philosophy is a guide to living life, what might be called "normative" philosophy, nationalistic (as well as other relativistic claims) are germane and proper.

In this way Wiredu's distinction and subsequent discussion suggests a way out of our difficulty. We must analyze our problems and determine which sense of 'philosophy' applies; this accomplished we may proceed to our analyses, bringing to bear the universal or nationalistic elements as relevant. Actually, it seems that it is precisely this approach which gives philosophy its immense richness. By seeing how different people, with different cultural backgrounds deal with these universal questions, we are all able to come away with greater understanding and insight. As W. A. Hart puts it, "the philosopher's interest in an alien and unfamiliar way of thought is in making it as a means of enlarging his conception of what thinking itself is."[13] Moreover, Hart continues,

> What the philosopher acquires by
> this means is not an alternative mode of
> thought, nor some mere adjunct to his
> original mode of thought; it is a mode of
> thought in which the two original elements
> are fused together....[14]

Thus, to do philosophy at all, we must be open to diversity in a way which Hountondji and Maurier would disallow. For this reason, their assertions are self-defeating and must be rejected. Instead, we must proceed as Wiredu and Hart suggest, trying to understand diversity of thought, trying to place it in the context of the whole of philosophy, trying to piece together the giant puzzle of human understanding.

Ultimately, then, the determination of perspective in African philosophy is seen to be couched in terms of a definition of philosophy, be it argued or implicit; and the ferreting out of such a definition is a crucial prerequisite to the full understanding of any work which purports to deal with philosophical matters. It thus becomes incumbent upon the reader to discern and analyze papers for their presuppositions, their entailed views, and their controversial assumptions. When a label is used, such as 'philosophy', 'religion', etc., one must be wary of its basis; when differences seem obvious, as between Lebeuf, Hountondji and Maurier over the existence of African philosophy, or as between Oguah and Wiredu[15] over the degree to which African and Western philosophy may be compared, we must try to determine the basis for the difference. Hopefully, the discussion of problems above will facilitate this analysis and lead to a fuller, richer understanding of the views presented.

At this point someone might object that the problems raised above in fact show the impossibility of studies such as those in the present volume. Contrary to presenting a case that no effort should be made to establish African philosophy as a study area, these points simply show the direction which such an effort must take. However, the arguments relevant to these problems are neither singular nor mutually exclusive; we thus see varied emphases, alternative solutions and diverse perspectives, as writers attempt to formulate a coherent rationale and methodology for further studies. So that such work might be understood more clearly, let us take a moment now to detail some of the additional considerations and presuppositions which they entail.

Methods and Materials

Initially, plausible reasons must be given for attempting an area study such as ours, and most authors hold three as of fundamental importance: (1) the thought of the African people is intrinsically valuable and should be studied for that reason, if for no other; (2) it is important to the history of ideas that we discover and understand the relation between (or influence of) African thought and the thought of the Western world. For, if Western civilization had its origin on the African continent, as many anthropologists now argue,[16] the correct pattern of intellectual development, and the proper relationship of influences, will only become clear as we begin to understand the basis and direction of that development. And, as mentioned earlier, (3) it is important in understanding practical affairs that we clearly delineate their underlying philosophical motivation.

At the same time, consideration of these matters is not isolated from the task of describing the subject area, specifying its data, or at least its data base, and establishing an appropriate methodology for use in the proposed studies. In fact, a fully plausible argument must cover all these matters. But, since space is necessarily limited, some considerations may be presupposed; accordingly, we need to look now at issues which are important to but not specifically discussed in most other papers.

Description of a subject area must include, or presuppose, the time span which will be covered. For example, are we going to consider the philosophical thought of Africa only in contemporary times, since the turn of the century, or for as far back in history as materials are available? This determination is crucial because if, for example, we were interested in the evolution of ideas, an indefinite time span would be appropriate, while if we were only concerned with the relation between technological development and changing philosophical viewpoints, a span encompassing only the era of technology might be adequate, although some work prior to that time would be necessary to establish norms against which the proposed analyses could be carried out. Moreover, the time element may determine the type, quantity, or range of materials to be considered in the study. Thus, in Olela's paper (in this book) the emphasis is on ancient thought, so the range of study is severely limited by available resources, whereas Neuberger's paper (also in this book) being concerned with contemporary issues might not be so limited.

To further complicate matters, the designation of time span may itself be influenced by another decision, viz., specific inclusion (or exclusion) of any given topic, such as slavery, political theory, or comparative studies based on dated Western ideas. On the other hand, a decision to deal with general topics, such as belief in God, the development of philosophically important concepts, etc., would necessitate an indefinite time span.

In addition to these obviously inter-dependent matters, there is also the question of geographical areas to be considered. Which peoples are we labeling 'African'? Are we going to deal with the thought of the Egyptians, Lybians and Ethiopians in our study of African philosophy? Or are we going to limit ourselves to Black Africa? A decision on this matter might be made in

49

terms of subjects of interest; for example, consideration of the political philosophy inherent in pan-African nationalism would preclude analysis of Egyptian political systems, at least as that subject is normally construed. In contrast, an interest in comparative studies of pre-scientific African thought and pre-scientific Western thought would, of necessity, sooner or later encompass Egyptian thought, since the early Greeks and the Egyptians (at least) were known to have interacted, as did the Egyptians and Black Africans.[17]

Just as time span, topic, and geographical considerations affect the description of a study area, they also affect the agreement of writers on precisely what is to count as acceptable material for study, since some materials relevant to one topic or geographical distinction, might be extraneous to another. In short, we need to consider one further matter, the sources for study and the methodology for the use of those sources.

Traditionally, philosophical studies are based on some systematically identifiable body of literature. A survey of philosophical literature will soon reveal extensive bibliography on Greek philosophy, Medieval philosophy, Anglo-American philosophy, Indian philosophy, etc., yet even the most diligent scholar will be hard pressed to find similar materials classified as African philosophy, despite the increased scholarship on Africa over the past decade. Moreover, omission of other than cursory attention to philosophical considerations within the normal range of African studies is no doubt intentional; but, given that these studies are usually undertaken by scholars with anthropological, sociological or historical interests, the omission is not completely unreasonable. To support African philosophy as a study area then obligates the supporter to produce such a body of literature. The difficulty is that there is no such literature available; in particular, there are no works by individual authors equivalent to, for instance, Aristotle's *Metaphysics,* Hume's *Treatise of Human Nature,* or Kant's *Critique of Pure Reason.* Does this mean that there can be no such thing as African philosophy?

One genuine concern in dealing with this question is the basic assumption that philosophy necessarily relies on published literature. We may grant that thought, which is the essence and substance of philosophy, must have an expression to be considered and analyzed. Further, this expression must be transmitted if analysis is to be other than solipsistic. The difficulty lies in trying to insist upon written, published expression as the only means adequate for philosophical purposes. The need for an expressive medium does not present a *prima facie* case for the exclusivity of written literature, especially if the latter is construed as original books and papers by specific authors. Such an assumption is clearly seen to be questionable if we note that this standard would remove Socrates from philosophical roles, since he apparently never wrote a single treatise. In short, this narrow approach to thought analysis demands in advance certain materials, thereby effectively stifling inquiry into diverse areas. When studying African thought we must rely on stories, oral tradition, ritual, social institutions, and so forth, as purveyors of thought.[18] These materials must be treated on a par with literature as traditionally considered for purposes of philosophical inquiry. These serve as the data for analysis of African philosophical thought, so that, when taken together with the analytical writings of other scholars, such as anthropologists, sociologists, and historians, we have a substantial basis for our studies. Admittedly, this still does not supply us with an African equivalent to Aristotle's *Metaphysics,* but it surely supplies us with a corpus for study from which a great deal may be learned.

Once a decision has been reached, even tentatively, concerning the description of subject area and the circumscription of materials for study, we must come to grips with the problems of methodology. How are we to approach our study of African philosophy? This is also a complex matter, with at least two major considerations. First, what is to be the framework for study. In order to work with the thought of the African people, do we have to go live among them, as Tempels suggested?[19] Or is it reasonable to say, as Hountondji proposes that, in the final analysis, only a native African is able to correctly study, analyze and interpret the thought of African people?[20] Or, may we take a middle position, viz., it is reasonable to assume that scholars outside the field area may legitimately and accurately study, analyze and interpret the materials gathered by others in the field area?

The first two views are initially plausible but ultimately unacceptable. Their plausibility lies in the obvious point that, if we are to use oral traditions, social institutions, etc., as our study materials, collection and initial interpretation must only be done by someone intimate with the source of the materials, i.e., in the field where one has long experience, only when one is bilingual, well versed in the customs and culture of the area, and so on. However, the limitation of all studies to such persons is ultimately too narrow a means of analysis, if for no other reason than objectivity. Materials must thus be disseminated to a wide range of scholars for examination. In this way, we may make use of work by those in the field, as well as those outside the field, no matter what discipline, provided only that they are dealing with the thought of the people in question. In this alone will the broader perspective of multi-disciplinary analysis be brought to bear on our understanding of African philosophical thought.

The second consideration, which arises when the source and distribution of materials have been decided upon, is how they are to be used and analyzed. Do we simply take the corpus of Western philosophy, for instance, as some sort of 'yardstick' against which to measure (in some way) the African philosophy? While such methodology does have the advantage of giving one a place to start, two distinct disadvantages result. By looking in African thought for manifestations of Western ideas, one subjects oneself either to the onerous possibility of 'finding' those ideas solely on the basis of looking, or overlooking significant differences through concentration on obvious similarities. Further, this approach, again as an initial methodology, promotes the fallacy of 19th century thinkers, that Africa has nothing to offer on its own except in so far as the offering is a reflection of the European/American 'civilizing' influence.[21]

At the same time, it is unreasonable to completely exclude the comparative studies which such a methodology facilitates. If we are to avoid the difficulties of this approach, yet retain its merits, an alternative method of concept analysis must be determined. Such an alternative may in fact be at the heart of the work by Tempels, Jahn, and Mbiti, for example.[22] Their approach is ostensibly to deal with concepts, either originally African, or somehow "universal" not in terms of fitting African to Western views but in terms of mapping out the African view on its own. As such, the writer may make a prior determination that the specific concepts will be analyzed, as Jahn does with *Ntu*, and Mbiti with "time." In any event, his object is to understand how, if at all, Africans utilize and understand that concept, all the while making an effort to accomplish the analysis solely in terms of the merits of actual usage, rather than on the basis of inter-cultural comparisons. In this volume, the papers by Minkus and Ayoade are further examples of this approach.

The immediate question, however, is whether someone who has a different conceptual background, such as Jahn or Tempels, as Europeans, and Minkus as an American, will be able to make such an analysis with any degree of objectivity. We might even ask if Africans who have received academic training in Western institutions, e.g., Oguah and Wiredu, will be able to completely divorce the two conceptual influences from each other. The question is open, however, and is in fact dealt with at length by Maurier in his paper; as such, it leaves us with still another problem to be resolved in our work of establishing African philosophy as a subject area. Yet we must have some methodology, and this does present one which allows us both approaches, the conceptual and the comparative, for better or for worse.

By now it must seem that the problems surrounding the study of African philosophy are so great that we are effectively prevented from any worthwhile work until their resolution. If we were to assume that our substantive work could not be accomplished until these issues were settled, we would indeed be unable to move on. But such issues are at the heart of philosophical inquiry and philosophers have long since learned to work around, over and through such problems. For the realization must come that we cannot wait for the settlement of such issues lest nothing at all be done. Why? Because these problems are so fundamental that their answers fully undergird the activity for which we are arguing, the study of African philosophy. If we are unable to reach tentative agreement, or at least air and define our disagreements, we will perpetually work on the substratum and never get to the substance. Thus, in a spirit of progress, while recognizing that revisions may be required sooner or later we must assume that there is a subject area correctly called "African philosophy," that its tenets may legitimately be found in the types of literature mentioned earlier, and that its fundamental conceptual framework and content may be profitably compared with "Western philosophy" on some grounds, at least. But we must keep firmly before us the fact that each writer on the subject will have resolved, for himself, the issues discussed above, and it should be instructive to note whether, and how, such resolution affects the results of his work. Only by taking this metaphilosophical position will we be able to properly assess their work and eventually determine the nature of African philosophy and its rightful place in intellectual history.

RICHARD A. WRIGHT

FOOTNOTES

1. For example, see the following articles, whose complete references are given in the Bibliography: Botolo (1974), Finazza (1974), Horton (1967) Hountondji (forthcoming), Mabona (1967), Oruka (1975), Postioma (1969 and 1972), and Ruch (1974)

2. W. A. Hart. "The Philosopher's Interest in African Thought." *Cahiers philosophiques africains* 1 (1972):62

3. Maurier's article appears in this book, while Hountondji's appeared in *Diogenes* 71 (1970):109-130

4. As quoted in Hart "Philosopher's Interest," p. 61

5. From a logical point of view, the validity of this argument requires both premises to be universal propositions, thus the only way Maurier's argument may be sound is if the premises are both true. If it is false that all philosophy is conceptual analysis, or if it is false that no African thinker engages in conceptual analysis, then regardless of the validity of the argument, it is unsound, thus of little value. Given the points made here concerning both claims, it would seem that the only remedy is to make either or both premises of the argument into particular propositions. However, this move changes the character of the argument, making it invalid. Thus the weight is upon Maurier to prove that his two universal claims are in fact true, thus making his argument sound. Without this proof, the argument is either invalid or unsound, neither of which is acceptable for the work at hand.

6. A. Johnson, in his book *What Philosophy Is,* presents materials detailing no fewer than *ten* different views on the nature of philosophy, while C. J. Bontempo's book, *The Owl of Minerva,* contains sixteen views, all cogently argued.

7. There is even a philosophical journal, *Metaphilosophy,*

54

devoted primarily to such discussion.

8.   Hountondji "Comments," p. 109

9.   J. E. Wiredu. "On an African Orientation in Philosophy."
      Second Order 1, No. 2 (1972):3-13

10.   Ibid., p. 9

11.   Ibid., p. 10

12.   Ibid.

13.   Hart "Philosopher's Interest," p. 68

14.   Hart Ibid., p. 72

15.   This disagreement is seen in their papers in this book.

16.   For specific references see the paper by Olela in this
      book; in a popular version, some aspects of this argument
      appear in Basil Davidson, *African Genius* (Boston: Little,
      Brown & Co., 1970)

17.   This point is argued, for instance, by W. K. C. Guthrie
      in his *History of Greek Philosophy,* especially in the
      discussion of Thales which occurs in Volume II.

18.   Kwame Gyekye in "Philosophical Relevance of Akan Prov-
      erbs," *Second Order* 2 (1973):45-53, argues well for
      acceptance of proverbs to this group of sources.

19.   P. Tempels, *Bantu Philosophy,* Presence Africaine, 1959

20.   Hountondji "Comments"

21.   For documentation of this view see again Davidson's *Afri-
      can Genius,* especially Chapter I.

22.   Tempels *Bantu Philosophy; J.* Jahn's *Muntu* (N.Y.: Grove
      Press, 1961); and J. Mbiti's *African Religions and Philoso-
      phy* (N.Y.: Doubleday, 1960). These are not the only
      ones we might consider, but they are well known and
      serve somewhat as pioneering works.

THE AFRICAN PHILOSOPHICAL TRADITION

Lancinay Keita

Because of the experiences of a recent past Africa's intellectual output has been rather meager, except perhaps in the area of literature where individual writers have not been slow to describe life in the precolonial or colonial period. But genuine intellectual work either of a philosophical or scientific nature has not kept pace with the output in pure literature.

The reason for this situation is that there is, perhaps, the belief that there is no genuine African intellectual matrix which could serve as a basis for African scholarship. This belief is fostered by the more current view that the African intellectual experience has been essentially "oral" and "prescientific" as compared, say, with the "literate" and "scientific" tradition of Europe.[1]

The end result of these beliefs has been to encourage African intellectuals either to search for the historical precedents of their own literacy in non-African sources[2] or to express great uncertainty about the definition of the concept of Africanity.

It is the purpose of this paper to present evidence that a sufficiently firm literate philosophical tradition has existed in Africa since ancient times, and that this tradition is of sufficient intellectual sophistication to warrant serious analysis. In this regard, then, this paper does not constitute an attempt to

57

discuss some particular aspect of the admittedly vague concept, African thought; it is rather a position paper--an attempt to offer a defensible idea of an African philosophy.

There have been recent attempts to describe the thought systems of individual African ethnic groups but such works can hardly be considered as genuine examples of African philosophy.[3] The way in which, say, the Ibo people view the world is of as little moment to African philosophy as the particular cultural ontologies of, say, the Vandals, the Vikings, the Basques or the Normans are to European philosophy. Perhaps the way in which the Vikings or Saxons viewed the world would be of interest to the anthropologist, but there has been no attempt to evaluate their respective world-views as examples of philosophical thinking.

A genuine African philosophy (like Chinese, European or Indian philosophy) should constitute the periods of Africa's most articulate efforts throughout its history. Viewed in this way the African philosophical tradition can be easily divided into three distinct phases: (1) classical, (2) medieval and (3) modern. A discussion of these three moments of African philosophy will constitute most of this paper. The discussion of classical African thought will be concerned with the thought systems of Ancient Egypt and their impressive influence on the Hellenic world and later on the highly significant European Renaissance. The discussion on medieval African thought will focus on the African interpretation of Islamic thought during the periods when the medieval African states of Ghana, Mali and Songhay were in existence. Modern African philosophy is, perhaps, less well developed than its two preceding moments, since philosophical traditions have become somewhat distorted as a result of the colonial experience. As a result, the best works, as is expected, are political and literary in nature. However, it should be pointed out that there have been two important intellectual phases in the post colonial period: (1) the Negritude Movement--romantic and ahistorical, (2) the Pan-Africanist Movement--empiricist and historically oriented. This modern period will also be discussed.

The Classical African Thought of Ancient Egypt

Granted that the colonial period in Africa was one in which European nations were in political and economic control of most of Africa, and enjoyed enormous benefits from the servitude imposed on Africans, it is understandable that most of the research done on Africa by European scholars would have tended to describe Africa as necessarily benefiting from colonialism. This approach entailed (a) distortion of African history to fit the belief that Africa was the continent of the uncivilized who should, no doubt, hope to benefit from being brought into contact with European civilization; (b) the usage of spurious anthropological techniques[4] to give the impression of scientific objectivity to the decidedly biased approach to African history.

It is for this reason that the history of Ancient Egypt was severed from the history of the African world and considered, henceforth, as part of the Oriental World--a world which encompasses cultures and peoples as diverse as the Turks, Chinese, Indians and Japanese. The aim, no doubt, was to create a world in which civilization was the patrimony solely of the Western and Eastern peoples with the African world being the receptacle of all that was uncivilized or "primitive"--to use the highly emotive though still current term. The result of this dogmatic approach to cultural history was that those Africans, considered civilized, were considered Oriental or at least were of Oriental origins.

However, sober historical research will not support this view.[5] According to the objective findings of researchers of African cultural history the cultural forms of Ancient Egypt were essentially African as expressed especially in the religion practiced by its inhabitants. For example, the strongly totemic characteristics of Egyptian religious practices are considered by many anthropologists to be essentially African. Furthermore, the written testimonies of Greek visitors to Ancient Egypt leave no doubt as to the ethnic and cultural backgrounds of the Ancient Egyptians. In fact, the belief that the Ancient Egyptians were a non-African people is relatively recent[6] and directly related to the period of European dominance in Africa.

Thus the basis for the thesis that the thought systems of the Ancient Egyptians warrant inclusion in the matrix of African thought systems has been established. It is fair to state that the earliest periods of Egyptian civilization produced thought systems that were, perhaps, excessively conservative (so dominant was the practice of ancestor worship), and it was not until the eighteenth dynasty that an intellectual revolution of some sort occurred. The cosmological revolution introduced by Amenhotep IV was an attempt to introduce a holistic interpretation of the universe guided and explained by one deity as opposed to the then dominant pantheism. The philosophical significance of this short-lived revolution is that it is highly plausible that Egyptian monotheism was of great influence in the shaping of two of the

59

important religions of the area: Judaism and Christianity. Any student of philosophy should know, of course, that philosophy in the Christian and Judaic world was greatly bound up with Christian and Judaic doctrine and, in fact, the main function of philosophy at that time was to justify the ontological claims of these two religious systems.

However, the major corpus of Egyptian philosophy was not made known to the outside world until the second or third centuries A. D. The body of Ancient Egyptian philosophy which became a source of interest to the outside world is generally known as the *Hermetica,* and the reasons for this interest, according to one scholar of the European Renaissance is as follows: "The world of the second century was weary of Greek dialectics which seemed to lead to no certain results. Platonists, Stoics, Epicureans could only repeat the theories of their various schools without making any further advances, and the tenets of the schools were boiled down in textbook form, in manuals which formed the basis of philosophical instruction within the Empire."[7]

The interest in the *Hermetica* derived from the fact that:

> This world of the second century was, however, seeking intensively for knowledge of reality, for an answer to its problems which the normal education failed to give. It turned to other ways of seeking an answer, intuitive, mystical, magical. Since reason seemed to have failed, it sought to cultivate the *Nous,* the intuitive faculty of man. Philosophy was to be used, not as a dialectical exercise, but as a way of reaching intuitive knowledge of the divine and of the meaning of the world, as a gnosis, in short, to be prepared for by ascetic discipline and a religious way of life. The Hermetic treatises, which often take the form of dialogues between master and disciple, usually culminate in a kind of ecstasy in which the adept is satisfied that he has received an illumination and breaks out into hymns of praise. He seems to reach this illumination through contemplation of the world or the cosmos, or rather through contemplation of the cosmos as

> reflected in his *Nous* or *mens* which sepa-
> rates out for him its divine meaning and
> gives him a spiritual mastery over it, as
> in the familiar gnostic revelation or expe-
> rience of the ascent of the soul through
> the spheres of the planets to become
> immersed in the divine. Thus that relig-
> ion of the world which runs as an under-
> current in much of Greek thought,
> particularly in Platonism and Stoicism,
> becomes in Hermetism actually a religion,
> followed in the mind alone, a religious
> philosophy or philosophical religion
> containing a gnosis.[8]

Clearly the strongly metaphysical nature of Hermetic thought would suggest its essentially African content. One traditional feature of African ontology (developed to its highest expression by the Ancient Egyptians) is that it is predominantly monist in outlook. The dualist cleavage between mind and matter which characterizes much discussion in modern European philosophy[9] did not exist for the Ancient Egyptian priest.

The neo-Greek interest in Egyptian thought at the time when "The mighty intellectual effort of the Greek philosophy was exhausted, had come to a standstill, to a dead end" did not develop, as Yates suggests, "because Greek thinking never took the momentous step of experimental verification of its hypotheses" but because (and it would appear somewhat paradoxical) pure empiricism has its limitations in that it leads to a simple-minded Baconian approach to the material world. Scientific progress and insights occur when science adopts a holistic view of the world, and attempts to go beyond the merely empirically given data to construct theories which contain elements which could be controversial to the pure empiricist. It is for this reason that metaphysical elements in the works of Newton, Leibniz and Einstein are understandable.

Thus the Greek return to the Egyptians is not without some logic, and it set the foundations for the all-important scientific breakthroughs of Bruno, Copernicus *et al*. As Yates writes, "The men of the second century were thoroughly imbued with the idea (which the Renaissance imbibed from them) that what is old is pure and hold, that the earliest thinkers walked more closely with the gods than the busy rationalists, their successors."[10] And more importantly:

Above all, it was the Egyptians who were
revered in this age. Egyptian temples
were still functioning, and devout seekers
after religious truth and revelation in the
Graeco-Roman world would make pilgrim-
ages to some remotely situated Egyptian
temple and pass the night in its vicinity
in the hope of receiving some vision of
divine mysteries in dreams. The belief
that Egypt was the original home of all
knowledge, that the great Greek philosophers had visited it and conversed with
Egyptian priests, had long been current,
and, in the mood of the second century,
the ancient and mysterious religion of
Egypt, the supposed profound knowledge
of its priests, their ascetic way of life,
the religious magic which they were
thought to perform in the subterranean
chambers of their temples, offered
immense attractions. It is this pro-Egyp-
tian mood of the Graeco-Roman world
which is reflected in the Hermetic Asclepius with its strange description of the
magic by which the Egyptian priests
animated the statues of their gods, and
its moving *prophecy* that the most ancient
Egyptian religion is destined to come to
an end.[11]

But the influence of Egyptian thought did not end with
the Greeks, it was of lasting influence on the shaping of European medieval and Renaissance thought. "It was on excellent
authority that the Renaissance accepted *Hermes Trismegistus* as a
real person of great antiquity and as the author of the Hermetic
writings, for this was implicitly believed by leading fathers of the
Church particularly Lactantius and Augustine."[12]

It has been established so far that the thought systems
of the Ancient Egyptians warrant attention in any discussion of
African thought. It has also been argued that certain features of
Egyptian thought were attractive to the Greeks (and later to the
medieval world) in a sort of neo-Egyptian philosophical revival.
Thus it is pertinent at this stage to discuss the essential features
of Egyptian philosophy as expressed in the classical work *Corpus
Hermetica.*

According to Clement of Alexandria, there were forty-two books written by Hermes, of which "thirty-six contain the whole of the philosophy of the Egyptians, the other six being on medicine."[13] These books possessed an extensively mystical tone which was a source of intense interest to the European scholar of the Renaissance. Again, according to Yates: "Nevertheless it is probable that Hermes Trismegistus is the most important figure in the Renaissance revival of magic. Egypt was traditionally associated with the darkest and strongest magic, and now there were brought to light the writings of an Egyptian priest which revealed an extraordinary piety, confirming the high opinion of him which the Christian Father, Lactantius, had expressed, and whom the highest authorities regarded as the source of Plato."[14]

This metaphysical interpretation of the world colored the Egyptian cosmology and philosophy of man and nature. The universe was perceived as being in perpetual animated motion, the expression of a single supreme creator.[15] The structure of this universe was indestructible since "nothing that is in the world will ever perish or be destroyed, for Eternity is imperishable." (*Ibid.*, p. 33)

Egyptian philosophy espoused not only the idea of the oneness and indestructible nature of the universe, (perhaps an intuitive prelude to the conservation laws of modern physical science) but also that the universe was a universe constantly energized and in perpetual motion.[16]

Concerning the nature of man, Egyptian philosophy expressed views that are quite sophisticated and are interestingly similar to those expressed by the Classical Greek thinkers on the nature of man. Man's intellect or rational faculties are derived from "the very substance of God." Thus the godlike characteristics of man are embodied in his rational faculties; and men who live by the fullest exercising of their intellects are close to the gods. On the other hand, when "man is not guided by intellect, he falls below himself into an animal state." (Yates, p. 33) The general thesis on the nature of man is that man partakes of the world of the gods by virtue of his intellect but yet is part of the animal world.[17]

Contrary to accepted doctrine, the philosophy of the Ancient Egyptians exercised great influence on the European Renaissance, for the name of "Hermes Trismegistus was well known in the Middle Ages and was connected with alchemy, and magic, particularly with magic images or talismans. The Middle

Ages feared whatever they knew of the decans as dangerous demons, and some of the books supposedly by Hermes were strongly censured by Albertus Magnus as containing diabolical magic. The Augustian censure of the demon-worship in the Asclepius (by which he may have meant in particular, decan worship) weighed heavily upon that work. However, medieval writers interested in natural philosophy speak of him with respect; for Roger Bacon he was the 'father of Philosophers,' and he is sometimes given a genealogy which makes him even more ancient than Ficino or the designer of the Siena mosaic thought."[18]

But perhaps the Egyptian thinker's most important legacy to modern science is the role the Hermetic paradigm played in the scientific revolution that took place in Western Europe in the seventeenth century. "Taking a very long view down the avenues of time a beautiful and coherent line of development suggests itself--perhaps too beautiful and coherent to be quite true. The late antique world, unable to carry Greek science forward any further, turned to the religious cult of the world and its accompanying occultisms and magics of which the writings of 'Hermes Trismegistus' are an expression... . In the long medieval centuries, both in the West and the Arabic world, the traditions of rational Greek science made progress. Hence it is now suggested, when 'Hermes Trismegistus' and all that he stood for is rediscovered in the Renaissance, the return to the occult of this time stimulates the genuine science." (Yates, pp. 449-50)

In other words radical changes in scientific reasoning initiated by such theorists as Bruno, Descartes and Newton were in some measure influenced by Egyptian thought.

However, Yates' interesting observations notwithstanding, there are grounds for further comment on the supposed opposition between Greek rationalism and Egyptian animism. It should be remembered that although the Greeks expressed an interest in scientific theories, they were not scientists in the true sense of the word. They did not seem aware of the fact that the validity of scientific theories depends on their capacities to undergo experimental testings.

The Egyptians, on the other hand, were well acquainted with empirical methods of research as their extensive architecture and medical reseaches signify. But purely empirical observations were not sufficient for the Egyptians; their empirical observations assumed explanatory status on being placed within the context of the Egyptian cosmology. Thus there are two aspects of the

Egyptian ontology: the empirical aspect based on the data of empirical observation, and the metaphysical aspect which sought to offer ultimate explanation for the physical data of the world.

It is of interest to note that in the Egyptian cosmology empiricism and metaphysics were complementary, the former affording facts about the world, and the latter serving as their ultimate explanation.   The Greeks, on the other hand, eagerly accepted the materialism of the Egyptians but tended to be less enthusiastic about their metaphysics, notwithstanding the Greek interest in the *Hermetica* in the second century.[19] However, the point being made is that European philosophy has inherited the tradition of the Greeks in which the material world is perceived as antithetical to the metaphysical rather than complementary to it, as was the case with the Egyptians.   And it was this reunion of the two ontologies that "stimulates the genuine science" in the seventeenth century.   The remarkable revolution of the seventeenth century could perhaps be explained by the timely fusion of the two major traditions of Egyptian thought; the empirist and the metaphysical, the one kept alive by the early Greeks, the latter nurtured by the later Greeks and nurtured by the Renaissance. According to Yates: "It may be illuminating to view the scientific revolution as in two phases, the first phase consisting of an animistic universe operated by magic, the second phase of a mathematical universe operated by mechanics.   An enquiry into both phases, and their interaction, may be a more fruitful line of historical approach to the problems raised by the science of today than the line which concentrates only on the seventeenth century triumph.   Is not all science a gnosis, an insight into the nature of the All, which proceeds by successive revelations?"[20]

The thought systems of the Ancient Egyptians represent the most literate expression of the African in ancient history. These thought systems were based on the essentially African view of the world as being both subject to empirical and metaphysical interpretation.   For the African the pursuit of metaphysics is an attempt to grapple with gnosis--to explain the life and motion that energizes the material world.   And this is basically the world view, not only of the Ancient Egyptian priest, but also of the African peasant.   The historical legacy of the classical thought of ancient Africa is modern science which began to develop in the seventeenth century.   It is of interest to note the indebtedness that Isaac Newton, the key scientific figure of the seventeenth Century, ascribes to the pioneering work of classical Africa.

It was the ancient opinion of not a
few, in the earliest ages of philosophy,

that the fixed stars stood immovable in the highest parts of the world; that under the fixed stars the planets were carried about the sun; that the earth, as one of the planets, described an annual course about the sun, while by a diurnal motion it was in the meantime revolved about its own axis; and the sun, as the common fire which served to warm the whole, was fixed in the centre of the universe.

This was the philosophy taught of old by *Philolaus, Aristarchus of Samos, Plato* in his riper years, and the whole sect of the *Pythagoreans;* and this was the judgement of *Anaximander,* more ancient still ...

The *Egyptians* were early observers of the heavens; and from them, probably, this philosophy was spread among other nations; for from them that it was, and the nations about them, that the *Greeks,* a people more addicted to the study of philology than of Nature, derived their first, as well as soundest notions of philosophy; and in the vestal ceremonies we may yet trace the ancient spirit of the Egyptians; for it was their way to deliver their mysteries, that is, their philosophy of things above the common way of thinking, under the veil of religious rites and hieroglyphic symbols.[21]

It is of some interest to note that Newton's major contribution to science (or natural philosophy as it was then called) was the creation of a theory that encompassed both terrestrial and celestial mechanics, but the Newtonian theory was put to the test most in its explanations of the motions of heavenly bodies. In other words the all-important principle of universal gravitation was essentially a principle of astronomy. It is in this context that one best appreciates Newton's confessed indebtedness to ancient Africa.

African Thought in Medieval Africa

The decline of Ancient Egypt as an independent center of African civilization began with the alien occupation by younger spheres of military power such as Greece, Rome, Persia and Byzantium, and culminated with the invasion by the Arabs in the seventh century. Islamic thought was subsequently introduced to North Africa, and subsequently to the Medieval states of Central Africa by means of trade and travel. Thus literate expression in Medieval Africa was strongly influenced by Islamic modes of expression. This particular situation could be compared with the spread of Christian thought from the Middle East into Europe during the European medieval period, or the spread of Buddhism from India to China.

However, contrary to what is commonly believed, Islamic thought did not introduce thought systems that were essentially Arabic into Africa. It can be safely said that the function of the nomadic Arabs were to serve as carriers or conduits of those ancient ideas of the African Egyptians, modified by the Greeks, into Southern Europe and Central Africa. The main original characteristic of the Islamic thought introduced to central Africa during the times of medieval Africa was that it was expressed in Arabic, in much the same way that scholars in medieval Europe communicated with each other in Latin and not in their respective natural languages. Even in the area of religious doctrine the Islamic contribution is strikingly unoriginal. It is mainly a synthesis of Ancient Egyptian, Judaic and Christian elements, but once again expressed in Arabic, which no doubt gives the Moslem's religion an appearance of authenticity.

Islam's simple role as carrier of the ideas developed in settled civilizations is well expressed thus: "In literature, in science, in Muslim canon law, in theology, and even in the scientific treatment of Arabic grammar, the Persians very rapidly surpassed the Arabs, so that we must be careful always to refer to Arabic philosophy, etc., remembering that, though expressed in the Arabic language, the common medium of all the Muslim world, only in a very few cases was it the work of Arabs: for the most part the Arabic philosophers and scientists, historians, grammarians, theologians, and jurists were Persians, Turks, or Berbers by birth, though using the Arabic language."[22]

As was mentioned above, the Arabic language was used, not to express new ideas but the Greek synthesis of the thought systems of Africa and Asia. Again:

One of the first and most significant
indications of the new orientation of
Muslim thought was the extensive production of Arabic translations of works dealing with philosophical and scientific
subjects, with the result that eighty
years after the fall of the Umayyads the
Arabic speaking world possessed Arabic
translations of the greater part of the
works of Aristotle, of the leading neo-
Platonic commentators, of some of the
works of Plato, of the greater part of the
works of Galen, and portions of other
medical writers and their commentators,
as well as of other Greek scientific works
and of various Indian and Persian writings.[23]

And the writings of the Greeks were taken not only to
Western Europe, but into the Sudanic states of Central Africa
where intellectual work of an impressive order was carried on.
In much the same way that non-Arabs constituted the majority of
the intelligentsia in the North African and Middle Eastern centers
of research, so too the scholars in Central Africa, though bearing
Muslim names, were African in the main. Witness the following
from C. A. Diop commenting on the same theme with reference to
the *Tarikh es Soudan:*

Dans le chapitre X de cet ouvrage, on
trouve les biographies de dix-sept
savants de Tomboucton avec l'indication
de toutes les matieres qu'ils avaient assi-
milees. Presque tous sont des dialecti-
ciens, des rhetoriciens, des grammairiens,
des juristes, etc. ... qui, en plus, ont
ecrit des ourvages dont les titres son
mentionnes, mais non encore retrouves
pour la plupart. L'un d'entre eux, le
celebre Ahmad Baba aurait laisse plus de
700 ouvrages.

...

Les savants soudanais du "Moyen Age"
africain etaient de la meme classe intel-
lectuelle que leurs collegues arabes; its
etaient meme parfois plus forts.[24]

The introduction of the thought systems of the Hellenic synthesis into medieval Africa served the function of reintroducing to Africa in a second phase the ancient original thought of the Africans of Ancient Egypt, this time with the nomadic Arab as carrier and Arabic the language of communication. The same phenomenon occurred in Western Europe: the Moslem invasion of southwestern Europe introduced, in an admittedly circuitous way, Greek philosophy and science to Western Europe and thereby paved the way for the important Renaissance. But what is of interest though is that in much the same way that the Islamic culture sought to indigenize foreign intellectual inputs by translations into Arabic, so too European culture accepted the Greek content of Islamic philosophy and science, but instead used the linguistic vehicle of Latin.

On the other hand the medieval African philosopher preferred to retain Arabic as the language of intellectual expression possibly because of trade and economic ties with the Middle Eastern centers of Islam, and because of the growing universality of Arabic in the Afro-Asiatic world. The European scholar could afford to reject Arabic because it was accompanied by a religion that could pose a threat to an already firmly entrenched Christianity; and Latin was already the language of the Church. It was Greek and Latin that nurtured to maturity the tribal languages of pre-Renaissance Europe. Thus although it was Islam that introduced modern Europe to Greek thought the European philosopher was able to remain within the Greco-Roma intellectual ambit by using Latin as the language of the philosopher, and by maintaining the memory of the Greeks in the terms and concepts of science and mathematics.[25]

The medieval African philosopher could have done the same by rejecting Arabic for the language of the Ancient Egyptians. But the memory of Ancient Egypt's monumental efforts were lost in history. And this phenomenon occurred despite the cultural and linguistic similarities between the important medieval African states and Ancient Egypt.[26]

The fall of the ancient states of Sudanic Africa announced a new era in the history of Africa. Africa was first victim of a long slave trade of more than four centuries duration, and then victim of a period of colonization by those same European powers grown economically and technologically powerful as a result of the surplus created by African labor in the New World. The result of these two phenomena has been a cultural anomie of the African transplanted to the New World and a state of amnesia of the contemporary African whose knowledge of history and

philosophy is limited to European thought systems. That pre-colonial Africa witnessed a classical and medieval period is not
common knowledge among modern day African thinkers.

Philosophy in Contemporary Africa

It would not be an exaggeration to argue that there is
no systematic body of knowledge expounded by African thinkers
today that could rightfully be labelled African philosophy. The
reason for this situation is easily explainable by appealing to the
colonial experience. The pressures of the colonial system rein-
forced with the cultural baggage of the dominant colonial powers
have not permitted the African time to reflect on the thought
systems of the African past, to theorize about such philosophical
concepts as the good society; the nature of mathematics, or to
comment on the writings of the ancient Africans of Ancient Egypt
and Medieval Africa.

There have been, of course, writings by African thinkers and poets of the Nigritude school,[27] but Negritude cannot
rightly be considered a philosophical movement--it is rather a
literary-poetic movement attempting to comment on, or explain the
plight of the transplanted or colonized African. The movement is
important in the sense that it points out the psychological problems confronted by the African intellectual who, as a result of the
colonial experience is made to believe in and apologize for a
historical past not as human or civilized as that of the colonizer.
The African thinker is goaded (with appropriate reinforcements)
to exult in a past that has been mainly aliterate and alogical and
excessively emotional. In a world in which the African thinker is
made to perceive himself as a tyro among the so-called civilized,
he is forced to justify his existence only by defending those
traits imposed on him by the colonizer. And the Negritude movement illustrates this point best. Even among those thinkers relatively untouched by the Negritude movement one perceives a
general advocating of the theory that systematic thought was
unknown in Africa until the advent of the colonizers.[28] The
European culture is literate, logical and scientific; African culture
is oral, superstitious, and aphilosophical.

Yet a sober appraisal of the facts will demonstrate that
of all the world's cultures the first to engage in any systematic
appraisal of the world was African--that of Ancient Egypt, and
that those cultures considered steeped in philosophy and science
were in reality great borrowers. The English philosopher seeks
inspiration from the Greeks, not from his direct ancestors who

inhabited Scandinavia. Chinese philosophy is not *sui generis* as is commonly thought. The Chinese accepted the thought systems of the Indians and modified them to suit their own cultural needs.[29] Witness the following from Hajime Nakamura, an authority on Eastern thought:

> The Chinese did not accept Buddhism in its Indian form. After it was introduced into China, it was modified under the influence of certain traditional ways of thinking of the Chinese, so that Chinese Buddhism diverged from Indian Buddhism to a very great degree. The following facts about that influence indicate the nature and extent of these divergencies:
>
> (1) The Chinese made complete translations of the Buddhist scriptures into their own language. They did not use Sanskrit or Pakrit as the sacred language of the Buddhist Church.
> (2) In translating, Chinese scholars and exegetes often gave peculiarly adapted interpretations of the original. Thus the Indian texts were not always faithfully translated. Interpolations were often added. The sentences were frequently embellished with Chinese literary ornament, thus taking on the appearance of Chinese literature.[30]

Thus it is a conservative statement to make that the great thought systems of the world's diverse cultures have not developed independently; there has always been exchange among peoples. Yet the African thinker is fortunate enough to have at his disposal a long tradition of systematic thought which he can study and modify to suit the modern world. The post-colonial period in Africa now affords the African philosopher the breathing space to structure the departments of philosophy in his universities as he sees fit. The student of African philosophy should be taught to appreciate the classical African though expressed in the *Hermitica* and the pattern and structure of ancient African mathematics. He should ponder the earliest beginnings of science in Africa and rethink the propositions of the ancient papyri. The student should be made aware of the function of Islamic thought as the conduit of African thought to European and African, yet understand the contributions of the

71

LANCINAY KEITA

African thinker in medieval Africa.

Although a modern African philosophy has no need to
live in the past, it must recognize it, and perceive it as a necessary support for the analysis and study of modern forms of
knowledge.

The above discussion on the African philosophical tradition constitutes an attempt to present a framework in which
discussion on the major thought systems of Africa could take
place. Consistent with the methodology of the formulation of the
dominant thought systems of a whole people, no attempt was made
to incorporate into the African philosophical framework the folk
ways of thinking of Africa's diverse people. Such an approach
leads to confusion and the paralyzing of any attempts at creating
a genuine structure of African thought. The ways of thinking of
Africa's diverse peoples are significant[31] from the philosopher's
point of view only in the sense that they resemble classical African thought in embryonic form. For a history of African philosophy is coherent only in the sense that it recognizes as a definite
stage in African thought the most literate moments of that particular era. The discussion focused on three distinct periods of
Africa's intellectual history. Its classical period was by far the
most remarkable in that it was essentially of independent derivation and exercised important seminal influences on Hellenic and
Medieval Europe, and medieval Africa.

What then are the distinguishing features of African
thought that emerges from the above analysis? African thought is
essentially holistic in the sense that it accepts the material world,
thus making possible empirical science, yet recognizing at the
same time that metaphysical elements constitute the ontological
support and motive force for movement and motion in the world.
Paradoxically, it was this holistic ontology that permitted the most
significant breakthroughs in empirical science in the modern era.

FOOTNOTES

1. From a strictly historical point of view the notion of an oral Africa and literate Europe is clearly forced. Literacy is a recent phenomenon in Europe--of course a very small minority of Greeks, and much later on, a small number of West Europeans learned to read and write Latin, but the vast majority of the inhabitants of feudal and industrial Europe were illiterate. Individuals learned to read and write during the recent advent of mass education. On the other hand some Africans knew how to read and write before the colonial era. Thus the term "oral tradition" as opposed to "literate tradition" should be employed guardedly. General usage, however, seems to imply that in some way "orality" is inherent to the African "essence" while "literacy" is a "physiological" trait of Europeans.

2. This position is most evident in the writings of the Senegalese poet Leopold Senghor, and the political theorist Frantz Fanon: See especially the latter's *Peau Noire Masques Blanches* (Paris: Editions du Seuil. 1952), pp. 201-208.

3. See J. Jahn, *Muntu* (N.Y.: Grove Press, 1961) and John S. Mbiti *African Religions and Philosophy* (N.Y.: Doubleday, 1970).

4. This tradition obviously antedates the colonial period, for it was during the period of the enslavement of the African in the Americas that notions about the supposed superiority of some races and the inferiority of others, especially the African, first warranted "serious" research. It should be noted that it was during this period that the term "negro" was first used, even by the scientifically minded European.

5. See C. A. Diop, *The African Origin of Civilization* (New York: Lawrence Hill and Company, 1974), p. 50.

6. Frances Yates, *Giordano Bruno and the Hermetic Tradition*

(Chicago: the University of Chicago Press, 1964), p. 4. Yates research on the influence of Egyptian thought on the Greek and Renaissance world relies heavily on A. J. Festugiere's research and text *La Revelation d'Hermes Trismegiste*, and takes into consideration the research done on the Renaissance by scholars such as P. O. Kristeller *et al*. Since limitations on space do not permit an exhaustive reference to the original sources, most of the supporting references will be from Yates' work.

7.   Yates, Ibid., pp. 4-5.

8.   It should be noted that many of the important European thinkers of the post medieval period wrestled with the problem of how to reconcile the mental world with the world of matter. The rise of empiricism was accompanied by the expunging of animistic concepts from any theorising about the material world. The writings of Newton, Leibniz, and Huygens, culminating in Hume's vigorous attack on metaphysics, demonstrate how important this attempt to reconcile a dualistic universe is in European philosophy. In other words, the conflict between materialism and idealism has been a most important characteristic of European thought.

9.   Yates, p. 5.

10.   Ibid., p. 5.

11.   Ibid., p. 6.

12.   Ibid., p. 12.

13.   Ibid., p. 18.

14.   Ibid., p. 31.

15.   Ibid., p. 31.

16.   Granted the influence of Egyptian thought on the Renaissance, it is plausible to argue that Galileo's notion of a dynamic universe (the natural state of matter in motion)--as opposed to the static Aristotelian ontology--could have been influenced by the former.

17.   It is of interest to note that this particular conception of human nature resembles that of the classical Greek think-

ers: Socrates, Plato, Aristotle *et al.*, in making the distinction between man's rational and appetitive faculties. It seems more likely, however, that this idea of man is of Egyptian origin if only from the point of view that the Egyptians expressed this view in their sculpture.

18. Yates, *Giordano Bruno*, P. 48.

19. Ibid., p. 2

20. Ibid., p. 452.

21. Isaac Newton, *Principia* (revised translation) (Berkley: University of California Press, 1960), p. 549. The passage is also interesting from the point of view that modern historians of science generally trace the contributions of Newton back to the Greeks yet Newton himself might want to question this.

22. De Lacy O'Leary, *Arabic Thought and its Place in History* (London: Routledge and Kegan Paul Ltd., 1958), p. 103.

23. Ibid., p. 105.

24. C. A. Diop. *L'Afrique Noire Pre-Coloniale* (Paris: Presence Africaine, 1960), p. 133-35.

25. The heavy usage of Greek letters in advanced mathematics and science may seem arbitrary, but it can be explained entirely by the role that the European assigned to Greece in European civilization.

26. C. A. Diop has done pioneering research in this area. See especially *L'Afrique Noire Pre-Coloniale - passim.*

27. The chief members of the Negritude school are Damas, Senghor and Cesaire, all of whom are poets.

28. See, for example, Kwame Nkrumah's well-meaning work *Consciencism* (New York: Modern Reader Paperbacks, 1964). The chapter "Philosophy in Retrospect" makes no attempt to explore systematic African thought systems; it is mainly a summary of European philosophy since the Greeks.

29. It is important to realize that societies need not be colonized or invaded in order that they accept new ideas. In

fact, new ideas seem to be best integrated into a recipient society when such ideas are freely accepted and not imposed. Thus the argument that the price of modernization is colonization etc. is a spurious one.

30. Hajime Nakamara, *Ways of Thinking of Eastern Peoples* (Honolulu: East-West Center Press, 1964), p. 175.

31. Of course the anthropologist will have an interest in studying the systems of, say, the Nuba, the Laplanders or the Welsh, but neither the folk beliefs of the Laplanders nor those of the Welsh constitute any chapter in European philosophy.

THE AFRICAN FOUNDATIONS
OF GREEK PHILOSOPHY

Henry Olela

Introduction.

The following discussion will attempt to justify the legitimacy of a Black philosophy from its historical African background. We further intend to demonstrate that such a philosophy
also serves as the basis of Ancient Greek Philosophy. This latter
claim is evidenced when one undertakes to examine the nature of
the intellectual influence on specific Greek philosophers of merit
by the Ancient African World-View.

Many sources have now dispelled the dogma of the
"compulsive originality" of the Greek mind. Any claims concerning the lack of precedence for Greek philosophy overlook its
historical development, although this insistence on the "purity" of
Western philosophy has successfully forged a place in academic
circles. The argument has been that the African mind is in no
way capable of any systematic philosophy. But if we agree that
basic assumptions about the Universe are points beyond which one
can say nothing; if we further agree that basic assumptions about
a world-view are by nature theoretical and Universal, then it
would be quite difficult to deny such assumptions in regard to
either Ancient Africans (Egyptians) or modern Africa. The
elements of these basic assumptions are, as it were, those

regarding the structure of reality, the nature of the origin of things, problems of justice, etc.

The question which we must perhaps settle before proceeding with our investigation is: Are basic assumptions in essence distinguishable from philosophical assumptions? It seems that if one were to insist in distinguishing between the two, such a distinction would not be that one is metaphysical and the other is empirical. The distinction would, furthermore, not lie in the fact that one is held by philosophers and the other held by laymen. The only distinction which may be rationally made would be the tradition in which the assumptions are made. Thus we are here forced to recognize the impact of culture on philosophy: philosophy was not and is not immune to the universal human process of sharing and assimilating of culture traits; philosophy was not, is not, culture free.

We are, in this essay, making a fundamental claim; the historical foundation of the Modern African World-View as well as that of the Greeks and Romans, came from Ancient Africans (Egyptians). Secondly, the most obvious claim, that the authentic theoretical foundation of African diaspora's experience is African, need not posit a difficulty.

In dealing with our topical subject matter, we will adopt a methodology which is familiar but has received little attention---the genetic approach. It may behoove us to give some attention to Theodore Comperz's analysis of the origin of the intellectual tradition in societies of antiquity; of special attention is his discussion of geographical determining. Gomperz believes that knowledge about geographical factors and influences are necessary conditions for the understanding of a people's philosophy.[1] The location of Greece was ideal for cultural influences from neighboring states and civilizations, thereby becoming an "apprentice of older civilizations."

The genetic approach, therefore, can establish some correlations between types of cultures; it presupposes that contiguity of either cultures or persons is important. The major problem with establishing such a thesis is the unfortunate situation professional philosophers themselves have created. There are very few philosophical texts devoted to the problem of the origin of philosophy. But a small number of these philosophical texts written on this issue have not received approval by Western philosophers. An example of such a work which has been regarded as non-philosophical (in the eyes of many philosophers) is George G. M. James' book, *The Stolen Legacy*. In fact the

78

book is quite rare, almost to the point of being out of print. We may outrightly suggest that this book should be a required text for courses in History of Ancient Philosophy.

A better understanding of Greek theology or philosophy must be preceded first by considering the "mystery of Crete, where primary Hellenic culture was born."[2] Crete is an island standing on the southern part of the Aegean Sea and the Archipelago. It is also the largest of the islands on the Mediterranean Sea. The question we must ask then is: Who were the Creteans? Various reliable sources do confirm that "the ancestors of Creteans were natives of Africa, a branch of the Western Ethiopians."[3] Long before the Sahara became a desert, these people were living on the grassland areas of North Africa. But by about 2500 B.C. when drought plagued the Sahara, they were scattered around, some of them moving toward the Mediterranean Sea. They became the most skilled seamen and established a powerful maritime culture in Crete. They carried on a flourishing trade with other Africans then living in Sais (the land which the Greeks later re-named Egypt), Sicily, and southern Italy. This prosperity lived on to see its destruction by 1400 B.C. by the "semi-barbarous Greeks from the North."[4] Along with this position is the implication that the questions of the Phoenicians or Canaanites were initially from Punt, situated in East Africa (what is now known as Somali and extending to Kenya). The ancient Greeks also knew them as Ethiopians. According to Leonard Cottrel, *Lost Worlds,* it is safe "to assume that Minoan Civilization throughout its development gathered ideas and techniques from both African and Asian sources."[5] But a slightly stronger position is taken by Willis N. Huggins, *Introduction to African Civilization.* He asserts that "No evidence exists to show that they were influenced from any other source other than African. Everything so far unearthed in Crete and the Sudan apparently indicate that in the Mediterranean area, there was a common race of men."[6] Thus far we have allowed ourselves to use Egyptian and Ethiopian civilization interchangeably. In ancient times all black men were called Ethiopian or Egyptian by others, also Ethiopians had a tremendous impact on Egyptian religion. We have noted that Egypt was originally called Sais. If we add the Egyptian prefix Ma (Ma simply means "of") to Sais we would have the Ma-Sais. Indeed, the ancient Egyptians were the descendants of the Gallas Somalians and the Masais (who today live in Kenya and Tanzania).

Modern philosophical speculation, however, has generated a tendency toward the neglect of truth in regard to many aspects of the foundation of philosophy. This is particularly

HENRY OLELA

indicative of the Hegelian idealism, which tended to underestimate African civilization. Hegel's dictum was basically that Africa was outside history because it had not achieved the "German" consciousness. Indeed, like most modern and contemporary Western philosophers, Hegel had consciously attempted to subscribe to the argument of the European or Asian origin of any cultural traits of merit found in Africa.[7] This ignored the fact that even the ancient Greeks themselves often credited Africa with being the source of foundations of philosophical knowledge.

There is one historical and archaeological note to which we must address ourselves--the relationship of Ancient Africa and Asia. Most Western philosophers who are liberal enough to admit to the Eastern origin of Greek philosophy, hold that it was a "trivial" influence, and it came from Babylonia. But according to historical, as well as archaeological findings, there was an African presence in Southern Mesopotemia (Babylonia and Sumer). These same Africans were also responsible for the construction of The Tower of Babel. Albert Churchward's position seems plausible when he claims that all that the Babylonians knew and speculated about was borrowed from the Africans. According to him, "The Babylonians copied and obtained all their knowledge from the Egyptians....what the Babylonians knew they borrowed either directly from the Egyptians or Sumerians--the latter obtained it from Egypt."[8]

The Elements of the Ancient African World-View

The Ancient Africans were well known for their tight cosmological views; Sais (Egypt) was the intellectual center of the world. Their speculation covered the whole realm of human knowledge including pure metaphysics, ethics, astronomy, mathematicians, science and medicine. Because of the small space allotted in this volume we can only briefly outline their systematic philosophy.

Mathematics

One of the ancient African mathematical texts which has survived to the present is the *Rhind Mathematical Papyrus.* This work became a property of the British Museum upon Henry Rhind's death, but it became known to modern scholars in 1858 when Rhind secured the rights to it. *The Mathematical Papyrus* was written during the reign of King A-User-Re, 1650 B.C., and copies of this work were made roughly about 1800 B.C. by the Scribe A'hmose. The entire papyrus contains eight sections of arithmetical problems dealing with forty problems. We also find in this work four sections of pure geometry containing nineteen problems.

Arithmetical problems were of varied nature--but most solutions partook fractional and decimal processes. The Ancient Africans were, therefore, the first to discover the use of both decimal points and fractions. To this day we use their method, with only slight changes. To say that the mathematical problems solved in the *Rhind Papyrus* are simple algebra and fractions is to fail to recognize that during the days that this was written, man was *inventing* such problems and their solutions--not just copying them out of textbooks. Besides fractions and decimal points, the Ancient Africans discovered methods of solving problems pertaining to volumes of pyramids and areas of cylinders. Their methods in these two cases are directly adopted by modern mathematicians.

The greatest achievements in the areas of mathematics was geometry. Without going into details, we may do well to state the basic African's geometrical maxims or theorems which were later directly adopted by the Greeks. There are at least five such basic propositions which found their way to Greece after the voyages of Thales, Pythagoras, and Euclid (the latter being the basis of Keat's philosophy) in Egypt, and their lessons from the Egyptian seers.

Proposition 1.

The square of the hypotenuse of a right angled triangle is equal to the sum of the squares on the sides containing the right angle.

The ancient Africans had a knowledge of possible combinations, in definite ratios, of the square of 3 and 4 which when added make 5. The acquisition of such knowledge made it possible, then, to construct a right angled triangle with sides of 3, 4, and 5. There were various versions of this theorem regarding strategies for the construction of the great pyramids. Problems of this type presupposed the knowledge of Isosceles triangles.

Proposition 2.

The three angles of a triangle are together equal to two right angles.

According to Charles Tylor, the "positive part of it must have been observed by the Egyptians, who must therefore have known that the three angles of an equilateral triangle are together equal to two right angles."[9]

Proposition 3.

The diameter of any circle bisects that circle.

It is worth noting that the ancient Africans gave pi the value 3 13/18. They calculated that if a diameter is marked or divided into 9 units, the circle drawn around it was equal to the square on a line with 8 units.

Proposition 4.

The vertical angles of two straight lines cutting each other are equal.

The proof of this theorem is found in any of today's standard texts of elementary geometry.

Because of their mathematical knowledge, the Ancient Africans of Sais were able to calculate the height of a pyramid as well as the distance of a ship in the ocean from a given point on land. But in the history of philosophy written by Western philosophers, these two discoveries have been falsely attributed to Thales. Euclid adopted the ancient African method of determining the distance of a ship at sea (Euclid Theorem 1.26).

The most common observation made by Western scholars about the nature of the Egyptian mathematical activities is that theirs was more of a practical inclination than a speculative endeavor. But contrary to this attitude the ancient people of Sais were also concerned with the theoretical demand of the acquisition of knowledge. They considered mathematical knowledge to be sacred and it was taught only to the intellectuals who were also the priests. The distinction between the intellectual and practical was rigidly enforced. The priests told laymen how to use this knowledge for their activities, but the actual theorems and proofs remained a sacred trust.

Science

The next discipline for which ancient Egyptians laid the foundation is science. We can rightly claim that they marked the foundation of modern science in the sense that modern science is a spin-off from the medieval scientific outlook which, in turn, took its direction from the ancient Greeks. The Greek science is a continuation of African science. There has been a tendency in Western scholarship to label African science as mere technical knowledge and not pure science. At any rate we may only point out that knowledge of whatever form does have an aspect pursued for its own sake--which would make it theoretical. Even if the distinction between *technique* and *pure science* was legitimate, there still is one phenomenon which is common to both; they are based on empirical observation. We may say that the pre-occupation of the laymen of Ancient Africa with solutions of problems of immediate concerns may appear to have dominated the thorough-going theoretical considerations of the priestly class. We must remember, however, that we are talking about a period far removed from our own--5000 B.C. to 2000 B.C. In our own times, scientists do not bother developing all their findings for laymen who may or may not be interested. Further, they are in disagreement over whether or not the scientists of the middle ages were *really* scientists or technicians; whether astronomy is science or magic; and what the cut-off point is between "pure" and "applied" science. It would not be surprising if, in a matter of a few generations, our so called "pure science" of today would be considered "technique"!

The text which contains one aspect of Ancient African science--mainly a medical treatise--is what is known as *Edwin Papyrus.* The observations made in this work form the core of natural sciences. As Breasted has pointed out, the authors of the text "were the earliest known natural scientists."[10] It would be incorrect, however, to say that African science was limited to the practice of medicine. In the other natural sciences--chemistry and physics--we find that as early as 4000 B.C. the discovery of metals in Egypt had already been made; glass-making was a major industry; and, the Egyptians had a definite knowledge of the ratios of elements, one of which was used to make bronze (a ratio of 12% tin makes the alloy harden).

Now if we agree that the exact sciences are theoretical by virtue of their basis in mathematical knowledge, then the Africans had mathematical capabilities of a far reaching nature which they definitely used to formulate working scientific theories.

HENRY OLELA

Philosophical Systems (Schools) in Ancient Africa

We need to distinguish about four distinct schools of thought in Ancient Africa or Sais. These were:

a) School at Heliopolis
b) School at Hermopolis
c) School at Thebes
d) School at Memphis

Of these systems, the one which fashioned the basis of Greek philosophy was that at Memphis. However, in this brief account we will only point out some of the important concepts which later became the concern of most Greek philosophers.

What is common to all these schools of thought was their consistent theory of Creation and the nature of basic elements. At Heliopolis, the account was that above everything else was Atum-Ra, the Sun-God or *Fire-God*. Atum-Ra was basic to all natures. It was self-created--thus we hear echoes from the *Pyramid Text* that: "O Atum, when you came into being you rose up as a high hill." Besides Atum-Ra, we also find four major gods or elements: Shu, *Air-God*. Shu was the spirit of life and eternity--"I am the eternity the Creator of the millions..." The ancient African theologians conceived a Universe of opposites; the opposite of Shu now became Tefnut--The living female. Tefnut is responsible for *World Order*. In the *Coffin Text* we read: "Order is her name...Life reposed with my daughter Order." The other major elements were Geb--the *Earth,* and Nut, the *Sky.* While Shu and Tefnut were children of Atum-Ra, Geb and Nut were his grandchildren. Thus we can arrange these elements in order of their priorities. We must add here that before anything else was created there was nothing but a Primordial abyss of *Water* (Nun).

Now we must hasten to see the consistency of thought between the Memphite School and that of the Heliopolis. According to the former, Ptah, the God of Gods, was actually the God of Creation. He first of all emerged from Nun (water) as a Primeval Hill. But while the Heliopolis school does not make mention of Ptah as the High God, the Memphite theology clearly states that after Ptah had posited himself as a Hill, Atum-Ra appeared from the Primoridal water and sat upon the Hill. The emergence of Atum was necessary because it was he who completed the creative process already started by Ptah. Atum was responsible for the being of *World Order* through his daughter Tefnut.

84

The Memphite Schools also posited a series of opposite gods--males and females:

Nun and Naunet (Water & Heavens)
Huk and Hauhet (Boundless and its oppo-
site--limited)
Amum and Amaumet (the invisible and the
visible)
Kuk and Kauket (Darkness and Light)

In the creative process Ptah merely uttered the *Word* for creation to take place. R. T. Rundle Clark writes that:

> The Memphite author has built his theory
> on the analogy of the *mind* controlling the
> motions of the body. This is the unique
> contribution of this text to cosmology.
> Whereas later philosophers--from the Ioni-
> ans down to Hegel--retreated into tautolo-
> gies before the problem of how the Word
> or the Idea actualized itself, the Egyptian
> constructed his theory on the model of
> mind and body.[11]

There was already a thorough-going sense of metaphysical ideal-ism. Ptah, therefore, was both *Mind* and *Word.* We may also remind ourselves here of Clark's further assertion that:

> When Kant looked upon the movements of
> the starry sky and then into the moral
> order within himself and recognized the
> two as the signs of one and the same
> God, he was closely following the thought
> of an anonymous Memphite more than four
> thousand years before.[12]

Creation was therefore done out of *thought* and *command* of Ptah. We can therefore summarize this discussion by stating that the Ancient Africans had already identified the following elements:

1) Water (Nun)
2) Boundless (Huk)
3) Air (Shu)
4) Fire (Atum)
5) The *Mind*
6) Chaos and *Order,* the latter in the
form of Tefnut.

85

HENRY OLELA

The Doctrine of Immortality of the Soul

We now need to say something about the nature of the human soul. Again because of the limited space, we can only list a few of the concepts which are relevant to our thesis. The Egyptian word for soul in general is *Ba.* But Ba has human characteristics and is distinguishable from *Ka,* which is a *double.* The other major concepts connected with the general theory of the soul are: *Khu,* the shining part of man which bridges the gap between human (man) and superhuman (God) beings; and the Body, Khat. Khat was subject to complete destruction upon the phenomenon of death. Ba does have some visible characteristics. In most African societies we find that it is to the Ba (soul of the ancestor) that libation is poured and food offered, in the hope that he will eat, drink and rejoice. Ka is not identical with Ba; it is more conceptual. Ka is the double of anything man can think of, of any conceivable object. In short, Ka is the conceptual replica of physical reality - created by Ptah, the *unmoved mover,* and completed by Atum, residing in the world of intellect.

A. H. Sayce believes that the notion of Ka was directly adopted by Plato in his theory of ideas. According to Sayce's interpretation,

> The ideas of Plato were the last develop-
> ment of the Egyptian doctrine of Ka.
> They were the archetype after which all
> things have been made. [13]

Plato believed that the real world is the world of ideas or forms. This borrowing of the sense of Ka is understandable since Plato went to study in Egypt when he was about twenty-seven years old.

According to the Egyptians, when a person dies, what remains is his real self--the Ka, but within the Ka there resides Khu which is the intellect or pure intelligence. The term "Khu" could be rendered as meaning "mind." Khu is the divine part of man; it makes the linkage between man and God possible. The Egyptians believed that the soul, being imprisoned in the body, found it difficult to achieve or attain pure intelligence. It is only upon death that man can grasp the nature of reality, because then he is pure intelligence. The salvation of man, which is the highest God, is the separation of Khat from Ka!

<u>The Ancient Greek Philosophers Influenced
by Ancient African World-View</u>

In this section, I will merely list Greek Philosophers who are identified with elements borrowed from the ancient African cosmology.

1. *Thales* -- After studying in Egypt for a considerable number of years, he came to believe that *water* was the fundamental stuff underlying the Universe. Thales was influenced by Egyptian theory that water (Nun) was the origin of all things--even the Gods.

2. *Anaximander* -- A student of Thales thought that the basic element was the *boundless.* This was an adoption of the Egyptian Huk (boundless).

3. *Anaximenes* -- Held that *air* was the basic stuff. The Egyptian teachers taught that Shu--Air God was the life force--Shu was life giving spirit.

4. *Hericlitus* -- Believed that *fire* is the basic element--taking the notion from the Egyptian--Atum--Fire.

5. *Pythagoras* -- Believed that the Universe is basically *mathematical.* He also taught the theory of transmigration of the soul, which was generally known as Orphic doctrine. Orpheus, like Pythagoras, had been to Egypt, where he learned from the Egyptian priests: Pythagoras studied in Egypt for about 22 years--learning mathematics and the mystery systems of the Egyptians.

6. *Xenophanes* -- the first Greek to teach the doctrine of the *One God.* His monism was of Egyptian origin. The ancient Egyptians as well as other Africans had a thorough-going doctrine of the One God, Ptah, who sways all things by the *thought of his mind.*

7. *Parmenides* -- The founder of the Eleatic School, believed in the One Being. He furthered the doctrine of the *One,* which Xenophanes theologically developed. Influenced by Pythagoras, from whom he learned his philosophy, he inherited the Egyptian belief that the Earth was spherical. According to Josef ben Jochannan, "Xenophenes, Parmenides, Zeno and Melissus (all of them natives of Ionia) migrated to Elea, Italy, after completing their education in Egypt."[14]

87

8. *Anaxagoras* -- He believed that the initiator of motion in the Universe was the *mind* (Nous). Mind was identified with the soul. We earlier noted that the Egyptian identified Khu with the mind. He also believed that *air* was the most pervasive of all the elements. He is also known to have gone to study in Egypt.

9. *Democritus* -- Taught that the atoms are the ultimate constituents of the Universe. He was widely traveled--went to Egypt and Ethiopia, where he is reported to have stayed for five years learning both astronomy and geometry. He is supposed to have brought back to Greece the atomic theory from the East--mainly for the Nyaya school, of India. According to George James, in *The Stolen Legacy,* "The original source of this doctrine however, is the philosophy of the Mystery System of Egypt...under the circumstances and in consequence of those facts, the Egyptian Mystery System was the source of the doctrines a) of the atom, b) of opposites. Leucippus and Democritus taught nothing new and must have obtained their knowledge of the doctrines from the Egyptians, directly or indirectly."[15]

10. *Plato* -- He traveled to Egypt where he studied under Egyptian priests. He picked up from Egypt some of the doctrines found in the Republic; that is to say, the three levels of society

    a)   the philosophers - kings
    b)   the soldiers
    c)   artisans

These doctrines were well established in the Egyptian social system. But before Plato, Pythagoras had identified these levels, which he called:

    a)   the Spectators - philosophers
    b)   Athletes - soldiers
    c)   Pedlers - laborers - artisans

Secondly, Plato adopted the Egyptian view of immortality of the soul. Thirdly, he adopted the Egyptian view of Creation--Atum is Demiurge--God of Creation. Fourthly, Plato's theory of ideas was influenced by the Egyptian concept of Ka. Fifth, the doctrine of the *Good* -- this is the further development of the Egyptian theory of Salvation. The release of the soul from the body was the highest good.

11. *Aristotle* -- He went to Egypt with Alexander the Great. He had access to Priestly material in the Temples--he freely acquired books from the Library at Alexandria. He adopted the Egyptian notion of the *unmoved mover.* Creative process developed from disorder (chaos) to order. This process was performed through *mind* and *word* -- or pure intelligence. He also adopted the doctrine of the soul as discussed in the *Book of the Dead.*

Conclusion

The preceding discussion has attempted to do three things. One most important supposition is that any discussion of "Black Philosophy" is reduceable to African Philosophy. Any philosophy must be evaluated from the context of its history. Contemporary Black Philosophy is moribund if it does not take as its starting point an African World-View--which is the basis of the Black experience. Similarly, the contemporary African philosophy is moribund if it does not take into account the "history of African philosophy" which takes us back to ancient Africa (Ancient Egypt, Ethiopia, etc.). Once the Black scholars have done this, their admiration of the Western philosophy will take a new dimension; the monopoly of philosophy by the Greeks will have a turn.

At this point we may do well to take James' recommendation:

> Now that it has been shown that philosophy, arts, and sciences were bequeathed to civilization by the people of North Africa and not by the people of Greece; the pendulum of praise and honor is due to shift from the people of Greece to the people of the African continent who were the rightful heirs of such a praise and honor.
> This is going to mean a tremendous change in world opinion, and attitude for all people and races who accept the new philosophy of African redemption, i.e. the truth that the Greeks were not the authors of Greek philosophy; but the people of North Africa....[16]

HENRY OLELA

What this position suggests is that systematic African/Black
Philosophy does not need to start from scratch. African philosophy or Black philosophy does not have to collapse into ideology--
-it has its legitimate basis. Similarly the newly developed "Black
Theology" must have its basis on an African World-View to
provide a history for it. Failure to recognize this demand merely
reduces it to ideology--in which case, after Black Liberation is
done with, the Black Theology (we may say the same thing for
Black philosophy) will have no relevance.

FOOTNOTES

1. Theodore Gomperz, *Greek Thinkers,* trans. L. Magnus and G. Berry (London: J. Murray, 1920), pp. 3-42.

2. Dibinger Wa Said, *Theosophies of Plato, Aristotle, and Plotinus* (N.Y.: Philosophical Library, 1970), p. 1.

3. Willis Huggis and John G. Jackson, *Introduction to African Civilization* (N.Y.: Negro University Press, 1969), p. 77.

4. Ibid.

5. Leonard Cottrel, *The Penguin Book of Lost Worlds* (Hamondsworth, Eng.: Penguin, 1966), p. 24.

6. Huggins and Jackson, *Introduction to African Civilization,* p. 4.

7. G. W. F. Hegel, *Philosophy of History,* passim.

8. Albert Churchward, *The Signs and Symbols of Primordial Man* (London: Sonnenschein, 1910), pp. 212-213.

9. Charles Taylor, *An Introduction to the Ancient and Modern Geometry of Conics* (Cambridge: Deighton, Bell & Co., 1881), p. xxxiv.

10. Edwin Brested, *The Edwin Smith Surgical Papyrus,* vol. 1, p. 12.

11. R. T. Rundle Clark, *Myth and Symbol in Ancient Egypt* (London: Thames and Hudson, 1959), p. 64.

12. Ibid., p. 66.

13. A. H. Sayce, *The Religions of Ancient Egypt and Babylonia* (Edinburgh: T & T Clark, 1902), pp. 48-49.

14. Yosef ben-Jochannan, *The African of the Nile* (N.Y.:

Alkebu-lan Books, 1970), p. 193.

15. George James, *The Stolen Legacy* (N.Y.: Philosophical Library, 1954), pp. 75-76.

16. Ibid., p. 171.

TIME IN YORUBA THOUGHT

John A. A. Ayoade

      The Yoruba speaking peoples are found scattered in three different countries in West Africa: Nigeria (where they are most populous), Dahomey and Togo. In Nigeria they inhabit what is now known as the Lagos State, the Western State and a good part of the Ilorin and Kabba Provinces of the Kwara State. In the adjacent country of Dahomey they are found east and north of the *Cercle* of Savalou. And in Togo they are found in the eastern sector of the *Cercle* of Atakpame. Within this large group of Yoruba-speaking peoples exist different dialects like Ekiti, Ijesa, Egba, and Ijebu in Nigeria. The Yoruba in Dahomey were referred to by European writers variously as Anago, Nago, Inago or Nagot while those of Togo were called Aana. One further comment is only in place here. And that is that apart from the names used for the various subgroups of the Yorubas in Nigeria, the Yoruba-speakers in Dahomey or Togo never call themselves Anago or Aana respectively. These were terms principally used for them by other peoples, just as the Yoruba repatriated slaves in Sierra Leone were referred to as the 'Akus', a name deriving from the Yoruba way of greeting. This study deals mainly with the Yoruba *in situ* as opposed to the Yoruba deracines found in the Caribbean or Brazil or even to the groups of scattered migrant Yoruba traders found as far afield as the Sudan. It must be noted, however, that the Yorubas of this study are themselves a mixture of the early inhabitants of the present habitat and later invaders. But our knowledge of the inhabitants is

93

at best very scanty.[1] And what we know about the Yoruba peoples themselves is gleaned from (a) the legends of the early rulers who became gods, (b) the stories of the rulers who did not become gods, (c) the travelogues of European itinerants and (d) recent written records, in an ascending order of credibility.[2] Therefore, as a consequence of the doubtful credibility of the oral traditions of the Yorubas, it is difficult to say with precision where the later invaders came from. Apart from the fact that these traditions might have suffered irreparably from the loss of human memory, they are also known to have been influenced by the two proselytizing religions of Islam and Christianity. The oral traditions vary widely between those claiming Ife as the centre of the world where creation began and those asserting that their ancestors migrated from a place northeast of their present positions.[3]

The Yoruba Environment

The area now occupied by the Yorubas falls broadly into three Zones parallel to the coast. Bordering the ocean is the coastal zone of about twelve miles wide consisting of Islands, peninsulas, sandbars, lagoons and swamps. This vegetational zone is covered with mangroves and forest. In addition it has a lagoon system running from Benin in the east to Dahomey in the West and providing a fairly adequate artery of inland waterway.

To the north the coastal zone gives way to the dense rain-forest belt in which are found Iroko, Rubber, Mahogany, Silk, Cotton and other forest trees. This area is particularly noted for its thick forest and scanty undergrowth. It is a very important agricultural zone as far as root crops like yams and cassava are concerned. However open parklands which support a different type of flora and fauna can be found even within this forest zone.

Further to the north of this rainforest plain is the interior plateau rising from 500-1500 feet above sea level. This plateau supports the deciduous forest that thins northwards until it is replaced by Savanna.

A brief discussion of the environment has been necessary because of the effects on man of the numerous climatic and biotic conditions around him. This is particularly the case of the Yorubas and all other peasant communities as far as their conceptualization of time is concerned, because they place a great emphasis on the observable phenomena of their physical environment.

The Nature of Time

Time is such a complicated phenomenon that is easier to describe than to define. Many Western philosophers have, at different times, grappled with this question and the issue is still all but settled. Both Aristotle and St. Augustine demonstrated the evanescence of time. To Aristotle time is itself not movement of which it is not independent. It consists of three interlocking parts of the past, the present and the future, although the present, while linking the past and the future, is an indivisible instant.[4] Thus the present is unlike the rest of time which is divisible. But as a temporal link between the past and the future it must somehow belong to both if time must be continuous. The above is interesting in the light of John Mbiti's reflection on the African concept of time. According to him time for the African is a two dimensional phenomenon with a long past, a present and virtually no future.[5] While it is possible that this may be true of some people about whom John Mbiti might have first-hand knowledge it is not remotely true of the Yorubas whose total perspective of time-future even extends beyond the end of this life to an after life.

Secondly, being a predominantly agricultural community they cannot avoid a long-term budgeting of their time in such a way that they can take advantage of the different seasons. Thus they are constantly engaged in a time scheduling which determines the allocation of work and of food as well as the storage of seed at harvest time for the next planting season. The future is therefore not only real to the Yorubas but is in fact given adequate place in their planning.

St. Augustine's philosophy regarding the present is similar to Aristotle's in the sense that it is an irreducible minimum unit of time that lacks duration. The past no longer is and the future is not yet but they can be measured. The future can only be measured in its passing, so that time in the ultimate analysis is that which passes from that which is to come through that which lacks extension into that which now is not.[6]

Berkeley on his own part cannot see the intelligibility of time when cut adrift of human activities.[7] Thus, although time is motion, it is no vacuum and becomes real only when it is considered as a property of things. This is what Newton classifies as relative, apparent and common time. However, Newton sees another type of time, i.e. absolute, true and mathematical time,

95

which "of itself, and from its own nature, flows equably without relation to anything external."[8]

One thing which is evident from the above survey of time in Western thought is that it is possible to ascribe a particular strand of thought to known individual philosophers. On the contrary this is not true of the African system of thought which is totally communal in origin. Thus it is not possible to identify any particular individual exclusively with any particular idea. But this is not to say that an idea does not have a beginning in an individual. All it means is that for any such idea to be acceptable to the generality of the people it must be founded on a previously accepted mores, ethos and philosophy of the people who are therefore pre-disposed to be socialized into that emerging trend of thought. It can be said that the absence of individual African traditional philosophers results only from the fact of an undocumented society because, at least in their elementary forms, any form of thought must have begun with an individual or individuals, although the permeability of such an idea is ultimately a function of its consonance with prevalent forms of thought. To some extent this phenomenon of an unindividualized philosophy lends greater credence to African philosophy in the sense that it represents a body of shared beliefs and hopes in contradistinction to Western philosophy which more often than not is shared only by a minority of the society. Thus, at least in this respect, African philosophy has a greater regulatory impact on the society.

Yoruba Time - Measures

The Yorubas have two main measures of time. The first is the human measure and the second the environmental cycle. (See Figure 1.) In a general sense these two ways of indicating time are in no way peculiar to the Yorubas. To a very large extent they are the attributes of all preliterate societies. This is more so of the human measure than perhaps of the cosmic cycle because at least in some respects the notion of time is a more indwelling human notion than the notion of spatial extent. Man can still reckon time even when completely cut off from all awareness of the external world, because events within his own body (nychthemeral rhythms, or inner dialogues) like his breathing and his heartbeat provide him with a standard of time reference, however crude it is as a unit of time measurement.[9] But as will be shown presently, the details of time measurement using the same human medium vary from one society to the other.

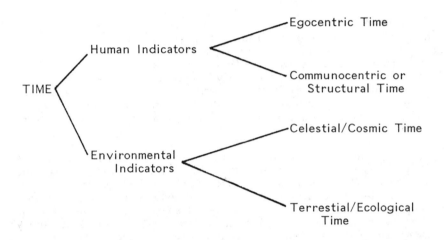

Figure 1

The Human Measure

As far as the Yorubas are concerned, the human person severally or the human person in interaction with others forms two ways of indicating time. This is also the case with the Nuer who differentiate between the egocentric time-scale and structural time which is based on the totality of inter-personal relations within the social structure. Structual or communocentric time (and this is also true of the egocentric time-scale) is linear and entirely progressive[10] whereas ecological time is cyclic.

An individual is the unit of reckoning under an egocentric time scale. The Yorubas periodize the age of an individual and this periodization is meant to be of universal application within the Yoruba community. A new-born baby does not take a name until the ninth day if male or until the seventh day if female, because the Yorubas believe that a male has nine ribs as opposed to a female's seven. And within the period the child is referred to as *Ikoko* or *Abiye* or *Aburo* even when the child's name is known immediately after birth because of the peculiar circumstances surrounding its birth.[11]

However after the naming of the child it is referred to in different ways roughly approximating particular stages of development. Apart from being generally referred to as *Arobo*

97

the child is also referred to as *Omo Omu* or *Omo Owo* as long as the child breastfeeds. Traditionally, a child is supposed to breastfeed for at least two years before it is weaned and it is only after a child is weaned that the parents can plan for the next child. And they can identify a recently pregnant mother by how frequently the recently weaned child weeps. There are, however, two sub-divisions of this developmental stage. These are the crawler stage (*Irakoro*) and the toddler state (*Omo Irinse*).

However, although a child within the above category is often referred to as young blood (*Omo Kekere eje Orun*), the Yorubas exhibit a verbal inconsistency by referring to a crawler or a toddler as grown up, particularly when such a child dies. Such verbal inconsistencies occur often because the infantile mortality rate is high. This inconsistency becomes particularly more glaring in the light of the fact that the child in the ensuing stage of development is still known as a child (*Omode*). It is after this stage that the individual is addressed as youth (*Odo*). Older people are known as *Agba*[12] or *Arugbo*. And those who are older still are referred to as *Agbalagba* or *Arugbo Kujokujo*.

It is very important to note that it is fairly difficult to use this egocentric time-scale because it only gives block ideas of the time implied rather than an exact time. But this is only because the Yorubas, as far as their thinking about time is concerned, prefer simplicity to exactitude. It is difficult to capitalize on this simplicity, however, because time as conceived above is only intelligible to the initiated. This is not to say that there are no visible indications of the respective stages of development. Indicating time with the human person as basis is principally dependent on indigenous factors. For example within the first stage of the child's development the Yorubas also identify the period of cutting the first teeth. Although this does not say anything for a precise time it no doubt gives an idea of the age of the child.

Similarly there are physical manifestations of youth. For example, the girl is said to have reached a stage in development when she develops the breast (*Gunmu*) and the boy at the same stage of development is regarded as undergoing a process of developing testicles (*Ro Epon*). However, in the case of the male, there are two sub-divisions of this stage of development: (1) the stage at which he has the physical manifestations of manhood although not sufficiently developed for the purposes of procreation; and (2) the stage at which he is fully matured in terms of procreation. The first sub-division is often accompanied by the appearance of fine brownish pubic hairs while the pubic hairs become black in the second stage and the male is regarded as fully mature. *(Balaga).* When referring to this stage of development the Yorubas telescope time by saying that a fully mature child is as old as his father,[13] although this is only in the respect that the child is as capable of procreation as the father. In other respects this cannot neutralize the anteriority of the adult over the child, for there are other attributes bequeathed to an individual by chronological age.[14] Two main examples of this are notable. The adult is particularly more experienced, an attribute which is highly treasured by the Yorubas. A second and more visible manifestation of old age is grey hairs. However, the Yorubas are themselves aware that some people have grey hairs earlier than others and therefore distinguish between the natural and the induced.[15] The awareness of the distinction notwithstanding, there is a confusion in the use of such external trappings for telling time or age. Nevertheless, this mode of indicating time combines theoretical consistency with practical significance. And above all, although time derived through this medium can be no more than a guesstimation, it shows that the people have a perception of an ordered sequence and duration, which are the two forms that any experience of time takes.[16]

There is another dimension to the use of an individual for the purpose of measuring time. Since individuals do not live in isolation but have relations with one another in the social structure, another form of time-measure, structual time, develops. This is particularly true of the Yorubas because very often time is told by a non-causal association of two events, whether or not they are isochronous. Thus, if a woman is asked when she got married, she replies by associating that event with more popular events like the enthronement of a king or the flooding of a river. Most Yorubas do not know how old they are, although they know that they are older than some other people. To some extent, this has to be the case because great respect is paid to age and seniority, so that time devoid of events makes little sense. This, therefore, sharpens their memory of the beforeness, afterness or simultaneity of events. The difficulty posed by this medium of indicating time is that, since communication was poor,[17] time was localized and only relative to structural space. However, for the locality, ambiguity in timing is solved by saying that an event *E* occurred at a time *T*, where *T* is some definite moment fixed by some dating from a well-known and presumably unique event.[18]

JOHN A. A. AYOADE

The Environmental Cycle

The mode of reckoning time clearly varies with the economy, the ecology, the ritual system, and the political organization, as well as with the technical equipment. But a peasant system like that of the Yorubas "has little need of elaborate scheduling, nor does it always possess the mechanical devices that permit accurate measurement."[19] Thus, in non-industrial societies the repetitive patterns of the world of nature, in addition to those of the human life, provide the basic measures of time reckoning. But the environmental measures of time are of two main types, (a) The celestial-cosmic cycle and (b) the terrestrial-ecological cycle.

Time indication with the aid of the celestial-cosmic cycle is based only on intuitively recognized regularities of the external world and the people's pre-scientific cosmologies. The day is based on the cosmological facts of day and night, and the divisions of the day by the Yorubas no doubt obeys the same rule. For example, they talk about *Afemojumo,* which is a period of the morning when one can hardly see the lines of one's palm. This period is followed by the period before sunrise which is usually referred to as morning. The period between sunrise and noon is called *Iyaleta* while noon is known as *Oorunkantari.* The afternoon is called *Osan* while the period roughly between 4 p.m. and 7 p.m. is known as *Irole* or *Ojoro,* which approximately marks the end of a day as evening then sets in. Evening lasts till people go to sleep and that does not normally come earlier than about 9 p.m., because the Yorubas often have late supper. The night starts after people go to bed, but the night is imprecisely divided into two, Night and High Night.

The next unit of time which the Yorubas derive from celestial-cosmic factors is the month, which is based upon the lunar cycle of 29.5 days. Special attention is paid to the waxing and waning of the moon, particularly to the first three days of the new moon. It is believed that insanity becomes more acute when the new moon appears, although they imply that each person has his own monthly cycle. Thus, whenever an individual misbehaves people around suggest that his month has appeared (*Osu re le*). It is therefore not possible to be precise about each individual's monthly cycle except at the points when such an individual misbehaves.

100

On the contrary, there is a definite monthly cycle which is arrived at in two main ways. The first set of months which is most probably autochthonous to Yorubaland is based on the meterological and climatological peculiarities of the different parts of the year. Thus, months derived in this way are organized segments of a seasonal cycle and are most probably much longer than the lunar month and occur more in Yoruba proverbs and expressions[20] than the second group of months which will be discussed presently. A reconstruction of the month based on metereological peculiarities is difficult, however, because they have been superseded by the Judaeo-Christian months. Thus, although the Yorubas have names for twelve months,[21] this mensal nomenclature is highly suspicious, for two main reasons: first, if the Yorubas depend on the waxing and waning of the moon for the reckoning of the months, then their lunar year would contain thirteen as opposed to twelve months, which means the name of one month is missing. Some authors believe that the Yorubas have a year of 360 days consisting of twelve months of thirty days with five epagomenal days to adjust the reckoning of the year.[22] But these authors have succeeded more in confounding rather than solving the problem of the imposition of the Judaeo-Christian year over the traditional Yoruba year.

Neither do they relieve our second reason for suspecting the names of the months, because, at least in one sense, the month of December known as *Osu Ope* (The Month of the Palm) would appear to be more Christian in derivation as the palm tree did not have universal respect among the Yorubas before the Christian story of the Triumphant Entry of Jesus into Jerusalem. Finally, it is possible to account for the assimilation of the Yoruba months into the Judaeo-Christian months by the fact that the Yoruba language was not written until the advent of Christianity. It is possible, therefore, that it was the missionaries who reduced Yoruba to writing who substituted the Judaeo-Christian months for the original Yoruba months.[23] This point is further buttressed by the fact that apart from the literate Yorubas who are marginally aware of these new names for the months, they are not commonly heard within the Yoruba universe and even to the literate elite sound pedantic.[24]

Terrestrial - Ecological Time

Apart from the day and the month, the Yorubas depend on their physical natural environment for indicating time. It must be noted, however, that units of time smaller than a day, particularly very short units, are variously determined. For example, they talk about the twinkling of the eye of a crab[25] which is regarded as the shortest unit of time. This is followed by the twinkling of the human eye.[26] And on other occasions a short time is also denoted by the time it takes the human sputum to dry up. For example older people among the Yorubas are fond of telling children whom they send on errands to return before the sputum which they have spat on the ground dries up. It will be noted that in each of the three instances given above there is no element of precision. The drying up of the sputum would depend on the amount, as well as the period of the day or even the season. Similarly some eyes twinkle faster than others. In fact small children stage competitions in literally holding back time by refusing to twinkle the eye.

Time is principally indicated with the aid of various ecological agents. The crowing of the cock signals the beginning of a new day,[27] and this is regarded as such an important function of the cock that whenever a cock crows at a wrong time it is regarded as failing in its duty and deserving of death. Similarly the early morning music of the dove is used for the purpose of indicating the morning, just as the end of the day is indicated by the perching of the chicken for the night.

Time during the day is indicated either by the sun or by an interpretation of the effect of the sun on people or objects.. The most important way in which this is done is by the interpretation of shadows. The shadow is long in the morning and progressively reduces in length until noon when an object does not cast any shadow at all. Noon is particularly the most explicit of the times indicated by the sun for it is the only part of the day for which the Yorubas have any specific name related to the movement of the sun, *Oorunkantari,* meaning that the sun is directly overhead. After this period in the day the shadow lengthens and becomes longest just about sunset. However one natural phenomenon can easily complicate time based on the sun. This arises from the fact that the setting of the sun varies from season to season. Thus there are periods of the year when the sun still appears bright in the sky yet it does not take a long time before darkness falls. People can easily be deceived by the sun at such a period of the year, hence the sun at such a time of the day and at such a season is called *Tanmooko.*

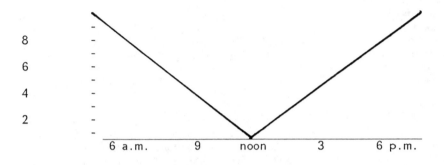

8
6
4
2

6 a.m.   9   noon   3   6 p.m.

Figure 2

The month as an ecological unit of time has been discussed.[28] It must be mentioned here, however, that if the month is an organized ecological segment of a seasonal cycle, the year constitutes the ecological cycle. This is because seasonal changes impress their rhythm on the productive process; the Yorubas, being a predominantly agricultural community, cannot avoid, time-budgeting based on the seasons. Since they all live within the tropical region, their year consists of two main seasons: the rainy season and the dry season. Following on this division, in most of the Yoruba country two maize seasons and one yam season make one year. The yam season sits astride the early and the late maize seasons. In addition to the crop seasons the Yorubas also use harvests to denote time. Thus they talk of the bumper harvest (*Ifo*) and the little harvest (*Igbaha* or *Agara*). The harvest and the crop seasons do not correspond to the Judaeo-Christian year, which definitely is a very recent inno-vation. Neither do the Yorubas have any means of distinguishing a leap year from the other years. The operative distinction which they have is between a male year (*Odun ti o ya ako*) and a female year (*Odun ti a ya abo*). The point of difference between these two types of years is in the level of peace and safety to life during the particular year. Thus, a year in which many disasters happen and many deaths occur is regarded as a male year, while a year of relative peace and plenty is a female year.

Ritual and Economic Units of Time

The week lacks any definite cosmological or ecological basis. It is an entirely social construct varying in length from society to society. The Yorubas now operate a seven-day week

103

and have names for the seven days.[29] It is highly probable, however, that the names of the days of the week, like the names of the months of the year, are of foreign origin. From all indications, it would appear that the figure seven occurs more in ritual worship than in everyday use. Thus the *Oro* ceremony lasts seven days *(Oro kije)*. Similarly the Egungun festival lasts seven days.

Furthermore, if what obtains in other parts of Africa is anything to go by, the basis of the week is likely to be economic. For example, the Lobagaa of modern Ghana designate the six days of their week by the name of the village where a market takes place on the day in question. Thus the very terms for day and market are the same *(daa)* and the week or the plurality of markets *(daar)*. To some extent the Yorubas also use the names of their markets for the same purpose, although these markets did not in any way constitute a week. If the market was the source from which the week originated the length of the week would be dictated by the number of places in the market round. Furthermore, it means that there can be neither uniform names of the days of the week nor of the length of the week, because the naming as well as the length would be subject to vicinal peculiarities, although this was not the case among the Yorubas.

The more plausible alternative is that the week has ritual origins; however, some authors argue that, since there was no interdependence between villages in cult matters, then the names of the days of the week as well as the length of the week would still vary from place to place.[30] This was not the case though, because there are three levels of deities among the Yorubas: (1) those worshipped throughout Yorubaland, (2) those worshipped by different villages, and (3) those worshipped by the different families. The deities which most probably give the names to the days of the week are those that prevail throughout the Yoruba universe. It would appear that only four such deities existed among the Yorubas: *Esu, Orisala, Odudua,* and *Jakuta.* They most probably have a four day week named after these deities.[31]

We have gone all this length to discuss names of the days of the week because the Yorubas believe that a man's character and destiny are determined by the day on which he is born. At the same time, the Yorubas (unlike the Ashanti in modern Ghana) do not name their children according to the days of the week on which they are born. They nevertheless have such names as *Abiose* (a child born on the rest day) or *Abiodun* (a child born during the annual Festival).

Absolute Time

To a large extent, the Yorubas distinguish between time and what is in time. Thus time is not inscrutably a property of events. It is a misconception of this possibility that produces the argument that the African has no concept of the future.[32] This assertion is often much too generalized to be true. What can be true is that, for a pre-literate society, lacking a sophisticated numeracy skill, the future is much too abstract and removed to be stated exactly. But for all peoples, the practical and cognitive relations towards the future are different from those towards the past.[33] Whereas the past has been experienced, the future can be known only indirectly by probable inference. Thus, any proposition asserting the occurrence of any future event must be true or false and cannot be both; unlike the past, the future has a limited certainty. But as far as the Yorubas are concerned, the future is more certain than the above. This belief is aptly put in several Yoruba expressions. For example it is often argued that a hundred years is not eternity.[34] In the same vein it is usually stated that the day after tomorrow is not a distant future because by tomorrow only one day is left.[35] These proverbs are often used to advise somebody who regards an activity as interminable; thus, they express the certainty of the future as an eternal truth and thereby caution prudence. Similarly, the Yorubas caution patience and longsuffering by advising that the harvest season (literally the next year) will come soon so that the farmer should not eat the yam he wishes to plant.[36] Neither do they overlook the inevitability of changes, as is well shown by their belief that the egg becomes the cock just as the child, barring death, becomes the adult.[37]

It would appear, therefore, that the Yorubas do not see themselves as completely ignorant of the future, although this does not derive from personal knowledge of that future. Yet they do not even believe that the details of the future are completely barred to them, because these secrets can be unravelled through divination. Neither do they accept that probable inferences can only by made from the past to the future. On the contrary, they believe that the future is encapsuled in the present in such a way that the future is only an outgrowth of the present and that a child normally shows traits of his adulthood.[38] Thus, the future co-exists with the present without being co-extensive with it.

The Yorubas balance this view of the certainty of the future by that of uncertainty, thereby casting a doubt on their certainty of the future. They assert categorically that it is only

JOHN A. A. AYOADE

possible to know the present and not the future,[39] particularly
because they are well aware that the future does not necessarily
follow the pattern of the present.[40] The practical implication of
this is that they are therefore mentally prepared for the uncertainty of the future in such a way as to mitigate its uncertainty.
As a result, there is only an apparent inconsistency between
their beliefs of certainty and uncertainty of the future.

By showing an awareness of the past, the present, and
the future, the Yorubas accept time as a locus of history. This
knowledge is exhibited in different dimensions. The first is that
of time in antiquity, as can be deduced from certain Yoruba
expressions which do not meticulously specify a point in time but
point to a period of time.[41]

Closely related to this belief in antiquity, and in fact a
category of it, is the notion of precedence. Thus the Yorubas
say that the chicken fed on certain food items before corn came
into the world. For the historian this expression is important in
two main respects: first, it is important because it shows the
precedence of the chicken over the corn; and, second, it more or
less confirms the assertion that the corn was introduced into this
area.

A similar view of antiquity and sequence is expressed in
the Yoruba saying that the *Ifa* and the Islamic religions antedated
them while the Christian faith came in their lifetime.[42] To some
extent this summarizes the history of religions in Yoruba-land.

In addition to their notion of time as a locus of history,
we find the notion of the irreversible and uninterruptible flow of
time. It is believed that time is very powerful because its
passage cannot be impeded, even temporarily.[43] This is in no way
arrested[44] as it is believed to be done by night travellers who
need the moon to lighten their paths. What is important to note
here is that they do not believe that they can induce the moon or
even its brightness. What they believe can be interrupted is not
the moon, which symbolizes time, but the brightness of the moon.

Since they do not therefore believe that time can be
arrested, they assert that things have to be done in their proper
time. Thus a theoretical problem arises with regards to the
precedence between time and event. Since it is events that must
keep pace with time and not vice-versa, it can be inferred that,
for the Yorubas, time antedates motion even though time was
unintelligible before motion. This is further complicated by the
belief that there are in fact events over which time has no

106

bearing at all because certain events can occur against all temporal laws.

Conclusion

What we have attempted to do in this paper is investigate an aspect of the life of the Yorubas with a view to providing an understanding of their life-styles through an analysis of their conceptualization and utilization of time. Certain conclusions can be drawn from this analysis of time. It is evident that the Yorubas reckon time in blocks of varying lengths and relative to the issues under discussion. Thus, time cannot be precise nor should the notion of punctuality and lateness be rigid. In effect, the prejudice masquerading as law, that the African (and this includes the Yorubas) is congenitally unpunctual, arises from a lack of understanding of their measurement of time. It is no less true that the same error of judgement is attributable to the failure to interpret time based on the human and material environment as charitably as possible.

Whatever else one might say about the Yorubas, it is clear that time is not only implicit in their thought and speech but is also a clear category of it. They are doubtlessly well aware that a proper understanding of time is a prerequisite to its judicious use. Thus, they do not see themselves as of necessity, helpless victims of time but as potential conquerors of time through a careful reflection on time-past, and a discreet scheduling of time-present as well as time-future. The importance of this factor is clearly borne out by the due emphasis which the Yorubas put on the timeliness of events. Of no less importance is the oft-sounded caution about the uncertainty of the future which paradoxically makes that future certain. And most important of all is the fact that the socialization process has made them so much time-conscious to a point that their cognizance of time is easily taken for granted.

JOHN A. A. AYOADE

FOOTNOTES

1. C. R. Niven, *A Short History of the Yoruba Peoples,* (London: Longmans, Green and Co., 1958), p. 3.

2. Ibid., p. 4.

3. Samuel Johnson, *The History of the Yorubas From the Earliest Times to the Beginning of the British Protectorate* (Lagos: C.S.S. Bookshops, 1969), p. 4.

4. Mortimer J. Adler and William Gorman, eds. *The Great Ideas: A Syntopicon of the Great Books of the Western World* (Chicago: Encyclopaedia Britanica Inc. 1971), p. 897. On the contrary however William James distinguishes between the knife-edge of the real present which is gone in the instant of becoming and the specious present with a certain breadth of its own. Ibid., p. 902.

5. John S. Mbiti, *African Religions and Philosophy* (London: Heinemann, 1969), p. 17.

6. St. Augustine, *The Confessions of the City of God,* bk. XI (Chicago: Encyclopaedia Britanica, Inc., 1971) pp. 94-95.

7. R. M. Hutchins, ed., *Great Books of the Western World: Locke, Berkeley, Hume* (Chicago: Encyclopaedia Britanica, Inc., 1971), pp. 431-432.

8. Quoted in Adler and Gorman, *The Great Ideas, p. 898.*

9. Norman Feather, *An Introduction to the Physics of Mass, Length and Time* (Edinburgh: Edinburgh University Press, 1968), p. 37.

10. E. E. Evans-Pritchard, *The Nuer* (Oxford: Clarendon Press, 1968) p. 95. This is also contrary to John Mbiti's view *(African Religions,* p. 17) that the linear concept of time in Western thought is alien to African thinking.

11. See also p. 82.

12. It must be noted that the word *Agba* has another use among the Yorubas. While it can denote an advanced age it can also be used to refer to witches and wizards. However there is a possible correlation between the two uses because witchcraft or wizardry is, in the main, a preserve of elderly people.

13. This is usually said in the form of a proverb *"Omo ro epon a ni ko to Baba, Baba so'pa ni?"* That is, a fully matured child has a similar physical sexual capacity as the father.

14. This feeling is usually put succinctly by the Yorubas in the saying *"Bi omode ni aso bi agba ko le ni ekisa bi agba,"* meaning that if a child has as many clothes as an adult he cannot have as many rags as the adult.

15. Usually the Yorubas make a distinction between *Ewu Ogbo* (natural grey hairs) and *Ewu Ose* (false grey hairs) which are believed to appear as a result of the frequent use of native soap.

16. David L. Sills, ed., *International Encyclopedia of the Social Sciences,* vol. 16 (New York: The Macmillan Company, the Free Press, 1972), p. 25.

17. Evans-Pritchard, *The Nuer,* p. 105.

18. C. D. Broad, "Time," in *Encyclopaedia of Religion and Ethics,* Vol 12 (Edinburgh: T. & T. Clark, 1971), p. 336.

19. Broad, "Time," p. 31.

20. A Yoruba proverb *("Iyawo ti a gbe ni osu aga ti nfi iyan mo ile yio ba nibe ni omo re yio ma je")* indicates the month of *Aga* as a month of plenty. Other months which occur in the Yoruba language are the months of *Oginnitin, Oye* and *Ewo.*

21.
Osu Sere	-	January
Osu Erele	-	February
Osu Erena	-	March
Osu Igbe	-	April
Osu Ebibi	-	May
Osu Okudu	-	June
Osu Agemo	-	July

Osu Ogun	-	August
Osu Owewe	-	September
Osu Owara	-	October
Osu Belu	-	November
Osu Ope	-	December

22. Northcote W. Thomas, "The Week in West Africa," *Journal of the Royal Anthropological Institute of Great Britian and Ireland* 54 (1924): 186.

23. Interview with Dr. Ignatius O. Ajimoke of the Department of Education, University of Ibadan on November 3, 1974.

24. Interview with Dr. J. O. O. Abiri, of the Department of Education, University of Ibadan on November 6, 1974.

25. The twinkling of the eye of a crab = *Iseju Akan.*

26. The twinkling of the human eye is called *Iseju* which is the same word now used for a minute.

27. The Yorubas always regard the cock as a sprightly bird that summons everyone to a new day's work. Thus they say that the lazy man hisses whenever the cock crows (*Akuku ko ole p'ose.*).

28. *Supra.*, pp. 11-12.

29.
Ojo Isegun or *Ojo Aiku* =	Sunday
Ojo Aje =	Monday
Ojo Asesedaiye =	Tuesday
Ojo 'Ru =	Wednesday
Ojo 'Bo =	Thursday
Ojo Eti =	Friday
Ojo Abameta =	Saturday

30. Thomas, "The Week in West Africa," p. 194.

31. Ibid., p. 200.

32. Cf. Mbiti, *African Religions,* noted on p. 73.

33. Broad, "Time," p. 337.

34. *Ogorun odun ki ise lailai.*

35. *Otunla ko jinna,*

110

Bo d'ola
The above proverb is sometimes rendered in another form:
Oni ni o bo ola l'oju meaning that it is only today that
stands between us and tomorrow.

36.　　*Amodun ko jinna k'eni ma mu ebu je.*

37.　　*Eyin ni d'akuko,*
B'omode o ku,
A t'agbalagba.

38.　　*Omo ti yio je Asamu Kekere ni o ti nj'eno samu samu lo.*

39.　　*Oni ni a mo ko s'eni to mo ola.*

40.　　The often say that time is unlike a straight line *(igba kii
to lo bi orere).* And neither does an individual have it all
smooth or all rough throughout life *(Igba kan ko lo ile
aiye gbo).*

41.　　Some of the expressions indicating antiquity include the
saying that there was a time when the eyes were on the
knees *(Igba ti oju wa l'orunkun).* Similarly antiquity is
also denoted in the expression that time was when somebody was beaten he beat the ground in return *(Aiye na mi
ki nna ileele).*

42.　　*Aije l'aba Ifa*
Aiye l'aba Imole
Osan gangan n'Igbagbo wo'le de.

43.　　This is often put succinctly in the saying *Enikan ko le mu
ojo so lokan* meaning that nobody can tether time.

44.　　They believe that the moon can be forced to keep its
brightness while the journey lasts *(Kika Osupa).*

111

CAUSAL THEORY IN AKWAPIM
AKAN PHILOSOPHY[1]

Helaine K. Minkus

The *Akwapim Akan* are members of the traditional political state of Akwapim, a federation of Akan and Guang speakers,
located in southeastern Ghana. Akwapim Akan religious beliefs
and practices, matrilineal social organization and hierarchically-
structured political organizations, are quite similar to those found
in other Akan states in Ghana although differing in some details.
The field-work upon which this analysis is based was primarily
conducted in Akwapim[2] and so can only speak reliably to causal
theory among Akwapim Akan but examination of the literature on
other Akan areas indicates that most of the statements would hold
with little variation for all Akan groups.[3]

It is evident that the economic, social and political
conditions of Akwapim Akan life have changed significantly within
the past one hundred years. Akwapim Akan are now citizens of a
nation-state and participants in a world economy. The first
mission station was established in the capital of Akropong in 1835
by the Basel Evangelical Mission Society. As well as introducing
a new religion, the missionaries established an educational system,
introduced many new crops, taught new technical skills and
organized commerce in imported goods. According to the 1960
census, 70.2% of Akwapim Akan claim to be Christian, 0.6%
moslem, 23.9% Traditional religion, and 5.3% No religion.[4] The
first primary school in Akwapim was built in 1843, followed by a

HELAINE K. MINKUS

seminary in 1848. The rate of school attendance is significantly higher for Akwapims than for most other groups of Ghanains, although formal education is still far from universal. Akwapims value education and boast of the highly educated men and women who come from the area. Akwapim farmers began growing crops for export in the nineteenth century and were among the first in Ghana to realize the value of cocoa as a cash crop.

Akwapim Akan life has undergone numerous changes and certain elements of the traditional culture have been lost or greatly modified. However, the basic assumptions of the cultural philosophy, including the causal theory, appear to have been maintained.[5]

The presentation of Akwapim Akan causal theory will begin with an examination of the basic premises, the causal efficacy of the various spiritual beings,[6] and the mode of operation of what can be termed "automatic forces," particularly medicines, charms and curses. The nature of the causal agents recognized and the way they operate will be examined in detail, chiefly in the context of explanation given for misfortune, illness and death. Beliefs about illness, the categories of illness and the treatment administered will then be discovered. This is followed by a discussion of man's ability to foresee and change events and the extent of individual responsibility for what occurs. The paper will conclude with a consideration of the premises of Akan causal theory and the ways in which the system is protected from doubt.

To the Akan, the created world, though composed of countless individual beings and objects, is viewed as unitary. The multitude of different types of existents are alike in having been created by the Supreme Begin and in owing their continued existence to His sustenance. They are similarly unified by their indispensable possession of *sunsum* 'spirit'. The *sunsum* is the essence of the being or object, its intrinsic activating principle or that which enables it to exercise power and to function in a characteristic manner. The concept of *sunsum* accounts for the basic similarity of all existents, which are alike in being spirited or active. The universe of traditional Akan thought contains no inert objects in the sense of matter incapable of awareness or action.

The term *sunsum* is used in a variety of contexts and serves as one of the principle concepts and unifying themes in Akan philosophy. As well as designating the activating essence of particular beings and things, it also refers to the general

114

power to act in non-ordinary, non-physical ways. In reference to human beings, *sunsum* denotes what can be described as the source of personality and strength. The term is employed in both a specific and a general sense. *Sunsum* may refer to the essence of a particular deity, man or plant, or refer generally to all beings and forces which man cannot perceive, or designate an aspect of reality and mode of causal operation.

Fundamental to Akan causal theory is the conception of an orderly universe in which all events are caused and potentially explicable. The following proverbs evidence the belief in an effective cause: *Biribi ankoka mpopa a, enye krada.* 'If nothing touches the dry palm branch, it does not make a noise.'[7] *Birebire amma a, amane mma.* 'If Birebire had not come, there would have been no calamity.'[8] (If the initiatory event had not occurred, the consequence would not have resulted.) As will be discussed below, most events also have ascribed reasons for their occurrence, an answer to the question *why* as well as *how.*

Events, as determined by the wills of spiritual beings, the operation of automatic forces, and the self-willed actions of men and animals, follow in orderly, comprehensible sequence. The world is not capricious, but neither is it subject to totally automatic determinism. Each thing as created by God has its own *sunsum* or activating principle which allows it to function in its specific manner; the inspirited universe maintains its orderly processes. However the Akan universe does allow for divine but still orderly intervention. God is always available an an ultimate recourse for those in difficulty. The aid of the more approachable spiritual beings--the gods, ancestral spirits and personalized talismans[9]--is frequently solicited. They all appear to deal with the same matters, although certain individual spirits specialize to some extent. The most common requests, enunciated in libations and during consulting sessions at shrines, reflect the matters of principal import to the Akan: fertility, health, strength, prosperity, and protection from evil forces. As conditions of life have changed, new requests have been added, e. g., for employment, success in examinations, freedom from motor accidents. Virtually any legitimate endeavor, and some perhaps illegitimate, may be bolstered by supplication to the spiritual beings.

The Supreme Being retains ultimate control over events and continues to sustain and rule over the world He created. However, the Akan God is also viewed as transcendent and in some respects remote from His creation. No living person can see or hear Him and His motives and modes of action are ultimately

HELAINE K. MINKUS

beyond human scrutiny and understanding.

God's attribute of transcendence and the concomitant belief that He has delegatd power to other agents that more directly interact with human beings pragmatically diminish His omnipotence. The other agents are treated in practice as if endowed with an independent ability to act. Sacrifices are offered to them in their postulation of a great number of beings empowered to affect events, joined with the acceptance of evil as necessarily co-existing with good from creation, obviates the problem of evil so burdensome to those monotheistic theologians who define the Supreme Being as both omnipotent and totally benevolent and attempt a rational reconciliation of these qualities with the existence of evil. For the Akan specific evils may be combatted, but there is no attempt to extirpate all evil. It must be accepted that witches do and always will exist to exercise their malignant powers, that the minor deities may at times harm the innocent, and that malicious and vindictive people may wreak their damage, while yet affirming that God and the world as a unity are benevolent. Belief in the metaphysical necessity of evil is accompanied by faith in cosmic justice. It is firmly believed that evil acts will be punished by evil consequences and good rewarded by good.

The reality of evil, although ultimately a part of and subject to divine justice, poses significant immediate problems for the individual. There is no doubt that life is dangerous and the individual always vulnerable: *Obra ye ko.* 'Life is war'. Attainment of success and prosperity and, in fact, mere continuance of earthly existence require spiritual and social protection. Throughout Akan thought, in the ideas concerning causality, human nature, social organization and values, the dependence of the individual upon others is emphasized. In social life, a man needs a strong benefactor who can support his cause, protect him from others and aid him in misfortune. One should strive to sustain amicable relations with all those who may be of assistance. The support and protection of spiritual beings and forces is indispensable. Each person by birth is a ward of his matrilineal ancestors and paternally related deity and must act in the ways they require so as to elicit their protection and obviate their punishment. An individual may choose to strengthen his spiritual resources by placing himself under the protection of a deity or personalized talisman or by acquiring some of the numerous protective medicines and charms available. His own 'soul' *(okra)*, conceived as both one constituent of the living person and as an extrinsic guardian peculiar to him, must not be neglected. The best protection against spiritual harm, particularly that which is

116

initiated by human agents, is a strong spirit *(sunsum).* The *sunsum* may perhaps be strengthened by medicine or training, but the relative differences in individual strength appear to be attributed largely to creation. The individual without a strong *sunsum* has therefore even greater need to rely on other, external sources of spiritual protection.

The Spiritual Beings

The spiritual beings are believed to bless those who behave well and to function actively to provide that which is sought, as the following examples indicate. A child who is conceived with a deity's assistance (i.e., whose mother, having long been barren, has been enabled to conceive and deliver safely) is often named after the god. The good fortune enjoyed by a family is frequently attributed to the good offices of their ancestral spirits. The ancestors, and particularly the recently deceased, are thought to reveal medicine that can be used to cure an ill kinsman. And yet as crucial as the ability of the spiritual beings to bring about what is desired is their power to prevent inimical forces from obstructing what would otherwise successfully unfold. The two conceptions are not mutually exclusive. Informants generally showed little interest in specifying whether the benefits conferred by well-disposed and powerful spirits resulted from their positive actions or from their protective influence. There may also be the idea that things will go well if the spiritual beings simply do not interfere, and so the petitions for aid may in part be requests for simple non-interference. Rattray had made the interesting but probably untestable suggestion that the belief system has undergone a change from an emphasis upon the dangerous nature of the spiritual and the need to placate and neutralize it to an admission (or hope) that the spirits may exercise positive benevolence.[10]

God, the gods and ancestral spirits and, in most contexts, the personalized talismans are conceived as personalized beings endowed with judgment, will, desires and temperament. Their actions and decisions are freely determined and not subject to coercive techniques. Human beings politely inform them of the situation for which help is needed, beg for their cooperation, honor them and attempt to secure their favorable intervention through the promise of sacrifices and offerings. Proper ritual attention must be proffered and the rules ordained by the spirits must be observed. They are expected to comply with the petitioner's request, not because they have been coerced by ritual, but rather because they are thought to be well-disposed beings

117

helpful to those who approach them respectively. Each lineage must remain on amicable terms with its own ancestral spirits. They may call the attention of the ancestors to a situation requiring rectification, which may have been worsened by the ancestors' neglect, but never chastise or scold their deceased elders.

By contrast, humans do exercise some leverage in regard to the deities and personalized talismans. The adherents of the deity or personalized talisman are not compelled to continue its worship and may always switch their allegiance to another being, thereby depriving the god or talisman of the homage and offerings it is thought to desire. Formerly, the inability of a priest to divine correctly or his consistent lack of success in the treatment of illness, which might be attributed either to the quackery of the supposed priest or the impotence of his deity, were met by the politically sanctioned killing of the priest and destruction of his shrine. Chiefs no longer exercise the death penalty, but an incompetent or unsuccessful priest quickly loses his following. The deities and personalized talismans, and their priests, are treated with respect as long as they provide what is sought; consistent failure is met with scorn and derision. New cults are frequently established and abandoned in favor of still newer ones.[11]

Automatic Forces

Reflective of the emphasis in Akan thought on personalized, powerful beings, most events are explained in volitional terms. However, the causal theory includes concepts of spiritual forces which operate automatically once their mechanisms have been set into operation. While some of these forces may be viewed as operating more automatically than others, few are completely independent of the actions and wishes of the personalized beings.

Two of the dominant types of spiritual objects or forces are *aduru* 'medicine' and *suman* 'charms'. The two categories are lexically and conceptually distinguished yet often overlap. Either or both terms may often be applied to the same material. This intergrading and frequent equivalence of the terms makes understandable their alternate usage in designating the personalized talismans. The term *aduru* denotes any liquid or powder not used as food or drink. Although its primary referent is medicinal, the root, sometimes with added suffixes, has come to denote such other substances as ink, paint and gun-powder. Medicinal *aduru* may take the form of liquid squeezed from boiled plant

118

parts *(odudo)*; herbal water, prepared by steeping plants in a basin of water, which is drunk or used in bathing *(kunkuma)*; a pill made by grinding the ingredients *(dufuaw)*; or black powder prepared by charring the combined ingredients *(boto)*. The primary constituents of medicine are plant parts--leaves, bark, roots and stem, and the term *nhaban* 'leaves' is often used in synedoche to refer to medicine. However, parts of animals and other things may also be included.

Medicine is categorized, according to the ends which it is expected to accomplish, as either good medicine *(aduru pa)* or else bad medicine *(adubone)* or poison *(aduto)*. Good medicine is used to treat illness and disease, to acquire protection from malignant human and spiritual agents, and to increase the chances of success in such ventures as trading, hunting and war. Some medicines work for the benefit of the user without inflicting damage upon any other individual; the only negative effect of a good medicine is to neutralize any evil power directed at the treated individual. In contrast, the essential function of bad medicine is to bring about the failure, misadventure, illness or death of those against whom it is employed.

All medicines--whether the simple herbal remedies used in the treatment of boils or a mixture that, strewn on a path, will cause the death of a particular individual should he step on it--operate by virtue of the combined *sunsum* of their ingredients. The Supreme Being created plants and other things with natural powers which may be utilized by man for his benefit or may be employed in malicious ways. Medicine which is properly prepared and administered will function efficiently by virtue of its own power, although its application is normally preceded, as are virtually all other ventures, by pouring a libation asking for the assistance of various spiritual beings.

As discussed above, medicine is classified as either good or bad. Although a spiritual-non-spiritual distinction appears in many Akan semantic domains, it does not seem to apply to medicines. Attempts to elicit criteria of classification beyond the good-bad distinction met with little success. Informants did volunteer or agree to the following two distinctions, but neither seems to be lexically marked or particularly salient. A distinction can be made according to whether the medicine must be brought into direct physical contact with the user or victim or may act at a distance. Some medicine is said to affect any individual, not protected by other medicines, who comes into contact with it, whereas others affect only the person against whom it is directed, or at least affect that person most severely. But the term poison

119

appears to apply equally to all bad medicines, with no distinction being made between those that might operate in a "spiritual" in contrast to a "non-spiritual" or "natural" fashion. In fact to describe Akan medicines as operating within either a "natural" or "supernatural or spiritual" realm would be equally distorting. All medicine, in common with everything else that exists and has power, functions by virtue of its *sunsum* 'spirit'. The *sunsum* is invisible, hence its workings cannot be directly observed. Yet, the *sunsum* constitutes the defining, i. e., "natural" properties of the object. All medicines thus work by "spirit," but are not "supernatural" or "miraculous." Some are more wonderful than others, not in the sense that they are outside the realm of what occurs lawfully in an orderly universe, but because they operate in ways that excite man's interest and amazement.

Closely related to medicines are the *suman* 'charms'. The criterial distinction between the two categories is that a *suman* is "something you hold." Its medicinal ingredients are placed within a material object such as a pot, leather pouch, beads, broom, headband, etc. which may be worn on the person or put in the user's house, or in the case of bad *suman* in the victim's house. Although most *suman* are individually owned, the protective ones are often acquired for the welfare of both the individual and his family, and some are regarded as exercising their protective influences for the benefit of the entire state.

The power of a *suman* comes from the *sunsum* of its ingredients and material form and the ceremony used in making and employing it. Man is said to have learned how to make *suman* from the minor deities, the "little people of the forest" (*mmoatia*) and through visions. Any individual may elect to purchase a *suman* from someone who knows how to prepare it. Unlike the deities and personalized talismans who have the power to reject potential adherents, a *suman* is purchased in the same way as any object and is expected to function for any user if properly handled. The simpler charms require little or no ritual attention. The more elaborate and powerful charms are given periodic libations and sacrifices and the care given a few of them approaches that for the minor deities.

Suman are not used in the treatment of illness, which is the exclusive domain of medicines. Either medicines or charms may be employed to secure protection, success or the downfall of one's enemies. Each charm or type of medicine is specific to a certain situation or desired end, although some of the protective ones may guard against a variety of dangers.

The two categories of *aduru* and *suman* although clearly distinct in certain contexts and with regard to some specific items merge in many cases. Black powder which is put into a leather pouch and worn around the neck might be called a *suman,* with reference to its nature as a total entity, or *aduru,* when attention is focused on the powder which enables it to operate. Treatment with medicine alone may enable a person to benefit from its power but to a lesser degree than if he also had a charm which contained the medicine plus other ingredients. The frequent similarity or virtual identity of *aduru* and *suman* is recognized in the Ghanaian English term "juju" used to cover all such automatic powers, particularly those that are considered harmful.

Both charms and medicines may be rendered ineffective if they are brought into contact with what is taboo or "hateful" to them. The activating spiritual power is negated or rendered impotent by contact with something which is inimical to it. Restoration of its power requires purification of the charm and renewal of the medicine. Failure of a charm or medicine to bring about its desired effects may also be explained by its being over-whelmed by a stronger power. If one man tries to harm another by use of a particular charm, he will fail if his intended victim has a similar charm as strong as his or has taken an antidote in medicinal form. Should the other have a stronger charm, the intended harmful effect may rebound on the evil-doer. Power must be fought with power: *Dade bi twa dade bi.* 'A cutlass cuts a cutlass'.

Certain acts are believed to have powerful consequences because of their own inherent power to affect events and/or because of the reaction they may elicit from the spiritual beings.

Thoughts and words have power to bring about the state which they symbolize. Evil thoughts or hatred for another may cause him harm. The concluding section of libations always asks the beings invoked to harm evil-doers, those who do not have good intentions but wish to cause the downfall of others. In general, it is expected that someone who hates another will either curse him, use bad medicine against him, spread malicious stories or in other ways try to undermine him. Hatred is regarded as dangerous primarily because it leads the one so disposed to actively harm his antagonist. But evil thoughts in themselves may cause damage. Stray thoughts of wishing that someone be harmed in some way do not seem to cause remorse in the person harboring them unless the envisioned misfortune is realized, in which case the one who wished it might well feel

121

responsible and guilty.

The efficacy attributed to words is illustrated by the proverb: *Eto Brewu a, owu.* 'If you name one 'come and die' he dies.'[12] Fathers are careful in choosing the names of their children, for it is believed that the child will come to resemble the person whose name he is given. This is explained in part by the belief that the *sunsum* of the person so honored will influence the child, but there appears to be as well a belief that the name by itself will exert influence. Certain dreaded diseases, e.g., leprosy *(kwata)*, are referred to only by euphemism *(mikura dua mu* 'I hold wood') for fear that mention of the true name of the disease will cause it to afflict the speaker.

The words of certain individuals are believed to exert extraordinary power, especially when uttered in blessing or curse. This quality, called *Anogya* or *Nkasaso,* is possessed particularly by the old but other individuals, with very strong spirits, are also able to exercise this verbal influence. The words of an aged person who has lived a good life are deemed especially potent, and their blessings are eagerly sought. But the bad words uttered on slight provocation by a senile or ill-tempered old person are equally thought to have effect, and mothers warn their children to avoid such people.

It is in the practice of cursing by invoking a deity that the power attributed to words is most strongly exemplified. Such curses are most commonly invoked in cases of theft, land disputes, adultery and defamation of character. A person who has lost something valuable may call upon a god to kill the thief. One who feels he has been falsely accused or his character unjustly defamed may employ a curse as a self-inflicted ordeal, by saying, for example, "If what X has said is true, may Akonnedi kill me." The formula may also be uttered in a conditional form, to order a person to carry out some action; if the order is obeyed, the threatened consequences are not realized. Formerly, witnesses to a court case were made to swear on a deity that what they were about to testify was true; it was fully expected that perjury would bring about death.

The verbal formula may simply be said or may be accompanied by the person's throwing water or an egg on the ground. To curse most effectively, however, requires that the person travel to the shrine of the deity invoked and pay the priest to conduct a ceremony. Revocation of the curse, regardless of the manner in which it was initiated, requires a ceremony at the shrine to purify the person who has suffered the effect of the curse, pacify and compensate the innocent party and inform the deity of the action taken and of the desire that it nullify the curse.

A curse wreaks havoc upon the family of the person against whom it is called. Not only the guilty person but many other members of his family may be killed by the deity unless the causes of the deaths are investigated and the ceremony of revocation performed. The injured party may demand a pacification fee far in excess of the original damage. Cases of exorbitant fees demanded and received were cited by a number of informants.

The effective power behind a curse is that of the deity whose name is invoked. The assumption of the deity's ability to judge the truth of the matter and identify the guilty party is attested by the belief that the curse will rebound upon a person who curses falsely, e.g., if he has himself spent his money but utters a curse accusing another person of stealing it in hopes of receiving compensation. Similarly, if a man accuses his wife of infidelity but she denies the allegation, he may categorically curse any who have committed adultery with her. If his wife is innocent of the charge, it is the husband who will suffer the effects of the curse. The formula, "If what X says is true, or if I did what I am accused of having done, may god X kill me," carries with it the implied addition, "If I am innocent, may god X kill those who have falsely accused or judged me."

Although the discriminating power of a deity is involved, a curse partakes of the nature of an automatic force. Once set in motion it acts as a malignant force that destroys without pity until nullified by the procedure of renovation. Even those in no way implicated in the matter may suffer if they share in illegally-gotten gains, e.g., by eating food bought with stolen money. A curse initiated by a simple utterance may continue to operate although the one who initiated it, motivated by temporary anger, may have forgotten having called it into force.

Certain conditions and situations, as well as words and acts, are regarded as inherently powerful, apart from and in addition to the response they elicit from the spiritual beings.... [For example] A person with six digits, either fingers or toes, is considered an abomination and must be kept segregated from ritual objects and their human attendants lest defilement result. Contact with a corpse also requires purification to remove the taint of death and prevent the evil associated with it from continuing to exercise its influence.

123

HELAINE K. MINKUS

Spiritual contamination, which results from exposure to certain situations and from the transgression of taboos, effectively lowers a person's spiritual resistance and makes him vulnerable to a variety of evil spiritual influences. Not only will his spiritual guardians, his own soul and his protective medicines and charms cease to shield him but witches, sorcerers and other evil agents and forces can more easily harm him. Purification plays a major role in almost all ceremonies, both those done for the benefit of one individual and those conducted for the welfare of a group or the entire town. Rites of purification cleanse a person or group from the effects of any contact with defilement, accomplish a release from the influences of a situation in which evil was operating, and prevent any threatening evil force from exercising its power.

Explanations of Misfortune, Illness and Death

Akan ideas concerning causality are most clearly manifested in the explanations given for cases of misfortune, illness and death. Beliefs about the nature and operation of causal agents cease to be theoretical but must serve as the basis for practical, remedial action. It is assumed that all events are caused, that there is 'something within them' (*biribi wom'*) or 'associated with them' (*biribi bata ho*) that accounts for their occurrence. Significant events do not occur without reason (*enye okwa*) and the cause may be determined if one investigates carefully or 'goes into the matter' (*woko mu*). When an event is of little significance in itself or not of much concern to the person speaking (though perhaps important to the one affected) or if the precise cause has not yet been determined, it may be described simply as a 'misfortune' or 'accident' (*abew, asiane, ahyiakwa*). Such a designation does not imply that the event happened fortuitously but calls attention solely to the unfortunate nature of the occurrence without specifying what brought it about....

The causes most frequently cited to explain serious cases of misfortune and illness and to account for death are the following: punishment by the ancestral spirits, deities and personalized talismans; the operation of witchcraft and sorcery; and the unfolding of a person's destiny. These as well as other subsidiary causes and forces will be examined in turn.

124

Punishment by the spiritual beings

The ancestral spirits hold their descendants and successors responsible for the proper conduct of lineage affairs, maintenance of the customs they established and proffering the ritual
attention they require. Punishable offenses include failure to
safeguard the property held in trust for all present and future
members, the commission of acts which bring disgrace upon the
group, dissension among members, and failure to show respect to
living elders. A chief, whose ancestors' authority encompassed
the entire state or town, is held liable for any failure to continue
the good rule which they established while in office. The protective influence of the royal ancestors is deemed indispensable for
the welfare of the community. The chief must, therefore, be
especially vigilant that the ceremonies for his ancestors are
performed correctly and that any acts which might be offensive to
them are speedily punished by the political authorities. The lineage head or chief is held liable by his ancestral spirits for all
that happens within his sphere of authority. Although direct
responsibility in certain areas may be delegated to attendants, the
successor in office is the one held accountable and punished for
any breach of custom or morals. It is commonly believed that the
ancestors can summon a person to the other world to answer a
charge of misconduct. Such a summons brings death to the
accused wrong-doer for: *Asaman, wonko nsan mma.* 'The spirit
world is not a place one can visit and return from again (as a
living man).'[13] However, the ancestors first make a person ill and
allow him time to investigate the matter and perform ceremonies of
pacification and purification. If the individual heeds the warning
and does what is required, he is able to escape the impending
death.

While the ancestors are clearly credited with the power
to cause death, some informants in attempting to explain the
precise nature of the action asserted that the ancestors themselves do not actually kill a person but simply remove their
protection, thus making the individual vulnerable to attack by
witches and other evil forces. According to some informants the
ancestors in effect use the witches as agents; others explained
the matter by saying that the ancestors "wash their hands" of the
person, and if there is a witch in the house desirous of killing
him, then it would happen. Whatever the exact mechanics, illness
and death can result from the action or withdrawal of protection
of the ancestral spirits. Similarly, failure to prosper may sometimes be attributed to the ancestors as agents. Barrenness,
however, is not an ancestral sanction. The ancestors wish the

lineage to grow and would not prevent this by stopping the fertility of its members.

The gods punish such actions as theft and murder primarily when they have been invoked by means of a curse. Although it is possible that a deity will punish--or more likely refuse to protect--one of his adherents who commits a serious breach of law or morality, the efficacy of deities in sanctioning immoral behavior is usually conceived as their ability to act when invoked by the victim or his relatives....

The ancestral spirits and traditional deities deal with moral as well as ritual infractions but to a more limited, less explicit extent than the personalized talismans. The rules enjoined upon new adherents, to which they must subscribe before being allowed to come under the protection of the shrine, comprise a list of moral injunctions. The adherent must agree to forswear stealing, adultery, using bad medicines or charms, having evil thoughts against others, employing the power of witchcraft, invoking a curse and engaging in other anti-social behavior. An argument could well be made that changing economic, social and political conditions have weakened the effectiveness of the traditional sanctions, both social and spiritual, and that the new cults with their explicit injunctions have to some extent filled the gap. Those who join the new shrines are motivated primarily by the desire to be protected from those who try to harm them in the ways listed above, but themselves become subject to punishment should they infringe the rules. As in the case with the ancestral spirits and the traditional deities, the principal sanction of the personalized talisman is the threat of death, preceded by a warning in the form of a dream or an illness of sufficient duration to enable the guilty person to confess his misdeed and pacify the personalized talisman.

Witchcraft

Not only illness and death but virtually any unfortunate event may be attributed to the actions of witches. A witch (obayifo) is a person, usually female, who harbors an evil spiritual power (bayi) within her. The power may be obtained at birth, for a pregnant witch can transmit her witchcraft to the fetus, but much more commonly is obtained later in life. The usual vehicle of transmission is food, especially palm oil soup, or a material object such as beads or other jewelry. A witch may not take her witchcraft with her when she dies; she will try to give it to a relative but if that is not possible she will leave it in a piece of jewelry, cloth or other article. The person who

126

inherits her goods will likewise come into possession of the witch-craft power. The company of witches may invite a person in a dream to accept meat or to travel with them; should the offer be accepted he or she then becomes a member of the company. Some people wish to become witches and seek to buy or otherwise acquire the power. But many people are not amenable; the prac-tice of witchcraft is inimical to their soul and the forced attempt to make them into witches causes mental strain and can lead to madness. A witch acting from spite may purposely transmit witchcraft power to a person she knows will become ill or mad from the struggle to resist it.

Witches are able to cause damage in a multitude of ways.... A witch may bore a spiritual hole in an individual's hand or pocket so any money he obtains is irretrievably lost. A student's mind may be dulled by a witch so he is unable to succeed on an examination or a job applicant's face clouded so he antagonizes any prospective employers. An herbalist may suffer because a witch spoils his medicine or makes him ill so he is unable to go into the bush to collect herbs. A witch may set out to challenge the powers of a traditional priest, herbalist, midwife or medical doctor by bringing a patient she herself is making ill or presenting herself as a patient. The failure of the practi-tioner to effect a cure, because he is unable to detect that he is confronted by a witch or incapable of overpowering her, damages his reputation and diminishes his chances of prospering in his profession. During the period of fieldwork, a man divorced his wife, of whom he remained fond, after learning that his mother-in-law, a witch, prevented him from accumulating any savings by repeatedly making her daughter ill, which forced him to expend any money he received on costly medical care....

Sudden or untimely deaths require explanation, and witchcraft is often cited as the cause.... Although witches may cause good deaths, i.e., those preceded by illness, they are held especially responsible for sudden violent deaths (*atofowu*). An event that more than most others is thought to merit imputation of witchcraft is the death of only one person in a car or passenger truck accident. It occasionally happens that a hunter accidentally kills a person because he mistakes him for an animal, having been led to this misperception by witches....

While the dominant conception of witchcraft is over-whelmingly negative and witches are considered quintessentially antisocial, some informants asserted that some types of witchcraft can be used for good (*bayi pa* 'witchcraft power used for good purposes'). Such a witch, who it seems does not also use witchcraft for evil ends, employs her power to look after her children and protect them from harm. Herbalists and priests were said by some informants, including some practitioners in reference to others, to have good witchcraft which they used to attract clients, enhance their reputations and, most importantly, to combat the effects of evil witches. As informants not unreasonably argued, how could a priest deal effectively with the witches and persuade or force them to release their victim unless he was himself a witch? *Kwaku Mframa,* an Ashanti medium-priest of many years experience, who converted to Christianity and submitted to a long series of interviews by members of the Institute of African Studies, University of Ghana,[14] stated repeatedly in the interviews that much of the power of a medium-priest rests upon the help provided by the good witches attached to his shrine. Two of my informants went further and denied that the gods have any power at all, declaring that the effects produced are due solely to a group of witches who combine their power....

The belief in witchcraft has resisted encroachment by Western scepticism and materialism more firmly than almost any other element of traditional Akan religion. The Christian Churches have been able to cast doubt on the existence and/or power of the ancestral spirits and traditional deities. Some informants, who obviously maintained the beliefs at least in certain contexts, did sometimes deny during interviews that such beings could affect man. But virtually no one interviewed, including the most highly Western-educated, expressed doubt concerning the reality of witchcraft. The more thoughtful agree that it is often helpless old women who are accused of being witches, that some individuals who confess to practicing witchcraft are mad, and that some people whose lack of success is due to their own stupidity find witchcraft a handy excuse. Yet all but one informant maintained firmly that the existence and operation of witchcraft provide the only possible explanation for certain events. One very highly educated, sophisticated man presented the following argument (only slightly rephrased) in support of the reality of witchcraft:

1) Confession of witchcraft is very embarrassing.
2) No one but a mad woman or one who is guilty of the charge would confess.
3) Sane women confess to being witches and to having caused certain deaths.
4) These deaths are inexplicable if witchcraft is denied.
   These women are witches and did cause the deaths.

Sorcery

Maintained as tenaciously as the belief in witchcraft is belief in sorcery, i.e., the conviction that bad medicines and charms possess effective malignant power. Whether the use of bad medicines and charms and the fear of witchcraft have in fact increased in recent years due to the stresses of culture change, as has been alleged by Ward and by Field,[15] would be difficult to verify. There is no doubt, however, that Akwapim Akan believe that both means of inflicting harm are widely utilized.

Witchcraft is thought to be practiced commonly but not exclusively by women. Its effects are produced by the invisible action of the evil power lying within the witch. In contrast, bad medicines and charms may be employed by either sex, although it appears probably that the tangible objects required for its use are obtained principally from male practitioners. Sorcery is able to effect the same results as witchcraft: various types of misfortunes, barrenness, madness, illness and death. Unlike witchcraft power which is versatile in its operation, the various bad medicines and charms are specific to one or at most several effects....

The users of sorcery are generally thought to be motivated by envy, malice and a desire to destroy the health, prosperity or life of their victim. They seek the destruction of the other person out of pure hatred, often engendered by their unwillingness to see any other individual prosper. The motive may, however, be that of revenge, in some cases partially justified by the ill-treatment or neglect received from the intended victim. Sorcery is able to affect the innocent, but the person who is guilty of some offense against the one who uses it is more vulnerable to its effects, in part because his protective medicines may cease to protect him.

Many of the death-dealing means of sorcery operate by spiritually shooting, tying up, locking or piercing the victim's soul. Each medicine or charm has its antidote, and any ailment caused through sorcery, except those that lead to sudden death, may be successfully treated if the sufferer is taken in time to a competent herbalist or priest. The practitioner can, by applying the antidote or the taboos of the medicine or charm, remove the spiritual needles or bullets from the victim or release his soul from the trap or lock used to bind it.

129

Bad medicines and charms are regarded as reprehensible, and their possession and use have been offenses punishable by the traditional political organization, the colonial and now the national government. There is no doubt, however, that they have been and still are employed. During a four-year period (July 1935-September 1939), the court records of the Paramount Chief's Tribunal at Akropong included thirty-four cases (of a total of 285) of persons charged with "possession and use of noxious charms with intent to destroy or endanger human life." Field, in her well-documented study of petitioners at the shrines of the new cults, records numerous instances of persons "caught" by the personalized talismans for their prohibited use of sorcery.[16] Several deaths occurring during the period of field-work were attributed to sorcery. In a few cases the evidence was very good that such means had in fact been employed. Given the context of Akan beliefs and the proven fact that people do employ bad medicines and charms, fear that one is subject to sorcery is not a paranoid reaction.

All herbalists interviewed denied that they ever use or dispense bad medicines and charms. They asserted that should they do such an evil thing they would soon suffer. Certain medicines may be used either to inflict damage or as an antidote; should the medicine once be used for evil purposes its power to cure is said to spoil, although it retains its efficacy for evil. According to the official line, an herbalist who assisted others in causing harm rather than restricting himself to his proper functions of curing and protecting would lose his power to heal and would soon die. Other informants--neither herbalists nor priests--maintained that the same person can use medicine to both cause a disease and cure it, thereby generating business, or at least may use certain medicines for evil ends while using other medicines to cure. They grant that a person who administers bad medicines and charms will eventually suffer, as will all other bad people. But it is regarded as prudent to be wary of those who know good medicines and charms for fear that they may also know how to make bad ones....

Evil spirits/forces/powers

When the precise cause of an unfortunate event has not been determined but it is suspected that the cause operated in a spiritual way, the event may be attributed to *sunsumone* 'bad or evil spirits'. The term encompasses all spiritual influences which prove inimical to the best interests of an individual, including the legitimate punitive actions of the spiritual beings as well as the

130

operation of agents and forces thought to be evil or at least hostile, e.g., the ghosts of those who died violent deaths, witchcraft, sorcery, bad thoughts. The term also covers other possible evil spiritual influences which may exist in the world but of whose exact nature man is unaware: the Akan does not claim that his knowledge of the world is comprehensive or exhaustive. *Sunsummone* includes these possibly existing unidentified forces as well as those that are known but whose precise nature is not specified in a particular case.

Two types of beings which may work for evil, and can in certain contexts be described as *sunsummone,* will be briefly mentioned. The first are the *mmoatia* "little people of the forest" who are usually invisible but when seen resemble human beings except that they are very short, are red, black or white, and have feet that point backwards. These elves (though "fairies" is the term most often used in the literature) are normally mischievous rather than harmful and are thought to help man by teaching him how to make medicines and charms. Some priests claim that they are aided in their work by the "elves." In the interviews conducted, the "little people of the forest" were rarely mentioned as being responsible for any event. They are invoked particularly when a person lost in the bush for several days or longer returns and reports either that he was beaten by them or more often was saved by their gifts of bananas and other foods. The second is *Sasabonsam,* conceived as a winged, hairy forest monster with a double snake as tail, who is inimical to hunters and priests but in league with the witches and *mmoatia.* *Sasabonsam* is mentioned in various popular songs and folk tales but does not appear to be invoked often as a causal agent, though certain circumstances no doubt are attributed to an encounter with him.

Throughout this chapter I have used without explanation such phrases as "evil influences" and "evil forces," which correspond to the Akan phrases *sunsummone* 'bad or evil spirits', *adebone bi* 'any evil thing', *bone bi* 'any evil' and, in certain contexts, *mmusu* 'misfortune'. Evil is thought to be ever-present and always menacing, whether exercised by identifiable agents or by more vaguely conceived influences. The Akan views himself as always subject to spiritually caused danger, which is the reason for his concern with purification and the acquisition of spiritual protection and power.

Contact with death and the experience of illness or misfortune place the individual in a vulnerable state, subject to the generalized evil associated with such unfortunate occurrences

and to the particular beings or forces which caused the event.
The compound where the deceased is laid in state as well as the
mourners and chiefs who attended the funeral must be purified to
free them from the evil taint of death. A person who recovers
from illness, is released from misfortune or experiences a narrow
escape from an accident undergoes a ceremony to release him from
the beings or forces which had him in their power and to cleanse
his soul, which has been exposed to the evil and weakened by
the contamination. (It was suggested by several chiefs that I
purify both myself and my car after it was repaired following an
accident).

Soul[17]

Events may be explained without recourse to agents and
forces external to the individual. Each person is endowed by the
Creator with a 'soul' *(okra)*, thought of as both an essential
constituent of the individual without which life is impossible to
sustain and as a somewhat separate guardian which 'stands
behind' *(di n'akyi)* the individual to guide and protect him. The
attainment of success in life is dependent upon the constant
ministrations of a soul motivated to help its ward by his consis-
tently good behavior. The soul is thought to be very sensitive to
disgrace and defilement and will neglect or even desert the individual, thereby causing him misfortune and illness and eventually
death, should his behavior alienate it sufficiently. Ceremonies
(kraguare, anohyira, asubo) may be performed to thank a soul
which has been active in seeking its ward's prosperity or to
purify and pacify a soul which has been neglectful because
angered by the person's disgraceful or sullying acts.

Destiny

Related to the concept of the soul is that of destiny
(nkrabea). Each person before he enters this world 'takes leave'
(kra) of the Supreme Being, at which time he either states or
receives the message that will determine the course of his life on
earth *(nkrabea* 'destiny', literally "manner of taking leave").
Informants were unanimous in stating that the time of a person's
death is stipulated by his destiny. Variant opinions were
expressed in regard to other elements possibly included in the
person's message. Most informants said that the manner of death
is also specified and thus some people are destined to die a
sudden and violent death. A woman may say before she comes to
live on earth that she will return when she is pregnant with her
fourth child or a person may indicate his wish to die by drown-
ing. Destiny was cited as a possible cause of sterility by most

informants, but some argued that God never sends anyone into the world to be barren. The number of children a person will produce was mentioned by several people as an element of one's destiny, supported by the alleged fact that a woman who chooses to be sterilized before she has borne the requisite number will become ill. The concept of destiny is invoked to account for the observed fact that some individuals are able to accomplish with ease whatever they attempt, whereas others seemingly as capable never manage to achieve their goals. Although the nature of a person's destiny is thought to explain the general tenor of his life, almost all informants, at least in an interview situation, steadfastly and emphatically denied that poverty results from destiny but claimed it is due to the person's own lack of industry.

Most informants denied that a bad destiny can be altered, although some maintained that a powerful priest could sometimes save a woman destined to die in childbirth or prolong the short life assigned to an individual. (A ceremony to change a bad destiny is described by Akesson.)[18] However, belief in the ability of witches and other evildoers to upset the good destiny arranged by God, for example, to kill a person before his allotted time has expired or to prevent a woman destined to bear children from doing so, was accepted by all informants. The deities are said to act as God's agents to deter the witches from upsetting the good destiny originally decreed by the Supreme Being.

Destiny may be invoked to account for the general tenor of a person's life, the unalterable elements of his character, and his seemingly irremediable failure to achieve something desired. Attribution of an unfortunate circumstance to destiny serves to reconcile the individual to his situation. But unexpected good fortune may also be ascribed to destiny. Should a person die in a motor accident, destiny is sometimes invoked as an explanation (*ne kra ye otofo* 'his soul is that of one who will die a violent death'). Yet, should he escape unharmed, the reason given is that his predestined time to die had not yet arrived.

Akwapim Akan believe that the message with which they entered the world determines what happens to them. Because the means of determining the content of the message are limited, attribution must, by necessity, be ex post facto. It seems likely that in general conversation and gossip, informants might assign certain events to a person's destiny while denying the relation in an interview situation.

HELAINE K. MINKUS

Informants' responses to questions concerning destiny indicated substantial variation in individual interpretations. Divergent positions were taken on three basic questions: 1) whether the individual states his message to God or receives it from Him; 2) whether the message can later be altered; and 3) whether bad things may be included. It is possible that some of the variation results from the merging of two formerly distinct concepts, that of *nkrabea* and *hyebea*. Interviews conducted during the summer of 1975 to explore this possibility yielded the following results. Some informants stated that the two terms are synonymous. Others claimed that *nkrabea* refers to the message the individual gives to God which can sometimes be altered and may include barrenness, while *hyebea* is the message given by God, which cannot be changed and does not include barrenness. Several informants explained matters differently by asserting that *hyebea* stipulates the time of death and *nkrabea* the other aspects of one's destiny. Distinctions between the two terms have been noted by Danquah and Hagan but the definitions they give do not agree with each other or with the ones cited above.[19] Sarpong differentiates the terms but claims that *nkrabea* is the divinely-imposed fate and *hyebea* the self-determined destiny[20] --a view none of my informants shared. Further research is needed to determine more precisely the possible sources or correlates of sub-cultural and individual variation in the usage of the two terms.

"Natural" causes

Despite the disagreement and vagueness with regard to certain aspects of the concept of destiny, what is fully affirmed is that each person must die and the time of his death is fixed by his destiny. Death having once been created by God became inevitable and inescapable; once the time for a person's death has arrived not even God can prevent or stay it. It is expected that for most people the death decreed by God will occur in old age and be preceded by a period of gradual weakening and illness, although most informants agreed that certain people are destined to die when young or in a sudden manner. The libation poured at funerals before the corpse is taken to be buried indicates the belief that some, but certainly not all, deaths are "natural." The corpse is told: "If your death is from God, then go peacefully. If it was caused by someone, you are a spirit and can see more. Do not let him rest but show him to us." An unexpected death calls for explanation and the family may consult a priest or diviner to determine its cause. They may be told that the death was caused by witches, bad medicine, punishment by a spiritual

134

being, or that the death came from God and no further action, of rectification or revenge, is called for.

All events are caused, but not all causes are said to operate in a spiritual way (*wo sunsum mu*). An individual's own bad character, ignorance, stupidity, carelessness, lack of industry, naivete or impetuousness suffice to explain many of the misfortunes he encounters. He himself may blame witches or sorcerers for his misadventures but more disinterested observers generally refuse to credit his accusations.

Illness

In a similar fashion, some illnesses are thought to be spiritually-induced (*sunsumyare*), but not all are. Some of the principal categories of illness and disease are the following: *honamyare* 'illness of the body'; *nsanyare* 'infectious illness'; *abusuayare* 'illness of the matrilineal group'; *mogyayare* 'illness of the blood';[21] and *sunsumyare* 'spiritually-induced illness'.[22]

Many ailments, e.g., malaria, headache, piles, boils, sores, rheumatism, dysentery, are regarded as quite common and elicit no particular concern if they respond readily to the ordinarily successful means of treatment. Although it is expected that most people who behave well will live to old age, no presumption is made of a life totally free from illness. Maintenance of good health requires good living habits and harmonious social relations. Anything that weakens the body or disturbs the mind, for example, insufficient food or sleep, overwork, worry, stress, fear, resentment or rancorous thoughts, may lead to illness or madness. Some diseases are thought to be contagious, e.g., yaws, measles, tuberculosis, and transmitted by use of an infected person's cup, towel, chewing stick, etc. and/or seasonal and so expected to befall a certain number of people at particular times of the year.

The terms *abusuayare* 'illness of the matrilineal group', and *mogyayare* 'illness of the blood', are applied to ailments thought to be hereditary. A woman who is suffering from an illness while pregnant may transmit the condition to the fetus. Apart from this direct transmission, some ailments are thought to be hereditary within a matrilineage. Not all members of the group will suffer from the condition but some in each generation undoubtedly will. A child suffering from a congenital ailment, passed on by its mother, may sometimes be cured, although it is considered more difficult to cure him than one who has acquired

135

the conditions later in life. Illnesses hereditary within a lineage, however, are within the blood and nothing can be done to remove them.

Designation of an illness as *sunsumyre* 'spiritually caused illness' indicates that the causal agent acted in a spiritual way. Such illnesses may result from witchcraft, sorcery, a curse, the effect of breaking a taboo, the punitive actions of the deities, personalized talismans and ancestral spirits, hatred and bad words, or contact with evil spirits. The particular nature of the symptoms sometimes indicates the spiritual origin of the ailment. For example, a person made mad through the use of a bad charm is said to behave differently from one who became mad through witchcraft, high fever, resentment, a fall or even from unjustified fear that someone was using the charm against him. However, what at first appear to be ordinary bodily illnesses may have a spiritual etiology, indicated by their prolonged or recurrent nature. Once an illness is determined to be spiritually induced, the cause must be dealt with before the symptoms can be treated with herbal applications....

The nature and presumed cause of an illness determine the treatment administered. Most people know some herbal remedies for common ailments. If they do not know which medicine to use or if the illness does not respond to their own treatment, they then commonly seek the advice of an herbalist. The herbalist will first pour libation asking that God, the deities and other spiritual beings bless his efforts to heal the patient. He may strengthen the patient's spiritual resistance by applying protective medicines to guard against attacks by witches, ghosts and other evil spirits and purify him from any spiritual "dirt" with which he may have had contact. Medicine specific to the disease is then prescribed. Should the medicine first prescribed prove unsuccessful, the herbalist will try others. The patient may simultaneously or successively consult a number of herbalists, medium-priests, medical doctors or prophets of the spiritual churches who have the gift of healing. The persons consulted and the order depends on the beliefs and prior experience of the patient and to some extent on the nature of the illness.

If it is suspected that the illness is not a simple bodily ailment but that "something lies behind it"--because the symptoms are particularly persistent or severe, the nature of the ailment in itself indicates a spiritual etiology, or the patient feels that his own wrong-doing or else malignant forces are responsible--the family of the patient will take him to consult a medium-priest or diviner to determine the cause. Should the illness be found to have a spiritual cause, the priest will specify what must be done to 'remove the misfortune' (*yi mmusu*) that is troubling the person. All medical attempts to cure the illness will prove futile if the precipitating spiritual cause is not first dealt with and the patient released from the misfortune that is threatening him.

The steps taken depend upon the being or force thought responsible. Should the person have offended a deity or ancestral spirit or been "caught" by a personalized talisman, he must confess fully, ask forgiveness, and offer sacrifices by way of propitiation. If a curse is operative, the ceremony of revocation must be performed at the shrine of the deity invoked, necessarily preceded by the pacification and compensation of the person who was wronged. The priest may advise the person to bring certain items to the shrine or else to leave them at some specified place in order to remove the misfortune. This seems to be done particularly when witchcraft is considered the cause; the gifts are intended to compensate the witch for any wrong the patient may have done to her and to secure her cooperation in the cure. A person suffering from the effects of sorcery is treated with the antidote of the bad medicine or charm. If the bad charm has been secreted in his house or buried in his yard, it is removed and its power for evil destroyed.

Once the cause has been correctly determined and effectively dealt with, the illness then becomes amenable to ordinary medical treatment. The priest may himself prescribe medicine (if done while the priest is possessed, it is said to be the deity or other spiritual being who indicates the medicine to use) or else may advise the patient to put himself under the care of an herbalist or medical doctor. Western-trained physicians are thought to do useful work, and herbalists and priests themselves sometimes go to hospitals for treatment. But Western medical science is considered woefully inadequate to deal with the true causes of spiritually-induced illness. Even with sophisticated X-ray equipment, doctors are unable to determine the precipitating cause of such an illness. For example, they cannot detect that the pains and wasting away of a patient are due to the spiritual needles which are pricking at his heart nor can they see that a case of barrenness stems from the removal by witches of the spiritual essence of the womb.

It is expected that if diagnosis is correct and appropriate action taken the patient should recover. However, if the illness is due to the person's wrong-doing and he refuses to confess completely, perhaps concealing certain acts out of embarrassment, the offended beings will continue to make him ill and eventually kill him. Delay in seeking treatment is dangerous because the illness may pass beyond the power of the spiritual beings to intervene and save the person from death. Herbalists, priests and the prophets of the spiritual churches are said to have the power to determine if a person is past the point of recovery. To protect their reputation as healers, they will reject such persons, telling them they will die regardless of the treatment administered. In other cases the healer may say that he does not know if the cure will be successful but he will try. If the patient does recover, he brings the offerings or money promised and undergoes a ceremony to release him from any taboos necessitated by the medicine used, to purify him from the evil influences associated with the cause of the illness and the state of being ill, and to thank his soul for his recovery.

Treatment for various forms of misfortune similarly depends upon diagnosis of the cause. If no spiritual influence is implicated, the person is so informed and may be advised to change his behavior in order to increase his prospects for success. For example, a man's failure to meet his financial obligations may be attributed to the extravagant sums he expends on drink or women, or he may be informed that an untrustworthy employee or relative has been falsifying his accounts. Quarrelsome, disrespectful behavior alienates those who would normally support the person and help him in his ventures. A person who thinks that everyone is against him may be told that it is his own behavior that is responsible. As determined by two diviners consulted on separate occasions, the repeated breakdowns of my car and the consequent expense did not derive from any evil spiritual influences but were due simply to its advanced age and weakened condition.

Ability to Forsee and Alter the Course of Events

Once an individual has been seriously afflicted by either illness or misfortune, it is imperative that he determine the cause and the appropriate remedial action. Some people, though apparently not very many, consult a priest or diviner at intervals to discover if any harmful influence is threatening them. Those under the protection of a shrine generally do not seek such preventative consultations but expect that the medium-priest will inform them of any potential danger and the action necessary to avert it. Consultations are commonly undertaken prior to any serious or risky venture such as marriage, establishment of a business or travel abroad to determine if the enterprise will be successful or if efforts may be made to improve the chances of success.

The pronouncements of the priests, diviners and prophets can be analyzed in terms of the possibility and efficacy of intervention to escape anticipated harmful events and/or insure a beneficial outcome.

The person who comes to consult may be told that regardless of the action he takes the bad state foreseen is inescapable. Such a pessimistic pronouncement is particularly likely when the assigned cause e.g., of an impending death or long-continued sterility, is diagnosed as due to the individual's destiny. Certain failure may also be predicted of a proposed marriage if the intended partner is declared to have an irremediably bad character or of a trading venture should the diviner forsee that the person was not meant to be a trader and will never be successful. In some cases the person may be told that the condition would have been remediable had efforts been made earlier, e.g., before the illness became so severe that it became incurable given the best efforts of both human and spiritual beings.

The outcome may depend solely on the acts of the person himself. If he performs a certain act, he will suffer; if he refrains, he will thereby avoid any bad consequence. For example, a priest may warn that traveling at night will surely result in being robbed or that continued heavy smoking or drinking will inevitably lead to an early death. Should the person follow the advice offered and avoid the stipulated behavior, he will obviate the anticipated evil. This mode of reasoning was exemplified by the course of action followed by one informant. He dreamt that he was surrounded by children to whom he was telling stories. The dream was interpreted by a prophet to mean that, should he continue his practice of telling stories to children, in future he would have many children. Although he is very fond of children he does not wish to have more than four, and so has since ceased his story-telling although he continues to play with children.

The outcome of an anticipated venture, for example, the prospects of passing an examination may appear favorable given the forces operative at a particular time but other inimical forces may later intervene and militate against success if they are not effectively counteracted. If the outcome is foreseen to be favorable but no ceremonies are done and witches or other evil forces not presently bothering the person attack, the actual outcome will be unfavorable. If the outcome is foreseen to be favorable and ceremonies are performed to counteract any possible evil influence (e.g., the person takes protective medicine, puts himself under the protection of a shrine, receives the prayers of a prophet, pours libation on his ancestral stools)[23] then, whether or not evil beings or forces try to interfere, the person will succeed.

The priest or prophet may forsee failure but believe that performance of some ceremony or other act may possibly alter the outcome. If no action is taken, the outcome will surely be unfavorable. This mode of reasoning is applied to the chances for recovery of a patient whose illness is attributed to the punitive actions of a spiritual being. If the patient does not confess fully or does not perform the necessary ceremony of propitiation, he will certainly die. However, even when the appropriate action is taken, his recovery is still only probable and depends upon the willingness of the spiritual being to forgive him and enable him to be cured.

Individual Moral Responsibility for Events

Although certain situations offer no hope of ameliora-tion, generally some action can be taken to attain the desirable or avert the undesirable. While the individual is necessarily depen-dent on others both his fellow men and the spiritual beings, he is not thought to be a passive victim or object of forces external to him and totally beyond his influence. A person's own actions are necessary although not sufficient, and much that happens to him is regarded as justifiably and predictably proceeding as conse-quence from his own precipitating acts. Misfortune, illness and death are generally ascribed to a person's own wrong-doing or else to the operation of malignant forces, but even in the latter case the sufferer is often thought to be at least partially respon-sible for having provoked the attack. Akwapim Akan causal theory asserts that the innocent may suffer and that man is vuln-erable to evil influences of all sorts. Yet in actual instances of misfortune, there is often a presumption of blame. For example, a man or woman unable to meet the minimum requirement of proper adulthood by producing a child is not respected and may suffer the sneers and contempt of others. Such people are said to be especially kind and generous to others in hopes that they will reciprocate. Barrenness and sterility are often attributed, at least by those not loyal to the person so afflicted, to the individ-ual's own bad behavior, e.g., promiscuity, adultery, induced abortions, or the forfeit of fertility for the sake of wealth (*Nzima bayi*). The presumption that the condition is due to the person's own acts justifies the poor treatment they receive, although it is

140

clear that other causes such as witchcraft, bed medicine and destiny may be responsible. Similarly, although a woman's death in childbirth may stem from several possible causes, it is often assumed that death during delivery is the result of the woman's having been unfaithful or in some other way having wronged her husband.

Although the afflicted person himself (or those with whom he shares collective responsibility) is often blamed for misfortune, the attainment of good fortune is not seen as dependent solely upon a person's own efforts. Achievement of the good life by Akan standards requires that the individual behave morally, respect others, observe his taboos, acquire the necessary ritual and practical knowledge, and avoid spiritual defilement and actions that would bring disgrace. However, such good behavior leads to good fortune only through the mediation of well-disposed benefactors, both spiritual and human. To blame oneself or another for misfortune is acceptable; to claim total responsibility for one's own good fortune or continued good health would be regarded as somewhat sacrilegious. Rewards are expected to match behavior and to be operative in this life, and Akwapim Akan have faith in justice on a cosmic scale. But it is necessary to acknowledge dependence on the perhaps expected but not automatic good offices of one's guardians.

Akan Causal Theory

Akan causal thought allows little room for chance occurrences. Each event has its effective cause and the concurrence of two events, if the effect produced is significant, is almost always attributed to some power which has brought them into conjunction. For example, if one person steps on a snake and is bitten, the occurrence may be ascribed to his carelessness and perhaps dismissed as happening without ulterior reason (*eye okwa*). But if he dies from the snake bite it is more than likely that either his own destiny or else witchcraft, sorcery or some other cause will be proposed to explain why such a thing should have happened. Certainly should several members of one family meet death or misfortune in a short time, there is little doubt that something lies behind the events.

The Akan belief system, sharing what is no doubt a widespread if not universal characteristic of traditional and probably more modern systems,[24] incorporates features that insulate it from attack and doubt. Failures of prediction can be accounted for without jettisoning the basic causal assumptions or the more

141

concrete statements concerning the efficacy of particular agents. As Horton has suggested, a system of convergent causality (in which causes A, B, C ... may all lead to result X) protects the belief system by disallowing a critical test of any particular causal connection.[25] If the ancestors, deities, witches and virtually any other agent or force, acting singly or in concert, are considered capable of causing illness, failure of treatment directed to the propitiation of one particular type of agent or counteracting of a particular force may always be attributed to a false diagnosis and does not negate belief in the efficacy of that agent in other situations. As most significant events are thought to be caused by spiritual, invisible agents of which precise knowledge is unattainable, diagnostic and hence curative failure is easily accepted theoretically. The emphasis in Akan thought upon personalized, powerful beings whose acts are freely determined provides an additional basis for readily-acceptable explanations of unsuccessful curative and remedial efforts. The Akan are not totally unaware of the self-protective features of their belief system. A chief who subscribes to the traditional view of causality commented that if a patient recovers then people say the spiritual beings have saved him but if he dies then the failure of treatment is considered to be explained satisfactorily by recounting the man's sins. His tone of voice made it clear that he appreciated the insulating effects of such reasoning.

Akan causal theory postulates a benevolent Supreme Being who retains ultimate, although not total, control of a great number of causal agents and forces which, removed from direct and constant divine supervision, are able to operate somewhat independently. It assumes the necessary existence of evil but affirms ultimate justice. The belief system is thus able to provide satisfactory explanations of particular events and allows an understanding and acceptance of evil while yet encouraging faith in the benevolence of the world as a totality. The causal theory subsumes all events within a general philosophic framework. Events or situations that threaten because they raise the problem of bafflement[26] are referred without much intellectual conflict to God and Creation as the ultimate explanation, i.e., if one cannot understand why something should be, then one must accept that it stems from creation, that it is as it is because God intended it to be so.

The causal beliefs have been no more immune from culture change than other aspects of Akan culture. Changes have occurred in the agents thought to have power (e.g., addition of the personalized talismans), the ways to deal with unfortunate events (e.g., addition of Christian prayer and spiritual healing), and the practitioners consulted (e.g., addition of prophets of the spiritual churches and physicians). Some people deny, at times, the efficacy of agents traditionally credited with power (e.g., the ancestral spirits and the traditional deities). Yet the basic causal assumptions appear to be as strongly evident among the most educated and Christian as among the most traditional Akwapim Akan. It is held by all that men are vulnerable and dependent upon others, that man is responsible for much of what befalls him and able to influence the course of events, that events are not fortuitous but have causes, that all that happens ultimately depends upon God, and that man's knowledge is limited but sufficient to deal with life's crises.

HELAINE K. MINKUS

FOOTNOTES

1. [This is a shortened version of the paper which appeared in earlier editions. Deletions are indicated by .... Ed.]

2. The fieldwork upon which this paper is based was conducted from July 1969 through August 1971, supported by a grant from the Council for Intersocietal Studies, Northwestern University, and a National Institute of Mental Health Pre-Doctoral Research Fellowship. Additional field research was done during the summer of 1975, made possible by a National Institute of Mental Health Small Grant and a University of Wisconsin-Eau Claire Research Grant. The support of these agencies is gratefully acknowledged.

3. See especially: William E. Abraham, *The Mind of Africa* (Chicago: University of Chicago Press, Phoenix Books, 1966, K. A. Busia "The Ashanti of the Gold Coast," in *African Worlds,* ed. Daryll Forde (London: Oxford University Press, 1954), pp. 190-209; M. J. Field, *Search for Security: An Ethno-psychiatric Study of Rural Ghana* (London: Faber and Faber, 1960); George Panyin Hagan, "Some Aspects of Akan Philosophy" (M. A. Thesis, Institute of African Studies, University of Ghana, 1964); R. Sutherland Rattray, *Religion and Art in Ashanti* (Oxford: Clarendon Press, 1927).

4. B. Gil, A. F. Aryee and D. K. Ghansah, *1960 Population Census of Ghana. Special Report 'E'. Tribes in Ghana* (Accra: Census Office, 1964).

5. A description of the complete cultural philosophy may be found in my doctoral dissertation: Helaine K. Minkus, "The Philosophy of the Akwapim Akan of Southern Ghana" (Ph.D. diss., Northwestern University, 1975).

6. There is no Akan concept which exactly corresponds with "spiritual beings" but for convenience I will use the term to designate God, the gods, the ancestral spirits and the personalized talismans.

144

7. C. A. Akrofi, *Twi Mmebusem: Twi Proverbs* (London: Macmillan and Co., 1962), p. 43.

8. Ibid.

9. The number of spiritual protectors available to the Akwapim Akan has been augmented in recent years by the introduction of new cults, imported from northern and eastern Ghana and the neighboring countries of Ivory Coast, Togo and Dahomey. These cults began to spread through southern Ghana about 1900 and reached their peak in the 1940s. The objects of the cults are designated as *suman* or *aduru.* Both terms designate traditional categories whose meanings have been extended to incorporate the introduced ideas. *Suman* traditionally referred to charms, amulets or talismans which are not personalized but are credited with spiritual power. *Aduru* comprises a wide range of 'medicines'. Applied to the new cults, the terms signal the difference in origin, nature and function between the old traditional deities and the objects of the cults. The deities are conceived as personal beings who descend to earth independently of human efforts. The medium-priest or priestess of a deity is said to be chosen by the deity himself, as evidenced by the deity's possessing the individual whom he wishes to serve him. The person who receives and responds to this call must serve an apprenticeship of three or more years under an established priest. The deities usually have a strong association with a local community and are regarded as tutelary guardians of the village or town. In contrast, the objects of the new cults, which I will term "personalized talismans," may, like any talisman, be acquired by any interested individual or group. In some cases the object of the cult was regarded in its original home as a traditional tribal deity rather than as a talisman. However, the Akan who have borrowed them view them as talismans which may be secured by purchase independently of any communication by the "spirit" of its wish to establish its cult. A medium-priest is selected for the talisman and sent for training but the apprenticeship is considerably shorter and less rigorous than that received by the traditional medium-priests. The popularity of the new cults is premised upon the supposed power of the personalized talisman to protect its adherents from evil forces. Rather than needing to be informed of harm suffered by an adherent, as is the case with the deities and ancestral spirits, it is able to respond immediately. In this respect the personalized talisman

145

evidences its origin as an impersonal, automatic force. The personalized nature of the objects of these cults is indicated by the conception of them as being *sunsum* (that is being composed entirely of 'spirit') rather than as having *sunsum* as one constituent, as is the case with the usual charms and medicines. The cults represent an addition to the being/forces recognized by the Akan, one intermediate between the fully personalized beings of the deities and the impersonal force of the usual charms.

10.   Rattray, *Religion and Art in Ashanti*, p. 182.

11.   Busia, "The Ashanti," p. 193; Jack Goody, "Anomie in Ashanti?" *Africa* 27(1957):359.

12.   Hagan, "Akan Philosophy," p. 52.

13.   R. Sutherland Rattray, *Ashanti Proverbs* (Oxford: Clarendon Press, 1916), p. 44.

14.   Kofi Asare Opoku and K. A. Ampom-Darkwah, *Akom ho Nkommobo (Kwaku Mframa)* (Legon, Ghana: Institute of African Studies, University of Ghana, 1969).

15.   Barbara E. Ward, "Some Observations on Religious Cults in Ashanti," *Africa* 27(1956): 47-61; Field, *Search for Security.*

16.   Field, *Search for Security.*

17.   [See K. Gyekye's paper in this book for further discussion of this topic . Ed.]

18.   Sam K. Akesson, "The Secret of *Akom* I," *African Affairs* 49 (1950): 244-46.

19.   J. B. Danquah, *The Akan Doctrine of God; A Fragment of Gold Coast Ethics and Religion*, 2nd ed. (London: Frank Cass & Co., 1968), p. 114; Hagan, "Akan Philosophy."

20.   P. Sarpong, "Aspects of Akan Ethics," *Ghana Bulletin of Theology* 4 (1972): 42.

21.   The term *mogyayare* is also applied to non-congenital ailments thought to result from impure or insufficient blood.

22. See Dennis Michael Warren, "Disease, Medicine, and Relig-
     ion among the Techiman-Bono of Ghana: A Study in
     Culture Change" (Ph.D. diss., Indiana University, 1974)
     for a comprehensive study of disease classification among
     the Techiman-Bono, an Akan-speaking group in west
     central Ghana.

23. The ancestral stools *(nkonnua)* are carved wooden benches
     used during life by the founder of the lineage of a cele-
     brated lineage head and consecrated or "blackened" after
     his death. The stool symbolizes the unity and continuity
     of the lineage, links its living members with their deceased
     forbears, serves as the shrine of the ancestral spirits,
     and sanctions the authority of the lineage head.

24. E. E. Evans-Pritchard, *Witchcraft, Oracles and Magic
     among the Azande* (Oxford: Clarendon Press, 1937) p.
     330; Robin Horton, "African Traditional Thought and
     Western Science, Part II," *Africa* 37 (1967).

25. Horton, "African Traditional Thought," p. 169.

26. Clifford Geertz, *The Interpretation of Cultures* (New York:
     Basic Books, 1973), p. 100.

HOW NOT TO COMPARE AFRICAN THOUGHT
WITH WESTERN THOUGHT[1]

K. (J. E.) Wiredu

Many western anthropologists and even non-anthropologists have often been puzzled by the virtual ubiquity of references to gods and all sorts of spirits in traditional African explanations of things. One western anthropologist, Robin Horton, has suggested that this failure of understanding is partly attributable to the fact that many western anthropologists "have been unfamiliar with the theoretical thinking of their own culture."[2] I suggest that a very much more crucial reason is that they have also apparently been unfamiliar with the folk thought of their own culture.

Western societies too have passed through a stage of addiction to spiritistic explanations of phenomena. What is more, significant residues of this tradition remain a basic part of the mental make-up of a large mass of the not so-sophisticated sections of Western populations. More importantly still, elements of the spiritistic outlook are, in fact, deeply embedded in the philosophical thought of many contemporary westerners--philosophers and even scientists.

Obviously it is a matter of first rate philosophical importance to distinguish between traditional, i.e., pre-scientific, spiritistic thought and modern scientific thought by means of a clearly articulated criterion (or set of criteria). Indeed, one of the most influential and fruitful movements in recent Western philosophy, namely the logical positivist movement, may be said to have been motivated by the quest for just such a criterion. Also anthropologically and psychologically it is of interest to try to understand how traditional modes of thought function in the total context of life in a traditional society. Since African societies are among the closest approximations in the modern world to societies in the pre-scientific stage of intellectual development, the interest which anthropologists have shown in African thought is largely understandable.

Unfortunately instead of seeing the basic non-scientific characteristics of African traditional thought as typifying traditional thought in general, Western anthropologists and others besides have tended to take them as defining a peculiarly African way of thinking. The ill-effects of this mistake have been not a few.

One such effect is that the really interesting cross-cultural comparisons of modes of thought have tended not to be made. If one starts with the recognition that all peoples have some background of traditional thought--and remember by *traditional* thought here I mean pre-scientific thought of the type that tends to construct explanations of natural phenomena in terms of the activities of gods and kindred spirits--then the interesting and antropologically illuminating comparison will be to see in what different ways spiritistic categories are employed by various peoples in the attempt to achieve a coherent view of the world. In such specific differences will consist the real peculiarities of, say, African tradition thought in contradistinction from, say, Western traditional thought. Such comparisons may well turn out to hold less exotic excitement for the Western anthropologist than present practice would seem to suggest. In the absence of any such realization, what has generally happened is that not only the genuine distinguishing features of African traditional thought but also its basic non-scientific, spiritistic, tendencies have been taken as a basis for contrasting Africans from Western peoples. One consequence is that many Westerners have gone about with an exaggerated notion of the differences in nature between Africans and the peoples of the West. I do not imply that this has necessarily led to anti-African racism. Nevertheless, since in some obvious and important respects, traditional thought is inferior to modern, science-oriented thought, some Western liberals have apparently had to think hard in order to protect themselves against conceptions of the intellectual inferiority of Africans as a people.

Another ill-effect relates to the self-images of Africans themselves. Partly through the influence of Western anthropology and partly through insufficient critical reflection on the contemporary African situation, many very well placed Africans are apt to identify African thought with *traditional* African thought. The result has not been beneficial to the movement for modernization, usually championed by the very same class of Africans. The mechanics of this interplay of attitudes is somewhat subtle. To begin with, these Africans have been in the habit of calling loudly, even stridently, for the cultivation of an African authenticity or personality. True, when such a call is not merely a political slogan, it is motivated by a genuine desire to preserve the indigenous culture of peoples whose confidence in themselves has been undermined by colonialism. But it was a certain pervasive trait of this same culture that enabled sparse groups of Europeans to subjugate large masses of African populations and keep them in colonial subjection for many long years and which even now makes them a prey to neo-colonialism. I refer to the *traditional* and non-literate character of the culture, with its associated technological underdevelopment. Being traditional is, of course, not synonymous with being non-literate. A culture can be literate and yet remain traditional i.e., non-scientific, as the case of India, for example, proves. India has a long tradition of written literature, yet it was not until comparatively recent times that the scientific spirit made any appreciable inroads into the Indian way of life. But, of course, a culture cannot be both scientific and non-literate, for the scientific method can only flourish where there can be recordings of precise measurements, calculations and, generally, of observational data. If a culture is both non-scientific and non-literate, then in some important respects it may be said to be backward in a rather deep sense. We shall in due course note the bearing of the non-literate nature of the traditional African culture on the question of just what African philosophy is.

What is immediately pertinent is to remark that unanalyzed exhortations to Africans to preserve their indigenous culture are not particularly useful--indeed, they can be counterproductive. There is an urgent need in Africa today for the kind of analysis that would identify and separate the backward aspects of our culture--I speak as an anxious African--from those aspects that are worth keeping. That such desirable aspects exist is beyond question, and undoubtedly many African political and intellectual leaders are deeply impregnated by this consideration. Yet the analytical dimension seems to be lacking in their enthusiasm. So we have, among other distressing things, the

151

K. (J. E.) WIREDU

frequent spectacle of otherwise enlightened Africans assiduously
participating in the pouring of libation to the spirits of our
ancestors on ceremonial occasions, or frantically applauding imita-
tion of the frenzied dancing of "possessed" fetish priests--all this
under the impression that in so doing they are demonstrating
their faith in African culture.

   In fact, many traditional African institutions and
cultural practices, such as the ones just mentioned, are based on
superstition. By "superstition" I mean a rationally unsupported
belief in entities of any sort. The attribute of being superstitious attaches not to the content of a belief but to its mode of
entertainment. Purely in respect of content the belief, for example, in abstract entities in semantic analysis common among many
logistic ontologists in the West is not any more brainy then the
traditional African belief in ancestor spirits. But logisticians are
given to arguing for their ontology. I happen to think their
arguments for abstract entities wrong -headed;[3] but it is not
open to me to accuse them of superstition. When, however, we
come to the traditional African belief in ancestor spirits--and
this, I would contend, applies to traditional spiritistic beliefs
everywhere--the position is different. That our departed ancestors continue to hover around in some rarefied form ready now
and then to take a sip of the ceremonial schnapps is a proposition
that I have never known to be rationally defended. Indeed, if
one were to ask a traditional elder, "unspoilt" by the scientific
orientation, for the rational justification of such a belief, one's
curiosity would be quickly put down to intellectual arrogance
acquired through Western education.

   Yet the principle that one is not entitled to accept a
proposition as true in the absence of any evidential support is
not Western in any but an episodic sense. The Western world
happens to be the place where, as of now, this principle has
received its most sustained and successful application in certain
spheres of thought, notably in the natural and mathematical
sciences. But even in the Western world there are some important areas of belief wherein the principle does not hold sway. In
the West just as anywhere else the realms of religion, morals and
politics remain strongholds of irrationality. It is not uncommon,
for example, to see a Western scientist, fully apprised of the
universal reign of law in natural phenomena, praying to God, a
spirit , to grant rain and a good harvest and other things
besides. Those who are tempted to see in such a thing as witchcraft the key to specifically *African* thought--there is no lack of
such people among foreigners as well as Africans themselves--
-ought to be reminded that there are numbers of white men in

today's London who proudly proclaim themselves to be witches. Moreover, if they would but read, for example, Treyor-Roper's historical essay on "Witches and Witchcraft,"[4] they might conceivably come to doubt whether witchcraft in Africa has ever attained the heights to which it reached in Europe in the 16th and 17th centuries.

It should be noted, conversely, that the principle of rational evidence is not entirely inoperative in the thinking of the traditional African. Indeed, no society could survive for any length of time without conducting a large part of their daily activities by the principle of belief according to the evidence. You cannot farm without some rationally based knowledge of soils and seeds and of meteorology; and no society can achieve any reasonable degree of harmony in human relations without a *basic* tendency to assess claims and allegations by the method of objective investigation. The truth, then, is that rational knowledge is not the preserve of the modern West[5] nor is superstition a peculiarity of the African peoples.

Nevertheless, it is a fact that Africa lags behind the West in the cultivation of rational inquiry. One illuminating (because fundamental) way of approaching the concept of "development" is to measure it by the degree to which rational methods have penetrated thought habits. In this sense, of course, one cannot compare the development of peoples in absolute terms. The Western world is "developed," but only relatively. Technological sophistication is only an aspect, and that not the core, of development. The conquest of the religious, moral and political spheres by the spirit of rational inquiry remains, as noted earlier, a thing of the future even in the West. From this point of view the West may be said to be still underdeveloped. The quest for development, then, should be viewed as a continuing world-historical process in which all peoples, Western and non-Western alike, are engaged.

There are at least two important advantages in looking at development in this way. The first is that it becomes possible to see the movement towards modernization in Africa not as essentially a process in which Africans are unthinkingly jettisoning their own heritage of thought in the pursuit of Western ways of life, but rather as one in which Africans in common with all other peoples seek to attain a specifically *human* destiny--a thought that should assuage the qualms of those among thoughtful Africans who are wont to see modernization as a foreign invasion. The relation between the concepts of development and modernization ought to be obvious. Modernization is the application of the

153

results of modern science for the improvement of the conditions of human life. It is only the more visible side of development; it is the side that is more immediately associated with the use of advanced technology and novel techniques in various areas of life such as agriculture, health education and recreation. Because modernization is not the whole of development there is a need to view it always in a wider human perspective. Man should link the modernization of the conditions of his life with the modernization of all aspects of his thinking. It is just the failure to do this that is responsible for the more unlovable features of life in the West. Moreover, the same failure bedevils attempts at development in Africa. Rulers and leaders of opinion in Africa have tended to think of development in terms of the visible aspects of modernization--in terms of large buildings and complex machines, to the relative neglect of the more intellectual foundations of modernity. It is true that African nations spend every year huge sums of money on institutional education. But it has not been appreciated that education ought to lead to the cultivation of a rational[6] outlook on the world on the part of the educated and, through them, in the traditional folk at large. Thus it is that even while calling for modernization, influential Africans can still be seen to encourage superstitious practices such as the pouring of libation to spirits in the belief that in this kind of way they can achieve development without losing their Africanness. The second advantage of seeing development in the way suggested above is that the futility of any such approach becomes evident. To develop in any serious sense, we in Africa must break with our old uncritical habits of thought; that is we must advance past the stage of traditional thinking.

Lest these remarks appear rather abstract, let us consider a concrete situation. Take the institution of funerals in Ghana, for example. Owing to all sorts of superstitions about the supposed career of the spirits of departed relatives, the mourning of the dead takes the form of elaborate, and, consequently expensive and time consuming social ceremonies. When a person dies there has first to be a burial ceremony on the third day; then on the eighth day there is a funeral celebration at which customary rites are performed; then forty days afterwards there is a fortieth day celebration (adaduanan). Strictly, that is not the end. There are such occasions as the eightieth day and first anniversary celebrations. All these involve large alcohol-quaffing gatherings. Contrary to what one might be tempted to think, the embracing of Christianity by large sections of Ghanaian population has not simplified funeral celebrations; on the contrary, it has brought new complications. Christianity too teaches of a whole hierarchy of spirits, started from the Supreme Threefold Spirit down to the angels both good and refractory down further to the lesser spirits of deceased mortals. Besides, conversion to Christianity in our lands has generally not meant the exchange of the indigenous religion for the new one, but rather an amalgamation of both, which is made more possible by their common spiritistic orientation. Thus, in addition to all the traditional celebrations, there is nowadays the neo-Christian Memorial Service, replete with church services and extended refreshments, a particularly expensive phase of the funeral process. The upshot is that if a close relation of a man, say his father, dies, then unless he happens to be rich, he is in for very hard financial times indeed. He has to take several days off work, and he has to borrow respectable sums of money to defray the inevitable expenses.

The extent of the havoc that these funeral habits have wrought on the national economy of Ghana has not been exactly calculated, but it has become obvious to public leaders that it is enormous and that something needs urgently to be done about it. However, the best that these leaders have seemed capable of doing so far has been to exhort the people to reform their traditional institutions in general and cut down on funeral expenses in particular. These appeals have gone unheeded; which is not surprising, if one recalls that these leaders themselves are often to be seen ostentatiously taking part in ceremonies, such as the pouring of libation, which are based on the same sort of beliefs as those which lie behind the funeral practices. It has so far apparently been lost upon our influential men that while the underlying beliefs retain their hold, any verbal appeals are wasted on the populace.

The ideal way to reform backward customs in Africa must, surely, be to undermine their superstitious belief-foundations by fostering in the people--at all events, in the new generation of educated Africans--the spirit of rational inquiry in all spheres of thought and belief. Even if the backward beliefs in question were *peculiarly* African, it would be necessary to work for their eradication. But my point is that they are not African in any intrinsic, inseparable sense; and the least that African philosophers and foreign well-wishers can do in this connection is to refrain, in this day and age, from serving up the usual congeries of unargued conception about gods, ghosts, and witches in the name of *African philosophy.* Such a description is highly unfortunate. If at all deserving of the name "philosophy", these ideas should be regarded not as a part of African philosophy simply, but rather as a part of *traditional* philosophy in Africa.

155

This is not verbal cavilling. The habit of talking of African philosophy as if all African philosophy is *traditional* carries the implication, probably not always intended, that modern Africans have not been trying, or worse still, ought not to try, to philosophize in a manner that takes account of present day development in human knowledge, logical, mathematical, scientific, literary, etc. Various causes have combined to motivate this attitude. African nationalists in search of an African identity, Afro-Americans in search of their African roots and Western foreigners in search of exotic diversion--all demand an African philosophy that shall be fundamentally different from Western philosophy, even if it means the familiar witches' brew. Obviously, the work of contemporary African philosophers trying to grapple with the modern philosophical situation cannot satisfy such a demand.

The African philosopher writing today has no tradition of written philosophy in his continent[7] to draw upon. In this respect, his plight is very much unlike that of say, the contemporary Indian philosopher. The latter can advert his mind to any insights that might be contained in a long-standing Indian heritage of written philosophical meditations; he has what he might legitimately call *classical* Indian philosophers to investigate and profit by. And if he is broad-minded, he will also study Western philosophy and try in his own philosophizing to take cognizance of the intellectual developments that have shaped the modern world. Besides all this, he has, as every people have, a background of unwritten folk philosophy which he might examine for whatever it may be worth. Notice that we have here three levels of philosophy: we have spoken of a folk philosophy, a written traditional[8] philosophy and a modern philosophy. Where long-standing written sources are available folk philosophy tends not to be made much of. It remains in the background as a sort of diffused, immanent, component of community thought habits whose effects on the thinking of the working philosopher is largely unconscious.[9] Such a fund of community thought is not the creation of any specifiable set of philosophers; it is the common property of all and sundry, thinker and non-thinker alike, and it is called a *philosophy* at all only by a quite liberal acceptation of the term. Folk thought, as a rule, consists of bald assertions without argumentative justification, but philosophy in the narrower sense must contain not just theses. Without argumentation and clarification, there is, strictly, no philosophy.

Of course, folk thought can be comprehensive and interesting on its own account. Still its non-discursiveness

remains a drawback.   For example, according to the conception of
a person found among the Akans of Ghana, (the ethnic group to
which the present writer belongs), a person is constituted by
nipakua (a body) and a combination of the following entities
conceived as spiritual substances:[10] (1) *okra* (soul, approximately), that whose departure from a man means death, (2)
Sunsum, that which gives rise to a man's character, (3) *ntoro,*
something passed on from the father which is the basis of inherited characteristics and, finally, (4) *mogya,* something passed on
from the mother which determines a man's clan identity and which
at death becomes the *saman* (ghost).   This last entity seems to be
the one that is closest to the material aspect of a person; literally, *mogya* means blood.   Now, in the abstract, all this sounds
more interesting, certainly more imaginative, than the thesis of
some Western philosophers that a person consists of a soul and
body.   The crucial difference, however, is that the Western
philosopher tries to argue for his thesis, clarifying his meaning
and answering objections, known or anticipated; whereas the
transmitter of folk conceptions merely says: "This is what our
ancestors said."[11] For this reason folk conceptions tend not to
develop with time.   Please note that this is as true in the West
and elsewhere as it is in Africa.

But in Africa, where we do not have even a written
traditional philosophy, anthropologists have fastened on our folk
world-views and elevated them to the status of a continental
philosophy.   They have then compared this "philosophy" with
Western (written) philosophy.   In other, better placed, parts of
the world, if you want to know the philosophy of the given
people, you do not go to aged peasants or fetish priests or court
personalities; you go to the individual thinkers, in flesh, if
possible, and in print.   And as any set of individuals trying to
think for themselves are bound to differ among themselves, you
would invariably find a variety of theories and doctrines, possibly
but not necessarily, sharing substantial affinities.   Since the
reverse procedure has been the only one that has seemed possible
to anthropologists, it is not surprising that misleading comparisons between African traditional thought and Western scientific
thought have resulted.   My contention, which I have earlier
hinted at, is that African traditional thought should in the first
place only be compared with Western folk thought.   For this
purpose, of course, Western anthropologists will first have to
learn in detail about the folk thought of their own peoples.   African folk thought may be compared with Western philosophy only
in the same spirit in which Western folk thought may be compared
also with Western philosophy, that is, only in order to find out
the marks which distinguish folk thought in general from

157

individualized philosophizing. Then, if there be any who are anxious to compare African philosophy with Western philosophy, they will have to look at the philosophy that Africans are producing today.

Naturally Western anthropologists are not generally interested in contemporary African philosophy. Present day African philosophers have been trained in the Western tradition, in the continental or Anglo-American style, depending on their colonial history. Their thinking, therefore, is unlikely to hold many peculiarly African novelties for anyone knowledgeable in Western philosophy. For this very same reason, African militants and our Afro-American brothers are often disappointed with the sort of philosophy syllabus that is taught at a typical modern department of philosophy in Africa. They find such a department mainly immersed in the study of Logic, Epistemology, Metaphysics, Ethics, Political Philosophy, etc., as these have been developed in the West, and they question why Africans should be so engrossed in the philosophy of their erstwhile colonial oppressors.

The attentive reader of this discussion should know the answer by now: The African philosopher has no choice but to conduct his philosophical inquiries in relation to the philosophical writings of other peoples, for his own ancestors left him no heritage of philosophical writings. He need not--to be sure, he must not--restrict himself to the philosophical works of his particular former colonial oppressors, but he must of necessity study the written philosophies of other lands, because it would be extremely injudicious for him to try to philosophize in self-imposed isolation from all modern currents of thought, not to talk of longer-standing nourishment for the mind. In the ideal, he must acquaint himself with the philosophies of all the peoples of the world, compare, contrast, critically assess them and make use of whatever of value he may find in them. In this way it can be hoped that a tradition of philosophy as a discoursive discipline will eventually come to be established in Africa which future Africans and others too can utilize. In practice the contemporary African philosopher will find that it is the philosophies of the West that will occupy him the most, for it is in that part of the world that modern developments in human knowledge have gone farthest and where, consequently, philosophy is in closest touch with the conditions of the modernization which he urgently desires for his continent. In my opinion, the march of modernization is destined to lead to the universalization of philosophy everywhere in the world.

How Not to Compare African Thought With Western Thought

The African philosopher cannot, of course, take the sort of cultural pride in the philosophical achievements of Aristotle or Hume or Kant or Frege or Husserl of which the Western student of philosophy may permit himself. Indeed an African needs a certain level-headedness to touch some of these thinkers at all. Hume,[12] for example, had absolutely no respect for black men. Nor was Marx,[13] for another instance, particularly progressive in this respect. Thus any partiality the African philosopher may develop for these thinkers must rest mostly on considerations of truth-value.

As regards his own background of folk thought, there is a good reason why the African philosopher should pay more attention to it than would seem warranted in other places. Africans are a much oppressed and disparaged people. Some foreigners there have been who were not even willing to concede that Africans as a traditional people were capable of any sort of coherent[14] world-view. Those who had the good sense and the patience and industry to settle down and study traditional African thought were often, especially in the 19th and early 20th centuries, colonial anthropologists who sought to render the actions and attitudes of our forefathers intelligible to the colonial rulers so as to facilitate their governance. Although some brilliant insights were obtained, there were also misinterpretations and straightforward errors. Africans cannot leave the task of correction to foreign researchers alone. Besides, particularly in the field of morality, there are non-superstition-based conceptions from which the modern Westerner may well have something to learn. The exposition of such aspects of African traditional thought specially befits the contemporary African philosopher.

Still, in treating of their traditional thought, African philosophers should be careful not to make hasty comparisons.[15] Also they should approach their material critically; this last suggestion is particularly important since all peoples who have made any breakthrough in the quest for modernization have done so by going beyond folk thinking. It is unlikely to be otherwise in Africa. I should like to repeat, however, that the process of sifting the elements of our traditional thought and culture calls for a good measure of analytical circumspection lest we exchange the good as well as the bad in our traditional ways of life for dubious cultural imports.

It should be clear from the foregoing discussion that the question of how African thought may appropriately be compared with Western thought is not just an important academic issue but also one of great existential urgency.

159

K. (J. E.) WIREDU

FOOTNOTES

1. This paper first appeared in *Ch'indaba* and is reprinted here by permission of the author and the editor of *Ch'indaba*.

2. Robin Horton, "African Traditional Thought and Western Science," in *Rationality* ed. Bryan Wilson (Oxford: Basil Blackwell). Originally published in *Africa* 37, nos. 1 & 2 (1967).

3. My reasons for this remark will be found in my series of articles on "Logic and Ontology," *Second Order:an African Journal of Philosophy* 2, no. 1 (January 1973) and no. 2 (July 1973): 3, no. 2 (July 1974); 4, no. 1 (January 1975).

4. *Encounter* 28, no. 5 (May 1967) and no. 6 (June 1967).

5. Note that "the West" and "Western" are used in a cultural, rather than ideological sense in this discussion.

6. I am aware that my insistence in the overriding value of rationality will be found jarring by those Westerners who feel that the claims of rationality have been pushed too far in their countries and that the time is overdue for a return to "Nature" and the exultation in feeling, intuition and immediacy. No doubt the harsh individualism of Western living might seem to lend support to this point of view. But in my opinion the trouble is due to too little rather than too much rationality in social organization. This, however, is too large a topic to enter into here.

7. The Arab portions of Africa are, of course, an exception, though even there what we have is the result of the interaction between indigenous thought and Greek influences.

8. "Traditional" here still has the pre-scientific connotation. Of course, if one should speak of *traditional* British empi-

160

ricism, for example, that connotation would be absent.

9. Since such effects do, in fact, occur, this threefold stratification should not be taken as watertight.

10. See, for example, W. E. Abraham, *The Mind of Africa* (Chicago: University of Chicago Press, 1967).

11. However, the circumstance that in Africa, for example, our traditional thought tends not to be elaborately argumentative should be attributed not to any intrinsic lack of the discoursive spirit in our ancestors but rather to the fact that their thoughts were not written down.

12. Hume was able to say in his *Essays* (London: George Routledge & Sons, Ltd), footnote on pages 152 and 153 in the course of the essay on "National Characters:" "I am apt to suspect the Negroes to be naturally inferior to the Whites. There scarcely ever was a civilized nation of that complexion, nor any individual, eminent either in action or speculation.... In Jamaica, indeed they talk of one Negro as a man of parts and learning; but it is likely that he is admired for slender accomplishments, like a parrot who speaks a few words plainly." Obviously considerable maturity is required in the African to be able to contemplate impartially Hume's disrespect for Negroes and his philosophical insights, deploring the former and acknowledging and assimilating the latter. A British philosopher, Michael Dummett, was recently placed in a not altogether dissimilar situation when, himself a passionate opponent of racialism, he discovered in the course of writing a monumental work on Frege *(Frege: Philosophy of Language,* Duckworth, London, 1973),--a work which he had, indeed, suspended for quite some time in order to throw himself heart and soul into the fight against racial discrimination in his own country, Britain,--that his subject was a racialist of some sort. (See his own remarks in his preface to the above-mentioned book). It would have argued a lack of balance in him if he had scrapped the project on the discovery. In the event he went ahead to complete the work and put all students of the philosophy of logic in his debt.

13. Marx is known once, in a burst of personal abuse of Lassalle, in a letter to Engels, to have animadverted: "This combination of Jewry and Germany with a fundamental Negro streak.... The fellow's self assertiveness is

Negro too." Quoted in J. Hampden Jackson, *Marx, Prou-dhon and European Socialism* (London: English Universities Press, 1951), p. 144. It is sometimes understandable for a man to chide his own origins, but to condemn a down trodden people like this is more serious. Would that black men everywhere had more of the self assertiveness which Marx here deprecates. The Akans of Ghana have a proverb which says: "If the truth happens to lie in the most private part of your own mother's anatomy, it is no sin to extract it with your corresponding organ." African enthusiasts of Marx, (or of Hume, for that matter) may perhaps console themselves with the following less delicate adaptation of this proverb. "If the truth happens to lie in the mouth of your racial traducer it is no pulillanimity to take it from there."

14. Coherent thought is not necessarily scientific thought. Traditional thought can display a high degree of coherence; and certainly African traditional thought is not lacking in coherence.

15. I ought perhaps to point out that the kind of comparison between African thought and Western thought that has been criticized in this discussion is the sort which seeks to characterize the given varieties of thinking as wholes. My remarks do not necessarily affect the comparison of isolated propositions.

THE CATEGORIES OF MTU
AND
THE CATEGORIES OF ARISTOTLE

Thomas J. Blakeley

Any effort to discover what relations, if any, there are
between the categories of *Mtu* and the categories of *Mzungu*[1]
--i.e., the extent to which one can correlate what can broadly be
called "Bantu categories" with the "categories of the West"[2] --has
to be considered very, very tentative.

As a matter of fact, there are those who would term the
whole enterprise nonsensical. For instance, I once had the
opportunity to discuss the matter with an African spiritual leader.
In answer to his query about what aspect of African existence
interested me most, I answered; "...the extent to which Aristotelian categories can be correlated with Bantu categories--once one
determines what the latter are--either directly or through the
intermediacy of some third, 'neutral', system of categories."
Whereupon he asked: "Has it occurred to you that it might be the
case that the Bantu have no categories?"--and he did not mean
"categories peculiar to the Bantu" but "any categories at all." At
the time, such a suggestion could only stun a naive *Mzungu* like
myself; in the interval, a study of Hegel's *Science of Logic* has
made it seem a little less inconceivable.

Even those who recognize some validity to the search
for such a correlation often look for it in some apparently strange

163

places. For example, at a meeting of an association of African students in a European university town, another African spiritual leader was heard to explain the difference between "European reasoning" and "Bantu thinking" as follows: "Whereas it is common knowledge that Europeans think in syllogisms, the Bantu think in what the European tradition called 'sorites'. Many misunderstandings would be avoided if only one did not expect Bantu discourse to follow the rigid syllogistic forms." In the classical syllogistic each syllogism can have only three terms: major, minor and middle. The most patently invalid syllogism is that with two middle terms--i.e., with four terms instead of three. The "sorites" is a syllogism which appears to contain two or more middle terms but which, on closer examination, proves to be several "stacked" syllogisms, abbreviated through a concatenation of middle terms, each of which represents a lesser or greater generality of the preceding.[3]

Further, were we to be satisfied as to the possibility of such a correlation to Western and Bantu categories and were we to have settled on the path to follow in pursuit thereof, there would remain the problem of who is the appropriate interpreter of the cross-categorization.

Such a problem would not exist (or, at least, would be less acute) if we were interested in, e.g., competing interpretations of political events or of economic facts; for such competing interpretations take place within a categorial framework which does not have to be agreed upon because it is taken for granted.

In the present instance, who is going to decide: a) what "Western categories" means; b) what the "Bantu categories" are; and c) how any possible correlation is to be detected or established? Is it to be a Western European philosopher? If so, what is a "philosopher" in the "Western European" tradition? Or, rather, which meaning of "philosopher" will be adequate for our purposes? The "metaphysician" of the "perennial" tradition? The "dialectician" of Marxist stripe? The student of the "logic of the language of science" in the analytic tradition? Or, do we have to find a theoretician of culture as a whole (a *Kulturkritiker*, so to speak), rather than a philosopher in the more narrow sense?

Further, would the task(s) be better done by a Bantu scholar? If so, will he use hermeneutic tools drawn from Western culture (with all the same problems as above) or those drawn from Bantu culture? If the latter, which "Bantu" (North, South, Central, etc.)?

In short, there is no lack of problems; or, at least, of questions that have to be resolved. It might be to the point to trace all such problems back to the central difficulty of all cross-cultural studies--which could be called the "paradox of the seat of the lexicographer's pants." In the initial encounters between two or more previously (at least, relatively) isolated cultures, some lexical equivalences have to be arrived at *ad hoc;* then, on the basis of these, the interlocuters can arrive at the establishment of more adequate means of "trading information", "sharing experiences", etc. Unless, of course, one wanted to assume that all languages have the same essential semantic referents (the same "object-range"). If this were the case, all language-users would be operating within the parameters of an identical system of categories--absolving us of the need to carry on our present discussion, but also making cross-cultural differentiations unintelligible.

Were these many serious questions as to the possibility of a correlative category-comparison on a cross-cultural basis answered to the satisfaction of one and all, there would then be the need to decide *how* to proceed. Here one can distinguish three possible approaches.

One could imitate a quite stylish mode of philosophizing by making an effort to proceed "presuppositionlessly," following the Hegel of the *Phenomenology of Spirit,* the Husserl of the *Ideen,* the Fichtean culture of the linguisticists, and/or a number of other models.

There is another, "more empirical," path which would have philosophers follow in the traces of ethnographers, cultural historians, etc., who have collected the most diverse myths, sayings, customs, etc. The data collected by these other disciplines are seen, in this account, as being "interpreted" by the philosopher who would "extract" or "abstract" from them the general notions, principles, etc., forming the philosophical infrastructure of Bantu theorizing.

It is hard to form precise objections to the presuppositionless approach but it is clear to all involved in philosophy that it cannot be subordinated to other, less general, disciplines without ceasing to be philosophy.

The third approach--that which has most often been taken in the pursuit of cross-cultural objectives--consists in taking one of the classical categorial systems of Western

THOMAS J. BLAKELEY

philosophy as the ground for asking what the categories of the Bantu are.[4] The main advantage of this procedure is that it obviates the need to search for a third, "mediating" set of categories which would serve to make possible correlation of Western with Bantu categories. The main problem with it is that there have been at least three distinct sets of categories in the history of Western thought (we will not worry at this point about the categories of Chinese thought, Hindu philosophy, etc.): the Aristotelian, the Kantian, and the Hegelian.[5]

The last of these could seem to be the most interesting for the task at hand for several reasons. First of all, Hegel's categories are fundamental not only to various Hegelianisms but also to Marxism, neo-Marxism, Marxism-Leninism and a number of related theoretical approaches. Secondly, it is the most recent of the three and has the greatest chance of being adequate to modernity, which is where Bantu culture is going, at least on one account. Finally, it is the only one of the three that tries to reconcile the notion of "ground" with a presuppositionless approach, generating all the categories out of the mere "desire to philosophize."

Of almost equal interest is the Kantian system of categories. Not only is it one of the historical grounds for the Hegelian system but it came onto the scene almost contemporaneously with the modern wave of colonization, as well as during the growing pains of industrial civilization. The last two traits should not be dismissed as mere accidents. They mean that the first serious European penetration into Bantu Africa was the work of Kantians, just as the industrialization which was to become the model for Africa was occurring in a Kantian context. Add to this the fact that the universities of the African continent were initially staffed predominantly by Kantians and neo-Kantians, and one can see the sense in which Kantian categories are very significant for our present occupation. Both the lexicographers and their first Bantu contacts operated *a la Kant*.

The strength of the Aristotelian categories lies not only in the fact that they represent the first scientifically formulated set of categories but more importantly is the fact that the other two--the Kantian and the Hegelian--were developed in Aristotelian language and continue to be expressed in a language which is essentially determined by the Aristotelian categories.

Taking our cue from this sameness in expository language and from Aristotle's specification of the categories as the highest genera, we may act as if there is indeed but one set of

166

Western categories--the Aristotelian. This means ignoring Trendelenburg's monumental effort to distinguish the three types of
categorization, and also his argument with Bonitz about the relationship between philosophic and linguistic categories.[6] Both of
these issues can await resolution of the immediate task.

As listed in their most complete form (in the *Topics*) the
Aristotelian categories are: Essence (or Substance), Quality,
Quantity, Relation, Place, Time, Position, State, Activity, Passivity.[7] Aristotle adds at the same place: "For the accident and the
genus and property and definition of any thing will always be in
one of these categories...".[8]

It would seem that all we need to do is to discover
whether Bantu speakers use substantives, qualifiers, quantifiers,
relatives, localizers, etc. But, that proves not to be the question because, on closer examination, it appears that almost any
language contains terms for doing these. Or, do they? How can
we decide whether or not relatives, quantifiers, etc., work in one
language the same as in another?

We are thus forced back to the paradox of the seat of
the lexicographer's pants but in the form of a more serious
dilemma: for, if the quantifiers, etc., work in the same way in
any language, our whole discussion is recondite; if not, then we
have to find a way of formulating quantity, quality, relation,
etc., in a way that makes clear the different ways they occur in
distinct cultures.

Obviously, there is no lack of work ahead for the linguist, ethnographer, cultural historian, etc.

While waiting for this help from other disciplines, the
philosopher should occupy himself with two remaining considerations. First of all, are there general ontological presuppositions
to the categories? And, are there questions of logic that have to
be decided prior to or alongside the questions about categorization?

The first of these is the problem of the so-called
"pre-categorials." In the perennial tradition, these are such
notions as "prior and posterior," "positive and negative," "active
and passive," and so on, which serve to delineate the context
within which the categories are formed. But, the most important
pre-categorials are the "transcendentals" which are said to be
"convertible with being." Though there are five in the usual
account,[9] we need deal only with the three more important ones:

167

the one, the true, and the good. In other words, all being is one; all being is true; all being is good; and whatever is categorized *is* being as one, as true and as good.

So, we can discover something about cross-cultural correlation of categories by discovering if the same pre-categorials are in effect and why they issue in diverse categories when and if they do.

Finally, we should come back to an issue raised earlier on--at least indirectly: that of the logical status of the categories. Any decision on this topic will, of course, depend on the type of logic one has at hand. If one is using classical, Aristotelian logic, then attention is focused on the categories ("the highest genera") as determining predictability: i.e., in their essentially semantic function. At the other end of the spectrum lie the diverse versions of contemporary formal logic, which seem to have little room for a theory of categories since they operate on what an Aristotelian would have to call a purely syntactic level. Between these two extremes, lie a number of interesting attempts at a "logical mix," where categories are seen as somehow "plastic" and/or "in motion." The most prominent of these efforts is the "dialectical logic" of Marxist-Leninist philosophy, which sees categories as "interpenetrant," "complexly interrelated," "in development," etc. [10]

Such are the questions that have to be answered and the problems that have to be solved if one is to come to grips with the challenge of cross-cultural category-correlation. Clearly, one is faced with a complex task requiring the collaboration of both *Mtu* and *Mzunga* across the whole range of cultural domains.

FOOTNOTES

1. *Mtu* (or *Muntu*) and *Mzungu* (or *Muzungu*) are the Kisw-ahili terms used for, respectively, a "person" and a "European". That two terms are needed poses, at the outset, an interesting problem of categorization.

2. To use "African", "Bantu", "Western", etc., as if there were not serious sub-distinctions to be made, is justified here only by the fact that "everyone is doing it" and it is the only way to make a first approximation.

3. For example, the syllogism "Joseph is human, To be human is to be rational, Therefore Joseph is rational" can issue in the following sorites: "Joseph is human, To be human is to be rational, To be rational is to syllogize, Therefore Joseph syllogizes". More often than not, the sorites occurs in abbreviated form; for example: "Joseph is human, To be human is to be rational, Therefore Joseph syllogizes".

4. Good examples of this approach are to be found in the works of Placide Tempels and John Mbiti. Fr. Tempels, in particular, makes no secret of the fact that he is looking for Bantu parallels to the main categories of the perennial philosophy.

5. Cf. F. A. Trendelenburg, *Geschichte der Kategorienlehre.* (Berlin, 1846). The categories of Chinese thought, Hindu philosophy, etc., pose exactly the same problem as those discussed relative to Bantu categories.

6. On categories as genera, see 998a20-999a23. See also H. Bonitz, "Ueber der Kategorien des Aristoteles," in *Sitz. Wien, Ak. histor.-phil. Kl.* 10(1853)591-645.

7. Cf. 103b22-24.

8. *loc. cit.* 24-25.

9. As listed by the tradition, the five transcendentals which are convertible with being *(ens)* are: the one *(unum)*, the true *(verum)*, the good *(bonum)*, *res* and *aliquid*-- the last two being hardly translatable (except as something like "thing" and "something").

10. For some works on dialectical logic by Soviet philosophers, see *Bibliographie der Sowjetischen Philosophie* (Dordrecht/Holland: Reidel, 1960-1970). See also, current listings in *Studies in Soviet Thought* (quarterly, by the same publisher).

PERSON AND COMMUNITY IN AFRICAN
TRADITIONAL THOUGHT

Ifeanyi A. Menkiti

My aim in this paper is to articulate a certain conception
of the person found in African traditional thought. I shall
attempt to do this in an idiom, or language, familiar to modern
philosophy. In this regard it is helpful to begin by pointing to a
few significant contrasts between this African conception of the
person and various other conceptions found in Western thought.

The first contrast worth noting is that whereas most
Western views of man abstract this or that feature of the lone
individual and then proceed to make it the defining or essential
characteristic which entities aspiring to the description "man"
must have, the African view of man denies that persons can be
defined by focusing on this or that physical or psychological
characteristic of the lone individual. Rather, man is defined by
reference to the environing community. As John Mbiti notes, the
African view of the person can be summed up in this statement:
"I am because we are, and since we are, therefore I am."[1]

One obvious conclusion to be drawn from this dictum is
that, as far as Africans are concerned, the reality of the communal world takes precedence over the reality of individual life
histories, whatever these may be. And this primacy is meant to
apply not only ontologically, but also in regard to epistemic
accessibility. It is in rootedness in an ongoing human community

171

that the individual comes to see himself as man, and it is by first knowing this community as a stubborn perduring fact of the psychophysical world that the individual also comes to know himself as a durable, more or less permanent, fact of this world. In the language of certain familiar Western disciplines, we could say that not only the biological set through which the individual is capable of identification by reference to a communal gene pool, but also the language which he speaks and which is no small factor in the constitution of his mental dispositions and attitudes, belong to this or that specific human group. What is more, the sense of self-identity which the individual comes to possess cannot be made sense of except by reference to these collective facts. And thus, just as the navel points men to umbilical linkage with generations preceding them, so also does language and its associated social rules point them to a mental commonwealth with others whose life histories encompass the past, present, and future.

A crucial distinction thus exists between the African view of man and the view of man found in Western thought: in the African view it is the community which defines the person as person, not some isolated static quality of rationality, will, or memory.

This brings us to the second point of contrast between the two views of man, namely, the *processual* nature of being in African thought--the fact that persons become persons only after a process of incorporation. Without incorporation into this or that community, individuals are considered to be mere danglers to whom the description 'person' does not fully apply. For personhood is something which has to be achieved, and is not given simply because one is born of human seed. This is perhaps the burden of the distinction which Placide Tempels' native informants saw fit to emphasize to him--i.e. the distinction between a *muntu mutupu* (a man of middling importance) and *muntu mukulumpe* (a powerful man, a man with a great deal of force). Because the word "muntu" includes an idea of excellence, of plenitude of force at maturation, the expression 'ke muntu po', which translates as 'this is not a man',[2] may be used in reference to a human being. Thus, it is not enough to have before us the biological organism, with whatever rudimentary psychological characteristics are seen as attaching to it. We must also conceive of this organism as going through a long process of social and ritual transformation until it attains the full complement of excellencies seen as truly definitive of man. And during this long process of attainment, the community plays a vital role as catalyst and as prescriber of norms.

172

In light of the above observations I think it would be
accurate to say that whereas Western conceptions of man go for
what might be described as a minimal definition of the person--
-whoever has soul, or rationality, or will, or memory, is seen as
entitled to the description 'person'--the African view reaches
instead for what might be described as a maximal definition of the
person. As far as African societies are concerned, personhood is
something at which individuals could fail, at which they could be
competent or ineffective, better or worse. Hence, the African
emphasized the rituals of incorporation and the overarching
necessity of learning the social rules by which the community
lives, so that what was initially biologically given can come to
attain social self-hood, i.e., become a person with all the inbuilt
excellencies implied by the term.

That full personhood is not perceived as simply given at
the very beginning of one's life, but is attained after one is well
along in society, indicates straight away that the older an individual gets the more of a person he becomes. As an Igbo proverb has it, "What an old man sees sitting down, a young man
cannot see standing up." The proverb applies, it must be added,
not just to the incremental growth of wisdom as one ages; it also
applies to the ingathering of the other excellencies considered to
be definitive of full personhood. What we have here then is both
a claim that a qualitative difference exists between old and
young, and a claim that some sort of ontological progression
exists between infancy and ripening old age. One does not just
take on additional features, one also undergoes fundamental
changes at the very core of one's being.

Now, admittedly, the whole idea of ontological progression is something in need of elaboration. Offhand it may not sit
very well in the minds of those unaccustomed to the view of
personhood being presented here. The temptation might be
strong in some quarters to retort that either an entity is a
person or it is not; that there can be no two ways about it. In
response to this misgiving let me note that the notion of an
acquisition of personhood is supported by the natural tendency in
many languages, English included, of referring to children and
new-borns as *it.* Consider this expression: "We rushed the child
to the hospital but before we arrived *it* was dead." We would
never say this of a grown person. Of course, with a child or
new-born, reference could also be made by use of a personal
pronoun, with the statement reading instead: "We rushed the
child to the hospital but before we arrived he/she was dead."
This personalizing option does not, however, defeat the point

presently being made. For the important thing is that we have the choice of an *it* for referring to children and new-borns, whereas we have no such choice in referring to older persons.

The fact, then, that a flexibility of referential designation exists in regard to the earliest stages of human life, but not in regard to the more established later stages, is something well worth keeping in mind. What we have is not just a distinction of language but a distinction laden with ontological significance. In the particular context of Africa, anthropologists have long noted the relative absence of ritualized grief when the death of a young child occurs, whereas with the death of an older person, the burial ceremony becomes more elaborate and the grief more ritualized--indicating a significant difference in the conferral of ontological status.

Before moving away from the foregoing observations made in support of the notion of personhood as acquired, let me note, in addition, that in African societies the ultimate termination of personal existence is also marked by an 'it' designation; thus, the same depersonalized reference marking the beginning of personal existence also marks the end of that existence. After birth the individual goes through the different rites of incorporation, including those of initiation at puberty time, before becoming a full person in the eyes of the community. And then, of course, there is procreation, old age, death, and entry into the community of departed ancestral spirits--a community viewed as continuous with the community of living men and women, and with which it is conceived as being in constant interaction.

Following John Mbiti, we could call the inhabitants of the ancestral community by the name of the "living dead."[3] For the ancestral dead are not dead in the world of spirits, nor are they dead in the memory of living men and women who continue to remember them, and who incessantly ask their help through various acts of libation and sacrificial offering. At the stage of ancestral existence, the dead still retain their personhood and are, as a matter of fact, addressed by their various names very much as if they were still at center stage. Later, however, after several generations, the ancestors cease to be remembered by their personal names; from this moment on they slide into personal non-existence, and lose all that they once possessed by way of personal identity. This, for the traditional African world-view, is the termination of personal existence, with entities that were once fully human agents becoming once again mere *its,* ending their worldly sojourn as they had started out--as un-incorporated non-persons. Mbiti has described this terminal stage of a person's life as one of "collective immortality" (in contrast to the "personal immortality" that marks the stage of ancestral exis- tence, a stage in which the departed are remembered by name by the living, and do genuinely form a community of their own).[4]

But the expression "collective immortality" is misleading and problematic. At the stage of total dis-incorporation marked by the term, the mere *its* that the dead have now become cannot form a collectivity of any kind; and, since by definition no one now remembers them, there is not much sense in saying of them that they are immortal either. They no longer have an adequate sense of self; and having lost their names, lose also the means by which they could be immortalized. Hence, it is better to refer to them by the term *the nameless dead,* rather than designate their stage of existence by such a term as "collective immortality," thereby opening up the possibility of describing them as "collective immortals," which certainly they are not. This emen- dation apart, however, Mbiti is quite right when he states that for African man no ontological progression is possible beyond the spirit world: "Beyond the state of the spirits, men cannot go or develop. This is the destiny of man as far as African ontology is concerned."[5]

The point can be made then, that a significant symmetry exists between the opening phase of an individual's quest for personhood and the terminal phase of that quest. Both are marked by an absence of incorporation and this absence is made abundantly evident by the related absence of collectively confer- red names. Just as the child has no name when it tumbles out into the world to begin the journey towards selfhood, so likewise, at the very end, it will have no name again. At both points it is considered quite appropriate to use an 'it' designation precisely because what we are dealing with are entities in regard to which there is a total absence of incorporation.

Finally, it is perhaps worth noting that this phenomenon of a depersonalized status at the two polarities of existence makes a great deal of sense given the absence of moral function. The child, we all know, is usually preoccupied with his physical needs; and younger persons, generally, are notoriously lacking in moral perception. Most often they have a tendency towards self-centeredness in action, a tendency to see the world exclu- sively through their own vantage point. This absence of moral function cannot but have an effect on the view of them as persons. Likewise for the completely departed ancestral spirits, who, at the terminal point of their personal existence, have now become mere *its,* their contact with the human community

175

IFEANYI A. MENKITI

completely severed. The various societies found in traditional Africa routinely accept this fact that personhood is the sort of thing which has to be attained, and is attained in direct propor- tion as one participates in communal life through the discharge of the various obligations defined by one's stations. It is the carrying out of these obligations that transforms one from the it-status of early childhood, marked by an absence of moral func- tion, into the person-status of later years, marked by a widened maturity of ethical sense--an ethical maturity without which personhood is conceived as eluding one.

John Rawls, of the Western-born philosophers, comes closest to a recognition of this importance of ethical sense in the definition of personhood. In *A Theory of Justice* he makes explicit part of what is meant by the general ethical requirement of respect for persons, noting that those who are capable of a sense of justice are owed the duties of justice, with this capabil- ity construed in its sense of a potentiality which may or may not have been realized. He writes:

> Equal justice is owed to those who have the capacity to take part in and to act in accordance with the public understanding of the initial situation. One should observe that moral personality is here defined as a potentiality that is ordinarily realized in due course. It is this poten- tiality which brings the claims of justice into play.... The sufficient condition for equal justice [is] the capacity for moral personality.[6]

I take it that an important implication of this claim is that if an individual comes to deserve the duties of justice (and the confirmation therein implied of the individual's worth as a person) only through possession of a capacity for moral personal- ity, then morality ought to be considered as essential to our sense of ourselves as persons. And indeed Rawls has argued in another context that a Kantian interpretation is possible in which the transgression of accepted moral rules gives rise not just to a feeling of guilt but to a feeling of shame--the point being that once morality is conceived as a fundamental part of what it means to be a person, then an agent is bound to feel himself incomplete in violating its rules, thus provoking in himself the feeling prop- erly describable as shame, with its usual intimation of deformity and unwholeness.[7]

176

If it is generally conceded, then, that persons are the sort of entities that are owed the duties of justice, it must also be allowed that each time we find an ascription of any of the various rights implied by these duties of justice, the conclusion naturally follows that the possessor of the rights in question cannot be other than a person. That is so because the basis of such rights ascription has now been made dependent on a possession of a capacity for moral sense, a capacity, which though it need not be realized, is nonetheless made most evident by a concrete exercise of duties of justice towards others in the ongoing relationships of everyday life.

The foregoing interpretation would incidentally rule out, I believe, some dangerous tendencies currently fashionable in some philosophical circles of ascribing rights to animals. [8] The danger as I see it is that such an extension of moral language to the domain of animals is bound to undermine, sooner or later, the clearness of our conception of what it means to be a person. The practical consequences are also something for us to worry about. For if there is legitimacy in ascribing rights to animals then human beings could come to be compelled to share resources with them. In such a situation, for instance, the various governmental programs designed to eradicate poverty in the inner cities of the United States could conceivably come under fire from the United Animal Lovers of America, or some other such group, with the claim seriously being lodged that everything was being done for the poor, but not enough for the equally deserving cats and dogs. Minority persons might then find themselves the victims of a peculiar philosophy in which the constitutive elements in the definition of human personhood have become blurred through unwarranted extensions to non-human entities.

Before bringing to a close the various comments made so far, it might be helpful to focus on two issues discussed earlier, in an effort to forestall possible misunderstanding. One issue is the acquisition of personhood, since the possibility exists of confusing the African viewpoint with the viewpoint known in the West as Existentialist Philosophy. The other issue is the articulation of the specific sense in which the term 'community' has been used in these pages, so as to avoid possible misinterpretation.

To begin with the first, it must be emphasized that the African concept of man contrasts in significant measure with Existentialism (which on the face of things appears to be its most natural ally among the various Western philosophers of the

177

person). Jean-Paul Sartre tells us that prior to the choice of his fundamental project an individual is "nothing [and] will not be anything until later, and then he will be what he makes himself."[9] Such a statement immediately evokes favorable comparisons between the African view of man and the Existentialist view, both views being regarded as adopting a notion of personhood, or self-hood, as something acquired.

But this, it must be warned, is a hasty conclusion to draw. For the Sartrean view that man is a *free unconditioned* being, a being not constrained by social or historical circumstances, flies in the face of African beliefs. Given its emphasis on individuals solely constituting themselves into the selves that they are to become, by dint of their private choices, such a view cannot but encourage eccentricity and individualism--traits which run counter to African ideals of what the human person is all about. Although in important ways existence does precede essence, it is not for the reasons that Sartre gives. We simply cannot postulate man's freedom and independence from all determining factors, including even reason, which is sometimes viewed by Sartre as unduly circumscribing the individual in his quest for a free and spontaneously authentic existence. As Professor William Abraham has pointed out in his book, *The Mind of Africa,* if possession of reason is part of our nature, then we cannot be enslaved by reason as Sartre sometimes seems to suggest; for no entity can be enslaved by its own nature.[10]

Nor is the above the only point at which Existentialist philosophy diverges from the African in the conception of man. Because of the controlling force of freedom, Sartre was led to postulate an equality of status between infant and child, on the one hand, and the grown adult, on the other. What all individuals have in common is that they choose; and choice is freedom, and freedom choice. As he puts it elsewhere, "Man does not exist in order to be free *subsequently;* there is no difference between the being of man and his *being free.*"[11] But this collapsing of the ontological distinction between young child and grown man is an illegitimate and absurd move. Even assuming that Sartrean freedom is a *sine qua non* of the metaphysics of persons, how can children with their quite obvious lack of intelligent appreciation of the circumstances of their lives and of the alternatives open to them, choose rationally? Is a choice undertaken in childish ignorance a choice that is truly free?

These misgivings are serious; and it is frankly quite difficult to understand what is meant by the type of freedom which Sartre insists both adults and children have in equal

178

measure, as a result of which it is then argued that they, and they alone, can define for themselves the selves that they are to be, each in his own way. As Anthony Manser has put it, and I entirely agree, "It would seem that little remains of the freedom Sartre has been emphasizing...; it is hard to see how an infant can be aware of what he is doing, and if not then it is odd to call him responsible."[12]

In the light of the foregoing observations, I take it then that the African view of human personhood and the Existentialist view should not be conflated. Even though both views adopt a dynamic, non-static approach to the problem of definition of human self-hood, the underpinning metaphysical assumptions diverge significantly. Above all, whereas in the African understanding human community plays a crucial role in the individual's acquisition of full personhood, in the Sartrean existentialist view, the individual alone defines the self, or person, he is to become. Such collectivist insistences as we find in the African world-view are utterly lacking in the Existentialist tradition. And this difference in the two approaches is not accidental. Rather it arises because there is at bottom a fundamental disagreement as to what reality is all about.

Finally, let me try to clarify the sense in which the term 'community' has been used throughout this paper. Western writers have generally interpreted the term 'community' in such a way that it signifies nothing more than a mere collection of self-interested persons, each with his private set of preferences, but all of whom get together nonetheless because they realize, each to each, that in association they can accomplish things which they are not able to accomplish otherwise. In this primarily additive approach, whenever the term 'community' or 'society' is used, we are meant to think of the aggregated sum of individuals comprising it. And this is argued, not just as an ontological claim, but also as a methodological recommendation to the various social or humanistic disciplines interested in the investigation of the phenomenon of individuals in groups; hence the term 'Methodological Individualism' so much bandied around in the literature.

Now this understanding of human community, and of the approach to its study, is something completely at odds with the African view of community. When Mbiti says that the African says to himself, "I am because we are," the *we* referred to here is not an additive 'we' but a thoroughly fused collective 'we'. It is possible to distinguish three senses of human grouping, the first of which I shall call *collectivities* in the truest sense; the second of which might be called *constituted* human groups; and the third of which might be called *random* collections of individuals. The African understanding of human society adopts the usage in description number one above, whereas the Western understanding would fall closer to description number two; the difference between the two being that in what I have called 'collectivities in the truest sense' there is assumed to be an *organic* dimension to the relationship between the component individuals, whereas in the understanding of human society as something *constituted* what we have is a non-organic bringing together of atomic individuals into a unit more akin to an association than to a community. The difference between the two views of society is profound and can be represented diagrammatically thus:

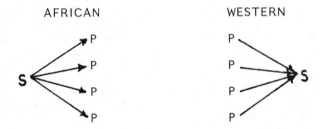

As can be seen from the diagram, whereas the African view asserts an ontological independence to human society, and moves from society to individuals, the Western view moves instead from individuals to society.

In looking at the distinction just noted, it becomes quite clear why African societies tend to be organized around the requirements of duty while Western societies tend to be organized around the postulation of individual rights. In the African understanding, priority is given to the duties which individuals owe to the collectivity, and their rights, whatever these may be, are seen as secondary to their exercise of their duties. In the West, on the other hand, we find a construal of things in which certain specified rights of individuals are seen as antecedent to the organization of society; with the function of government viewed, consequently, as being the protection and defense of these individual rights.

FOOTNOTES

1.   John Mbiti, *African Religions and Philosophies* (New York: Doubleday and Company, 1970), p. 141.

2.   Placide Tempels, *Bantu Philosophy* (Paris: Presence Africaine, 1959), p. 101.

3.   Mbiti, *African Religions, p. 32.*

4.   Ibid., p. 33.

5.   Ibid., p. 34.

6.   John Rawls, *A Theory of Justice* (Cambridge, Mass: Harvard University Press, 1971), pp. 505-506.

7.   Ibid., p. 445.

8.   See, for instance, Peter Singer, *Animal Liberation* (New York: Random House, 1975); as well as Tom Regan & Peter Singer eds., *Animal Rights and Human Obligations* (Englewood Cliffs, N. J.,: Prentice Hall, 1976).

9.   Jean-Paul Sartre, "Existentialism Is a Humanism" in Nino Languilli ed., *The Existentialist Tradition: Selected Writings,* trans. by Philip Mairet (New York: Doubleday-Anchor Books, 1971), p. 399.

10.   William Abraham, *The Mind of Africa* (Chicago: The University of Chicago Press, 1962), pp. 20-21.

11.   Jean-Paul Sartre, *Being and Nothingness: An essay on Phenomenological Ontology,* trans. with an introduction by Hazel E. Barnes (New York: The Philosophical Library, 1956), p. 25.

12.   Anthony Manser, *Sartre: A Philosophical Study* (London: The University of London Press, 1966), p. 122.

THE HUMAN PERSON AND IMMORTALITY
IN IBO (AFRICAN) METAPHYSICS[1]

Richard C. Onwuanibe

The theme of the human person and immortality, though a watershed of philosophical discussions in the past, has currently and forcefully become an issue in the face of modern materialism and dehumanization. Most philosophical discussions on this theme have centered on western and eastern conceptions without touching on the African ideas in this area. I intend in this paper to make a contribution towards filling this gap by investigating the conception of the human person with reference to immortality in Ibo metaphysics as an example of African metaphysics[2] and by addressing myself to the philosophical issues involved.

It will be argued that the Ibos subscribe to a metaphysic which adequately expresses their view of the human person and immortality by analyzing their philosophical matrix which is not totally materialistic; their expression of the human person in terms of subject rather than object shows a conception of human transcendence. An investigation of their conceptual framework with regard to primitive notions about the soul (mkpuru obi), presence, death as passage, belief in reincarnation, cult of the ancestors and veridical dreams shows evidence of their native sense of personal immortality. In conclusion, a warning is given against imported materialism which poses a threat to the Ibo holistic view of man since a major problem today is how to integrate modern scientific and technological achievements with Ibo traditional values without losing sight of the vital transcendence of the human person.

The Human Person

The traditional African philosophy of the human person is more existential and practical than theoretical. It is based on the conviction that the metaphysical sphere is not abstractly divorced from concrete experience; for the physical and metaphysical are aspects of reality, and the transition from the one to the other is natural.[3] In this regard, some writers have made derogatory remarks to the effect that Africans have no speculative bent; but this misrepresentation stems from ignorance of the true nature of their philosophical thinking. The Ibos are not total materialists in their fundamental views of reality, especially with regard to the human person as it can be argued from their view of soul (*mkpuru obi*) and presence.

An essential aspect or source of the human person is the soul (*mkpuru obi*), spirit (*mmuo*). The philosophical problem here is whether these are identifiable with the body. These primitive notions which are embedded in Ibo language and other African languages are not identified with the body, though related to it.

How is it that in virtually every language of the world, not only African languages, people say, "I have a body," "This is my body" or "This body is mine," and not "I am this body," --meaning by this, "I am totally this body"? It is absurd to identify oneself totally with one's body, for example, to say "I am totally identified with this body"; for one is *prima facie* aware that one is more than one's (this) body. One might object to the nonidentifiability of oneself totally with one's body by saying that when somebody pushes one, one could react by saying, "Don't push me," It seems that here one is identifying oneself with one's body which is pushed. However, within one's consciousness, this does not mean total identification of oneself with one's body but an identification of a relation of one's body to oneself. The seemingly complete identification of the expression, "Don't push me," is due to the vagueness of ordinary language. The possessive case phenomenologically and linguistically indicates that there is more to one than one's body.

The Ibo notions of soul (*mkpuru obi*) and spirit (*mmuo*), as essential aspects of man, bear out the transcendence of the human person from the metaphysical point of view. When one says *"O meturu m na mmuo"* (It touches my spirit), one is acknowledging that what has happened, or is at stake, touches the deepest part of oneself. We shall see later how this aspect of man is the vehicle of immortality. By maintaining the irreducibility of this core of the human person to materialistic basis, the Ibos subscribe to a view of transcendence in their metaphysic of the human person. It can be argued that materialist or physicalist views are not adequate for a total conception of man; for man's aspirations, values and relative achievements in the arts and sciences do not make full sense when discussed only from the backdrop of materialism and physicalism.

Another pointer to the Ibo view of the transcendence of the human person in view of immortality is <u>presence</u>. The Ibo conception of the human person involves the notion of presence. High regard for the human person in terms of presence is displayed in everyday living in warm greetings. It is offensive not to be greeted. In Heideggerian terminology, man in-the-world is not merely ready-to-hand, that is, functionalized. Man's existence (*dasein*) transcends the level of a role to be played or used. In Ibo metaphysics, living is a form of participation in which a fundamental distinction is made between the ontological and the ontic, between humans and animals. To be said to be an animal is to be depersonalized. The distinction between humans and animals is shown in corresponding attitudes: for one does not greet animals even if they are highly regarded pets. Not to be greeted among the Ibos can be construed as a form of depersonalization. When one looks at you, one may see you as an object or a subject. Looked at as an object by another in terms of Sartre's notion of "gaze", you lose the transcendence of subjectivity. In Buber's terminology, the relation here is an I-It relation; but what the Ibos mean in greeting another person is an I-Thou relation. The greeting is genuine, and you can feel its authenticity through the concomitant smile of the one who greets you. A foreigner from the western world will be surprised at the shower of warm greetings he or she will receive when staying in an Ibo community, and at the loud and warm conversations that go on among passengers in public vehicles. This is a contrast to the silence one often experiences among passengers in public vehicles in the western world. An American alone taking a bus from Cleveland to Washington D.C. will enter the bus, go straight to his seat, take up a paper to read, and most probably will not greet any fellow passengers. He or she is lonely in the midst of a crowd of passengers. He or she is not really a "fellow

185

passenger" for fellowship at its lowest level of meaning of communication is absent; and others in this case are not present. Silence or lack of communication constitutes an accute problem of alienation in the western world today.[4] Where there appears to be communication it is mostly object-oriented rather than subject-oriented.

A metaphysical analysis of the presence of the human person shows the distinction of the human person as subject and not as object. Object-oriented thinking aims at controlling and exploiting the other, while subject-oriented thinking feels the demand of the freedom of the other. The human is not basically resolvable into physical data. The presence of a person as subject is not ultimately objectifiable. Even when one attempts to objectify the self which is the source of personhood in the process of introspection, one sees that the attempt is illusory in that the attempt to posit the self ultimately as an object is countered by a concomitant negation; for there is a dialectical movement of affirmation and negation in the process of introspection to save the transcendental aspect of the human self, that is, when one holds the self as an object of consciousness, there is always in the background the receding and incomplete self which negates ultimate objectification of the total self. This is a primitive movement that is amenable to metaphysical reflection. The human self transcends the objective category. That is why in his philosophical reflection, Immanuel Kant indicates the self, in this case, Transcendental Ego, as pure subject, as Transcendental Apperception.[5] And in his phenomenological investigations, Edmund Husserl criticized Descartes for not making a transcendental turn when Descartes posited the self as a "thinking thing". On the contrary, the self or personhood involved "no-thingness". For this reason, Sartre rejects the idea of a transcendental ego which he thought makes the self a transcendental something (it). He prefers to denote the self, *For-Itself* as Nothing as opposed to *In-Itself* which is a mass of being, an "It".

True personhood, as pure subject, is not something that can be analyzed into anything. Hence, for example, Kant could not get at himself as object of awareness; nor could Hume find his "self" either. Personhood is a manifestation or presence even through a body, but never identifiable with it. Since "person" is primitive, the inability to analyze person (qua subject or soul) is not an argument for its non-existence but for its "transcendence" or "no-thingness" ("Thou"). In Ibo greetings, the "Thou" is manifest and emphasized. Nobody greets a body but "what" is manifest through the body.

186

In Ibo philosophical reflection, the self deriving from the soul and spirit indicates the personhood. To talk of human person makes sense only when to be human includes not only the physical aspects but also the transcendental aspect. Here the transcendental aspect includes the mental to a certain extent, the spiritual aspirations and values of man.

In this context, it is worthwhile to note that the essential greatness of a culture consists of the commitment to personhood and to all that it stands for, viz., in terms of human rights, human aspirations and development; and conversely, a decline in the consideration of personhood is symptomatic of a decline of a culture. Periods of high culture, philosophical options included, give expression to the transcendence of the human person, for culture is not essentially materialistic. In Ibo culture the transcendence or subjectivity of the human person finds expression in egalitarian spirit. On the contrary, a culture which emphasizes materialistic attainments can achieve mechanical perfections without adequate idea of personhood.

While, on the one hand, what is empirical and objective carries a sense of clarity and comprehensibility, on the other hand, the subjective sphere is fraught with a certain opaqueness, incomprehensibility and mystery because the subjective domain cannot be totally subsumed under the categories of reason. Human existence is metaproblematic because it is not totally discoverable, and consequently, it allows for philosophical faith, which is not a denial of reason but a recognition of its limits, and an option for the domain of transcendence which goes beyond death and includes immortality.

Death

Since human existence embraces both physical and metaphysical aspects, death poses a problem. Is death an ultimate situation? The answer given to this question shows the adequacy or inadequacy of a person's view of the human person. Death carries a sense of mystery with it.

The Ibos express the inescapable nature of death by rhetorically asking *"Onwere anya ebe onwu?"* (Who has eyes that will not see death?) The conception of death as part of the human condition is universal. There is a certain fear attached to death because it is not totally known, and consequently, not wholly accepted. A spate of literature has now appeared on the literary scene, the upshot of which is to reconcile people to the

187

acceptance of death; and this acceptance is considered by some writers as a source of personal growth.[6] In the context of existential phenomenology, the acceptance of one's death is indicative of one's authenticity.[7]

To a materialist death poses as man's ultimate situation which carries a sense of absurdity in man's total frame of reference; but to a mind imbued with human transcendence with regard to personhood, it is a passage to the world beyond.

In the Ibo existential frame of reference, as in other African cultures, although death instills fear in the minds of men, its redeeming feature is that it is a "passage", a "going home" to the world beyond. Death does not destroy the tissue of human possibilities and aspirations because of the native sense of immortality.[8] Just as a seed partly dies in the ground and springs to life, so does man die and take on refurbished life. This follows a kind of conservation law. However, the time of a person's death is an occasion of mourning, especially if he or she is young. The death of old people is regarded with mixed feelings of sadness and smouldering joy, in that the physical presence of the deceased is lost, and in that the deceased person is going home to be with the ancestors. The death of the young is not easily accepted, and it is considered "unnatural" in the sense that in the order of nature for a young person to die is not to follow in the natural order in which the old die first. This is in accord with the worldview universe in which the natural, moral, and metaphysical spheres blend into a system. The deceased have changed condition, and they are no longer in the company of the living as they used to be.

Immortality

A fundamental question to be asked is whether personal immortality is so elemental in man that it is based on a kind of intuition, and does not require rational justification by long argumentation. The universality of the belief in personal immortality in all cultures weighs in favor of the innate sense of personal immortality. In searching for evidence or proof one should bear in mind that they are relative to the subject-matter as Aristotle has pointed out. What kind of evidence should count is an important consideration. Scientific evidence should count in a scientifically verifiable subject-matter, but should not be demanded as a paradigm in all cases. Various kinds of evidence for personal immortality have been given in the history of this topic.[9] We shall see later on the kind of evidence the Ibos have for personal immortality .

Among the Ibos, personal immortality takes the form of continued existence in the world beyond and in reincarnation. The problem is knowing what servives the physical decay of the body. If the self or soul survives, is it totally disembodied or does it have a body of a certain kind since food, clothing, money, jewelry are put in the grave for the use of the departed? And in former times in the case of chiefs and Kings, slaves were killed to accompany and serve their masters in the other world. What emerges in this grey area of the physical and transcendent is that the departing being soul (self),[10] spirit *(mmuo)* has a kind of body - a spiritualized body - for the other world; and in the case of a reincarnated soul, the soul has the potentiality of its body purified from the bodily ills which were a bane in this life.[11]

The deceased are said to go home. Immediately a person expires, some close relative announces the death aloud: *Ole ole o la looo, ole ole o la looo!* (Oh he/she has gone home). The deceased person is therefore a "living-dead." He is present in a different mode; and he is addressed personally to depart in peace and not to trouble the living relatives, especially children, to be propitious to them, and to bring harm to the person who may have caused his death. Here even in death the person is still addressed as present, as a "Thou" though there is a kind of fear surrounding this communication. The underlying idea in the native mind, as I have mentioned before, is that personhood is a manifestation, a presence that can shine through the body in the case of incarnate beings. The personhood, or "Thou," survives the decay of the physical body.

The Ibos do not bury their dead abroad. It is considered undignified to be buried abroad, away from home. Except in cases where a person dies of abominable disease, the dead are buried in graves around the home, even in the courtyard of the home; for the deceased members of the family, especially fathers, are said to be present, and are invoked on occasions especially in time of crisis.

The sense of the "presence" of personal immortality of the deceased members of the community is partly expressed in the cult of the ancestors *(ndichie)*. The most important symbol of their participating presence in Ibo extended family structure is *Ofo* which is a portable three stick symbol from a branch of the *Ofo* tree. In a special ceremony the *Ofo* is endowed with the spiritual power of the ancestors and it is transmitted through

inheritance to heads of extended families. It symbolizes authority, the guarantee of truth from God and the transmission of
sacred orders.[12] The ancestors are guardians of the welfare of
the community. As intercessors in the transcendental world, they
are invoked to bring blessings and avert dangers from the family
or community. Those who have recently passed to the other
world are invoked by name to show their personal immortality,
while those whose memories are lost in the long past or time
immemorial are said to belong to the class of ancestors. The
"living-dead" are said to be powerful.

Indications of the sense of personal immortality can be
seen from analyses of some dreams. There appears to be some
truth in the saying that death is like sleep in which one dreams.
Some dreams are so vivid that one thinks that one's dreams are
happening in waking life. In some dreams, one makes a journey
to familiar or unknown places, encounters strange people, meets
accidents, and sometimes sees and communicates with dead relatives and friends. While the body of the dreamer is stationary in
sleep, some part of the dreamer, the soul, spirit, is active in
dream "experiences." The natives hold that this active part with
a "spiritualized body" is the immortal self.

One may argue that the content of dreams is nothing
more than the concoctions of the imagination from the memory of
waking experiences in real life; for in some dreams the impossible
can happen; for example, I have dreamt that I was flying.
However, the content of some dreams cannot easily be dismissed
as concoctions of the fertile imagination. Some dreams are veridical. Some have dreamt of things that eventually came true in
real life. We have heard of the Pharaoh's dreams about the
famine which eventually scourged Egypt, of Nebuchadnezzar's
dreams which Daniel interpreted. Some people have been inspired
by supernatural powers in dreams, for example, in the New
Testament, St. Joseph was inspired in his dream by an angel to
take Mary back as his wife because she had conceived by the
power of the Holy Spirit. In some dreams I "have seen" some
dead relatives and played with them. However, this dream experience can be explained by saying that my imagination drew from
my waking experience when these dead relatives were alive.
Although most dream experiences of communicating with the dead
can be explained this way, but not all. One striking example is
a case in which a friend of mine told me about a certain widow.
She saw her dead husband in a dream, who told her that he was
lonely and wanted her to follow him. The wife agreed and
prepared to follow the dead husband. She called her children
and asked them not to cry for her because she was soon to follow

her husband. A year later, she died at exactly the same hour and day her husband died. This case points to the validity of maintaining that dreams can be ways of reaching out to the world beyond. Some dreams thus contain paranormal elements which are indicative of the world beyond, and the Ibos take these seriously.

The appearances of ghosts of dead relatives or friends are a kind of evidence of personal immortality. Regarded as paranormal, they can reasonably be held to be philosophically tenable in view of a non-materialistic metaphysic of man, though they are scientifically open questions. [13]

The world beyond is considered to be like this world, and the "living-dead" are said to conduct their life activities in ways similar to this life. This is why the dead are buried with material goods such as money, clothing, and jewelry for their use. [14] The significance of the second burial [15] is the reception of the deceased person by peers in the next world. There is thus a natural transition from the present life to the other.

In view of the fact that the Ibos believe in reincarnation (*eyo uwa*) as a way of personal immortality, a philosophical problem arises in instances where a deceased member of a family is said to have been reincarnated and is still invoked among the ancestors. There appears to be a contradiction here. A solution for this apparent contradiction is that the human soul (*mmuo*) sustains a multiple personality: as one manifestation, "Thou," it is not restricted as an object. Hence, one personality could be reincarnated while the rest remain among the "living-dead" in the world beyond.

The Ibo expression *"Inyi na-eje inyi na-ayo"* (Many go, many return) epitomizes the metaphysical principles underpinning continuity in personal existence, immortality, and especially reincarnation. Humans do not reincarnate as subhumans except as a form of punishment for evil lives. Belief in reincarnation is so strong that dying parents or relatives console their children or relatives that they will come back to them. The dying parents often tell the family what kind of life and personality they hope for when they reincarnate. There are instances where the predictions of dying relatives with regard to their reincarnation are said to have come true. An interesting case is one which my friend, Dr. Felix Ekechi, a professor at Kent State University, told me about a relative who reincarnated in his body. He said that those who knew this relative of his said that when this relative was about to die he told the family that when he reincarnated he would be intelligent, scholarly, and be born in the family of a

191

relative who is well-to-do. When Dr. Ekechi was born and was growing up as a boy, he was said to resemble exactly the dead relative in gait and intelligence. Could this not be a case of genetic survival and not of personal immortality? My grandfather, Ahanaonu is said to have reincarnated in one of my cousins because my cousin exhibits some of my grandfather's qualities; for example, my grandfather used to blink in one of his eyes.

Reincarnation[16] is in the realm of the paranormal, and conclusive evidence by way of empirical verification may not be reached. However, it would be fallacious to lump reincarnation in the limbo of superstition since its verification is still an open question. A crucial objection to reincarnation is that those who are supposed to have been reincarnated do not recall their previous life. Could we hope that one day a psychological technique will be found for unravelling the mystery of reincarnation? Personally, I do not believe in reincarnation, because I do not want to start life's struggle all over again. However, it can give somebody another chance to redeem an unfortunate life, and actualize more life potentials.

In dealing with the problem of immortality, I have not touched on it with reference to procreation. It is not necessary to treat it here since we are concerned with personal immortality. However, a person can become immortal in the memory of generations of descendants. This kind of immortality is recognized in Ibo philosophy, for there is a high premium on marriage and begetting of children. Sons are wanted more than daughters because sons succeed their fathers and carry on the family name and tradition. The status of daughters is now on the increase as they are given the opportunity to actualize their human potentials, and may be better than some boys in this respect.

The problem of the human person and immortality necessarily involves human transcendence. Man is part of nature, but also transcends it. This is an important presupposition of the Ibo view of the human person. This view avoids materialism as the fundamental basis of reality, and allows for the realm of the immaterial, of mystery and faith in a holistic conception of man. The realm of the immaterial, of mystery and faith, includes the divine, and metaphysics is not complete without the treatment of God, the highest Being and His relationship to lesser beings such as humans. Here metaphysics is complementary to theology. In the Ibo conception of man, man is oriented to the divine. This is the reason why most Ibo names express man's relation to God, specifically in terms of God's creation and providence. For example, popular names such as *Chukwukere* (God created), *Chinyere*

(God has given), *Chukwuemeka* (God has done marvelously), *Chinedu* (God leads), *Chiedozi* (God preserves), *Onyebuchi* (Who is God? No man is God.) show man's orientation to God. This orientation of man to God constitutes an important facet of the human person and immortality because God (*Chineke, Chukwu*) who is immortal confers immortality. A major reason for the establishment and growth of Christianity among the Ibos is the fertile soil of the Ibo metaphysics of the human person which includes orientation to God, or connatural knowledge of God.

To conclude, the transcendence of the human person with reference to personal immortality is central to the Ibo holistic conception of man. Without human transcendence with regard to personal immortality, according to Ibo wisdom, life would not be fully meaningful. By avoiding materialism which, as the substratum of reality, does not give a backdrop for fully meaningful discussion of holistic view of man, and by subscribing to the realm of the immaterial, of mystery and faith, which includes relationship to the highest Being in ordinal metaphysics the Ibos, according to our argument, have a metaphysic which adequately expresses their view of the human person and immortality. The danger facing the Ibo view of man today is imported materialism; and the problem is how to integrate modern scientific and technological achievements with the traditional values without losing sight of the vital transcendence of the human person.[17]

193

RICHARD C. ONWUANIBE

FOOTNOTES

1.   This is a revised version of the paper which was read at
      the East Central Conference of the American Catholic Phil-
      osophical Association, November 11, 1979, Cincinnati,
      Ohio, U.S.A.   It was published in the present form in
      Philosophy Research Archives, Bowling Green State
      University, Ohio 43403, and is reprinted here with the
      permission of the author, editor and publisher.

2.   It is important to note here, at the outset, that African
      thought, and specifically Ibo thought, on the human
      person and immortality has presuppositions that have
      metaphysical implications.   Hence the justification of the
      title of the paper is in order.   My approach will be partly
      interpretive and partly analytical of the cultural ideas in
      this context.

      The comment of Reverend Frank M. Oppenheim, S. J.,
      Professor of Philosophy at Xavier University, Cincinnati,
      Ohio, U.S.A. on this paper when it was read at the East
      Central Conference of the American Catholic Philosophical
      Association, November 11, 1979 in Cincinnati is in order:

                    We can search for wisdom in any
                    form--just as intently as an African
                    nomad searches for water in whatever
                    creekbed, hole, or oasis he encoun-
                    ters. If so, we will be led back to
                    that vital nerve of perennial philoso-
                    phy's listening for Wisdom coming from
                    any wise people and receiving it in
                    THEIR way of refining it--be this
                    through proverb or ritual, through
                    Zen meditation or simply smiling in
                    one's love of life. Onwuanibe offers
                    us the great service of opening our
                    minds to an incipient dialogue between
                    North and South rather than letting
                    us settle for an interchange merely

between East and West.

3. This idea of the connection between the physical and metaphysical in African thought has been emphasized by John
S. Mbiti when he said that "the spiritual universe is a
unit with the physical, and that these two intermingle and
dovetail into each other so much that it is not easy, or
even necessary, at times, to draw the distinction or separate them," (*African Religions and Philosophies*, New
York; Doubleday and Company, Inc., 1970, p. 97.) See
also Placide Tempels' idea of Vital Force as the ontological
medium of the physical and metaphysical (*Bantu Philosophy*, Paris Ve: Presence Africaine, 1969). It is important
to note that the sense of "metaphysical" as "ontological" is
in place here because the ontological is more than the
concern with beings of a physical nature.

4. The problem of alienation constitutes a central theme among
existentialist thinkers, such as Gabriel Marcel, Karl
Jaspers, Martin Heidegger, Jean Paul Sartre, to mention a
few.

5. Immanuel Kant, *Critique of Pure Reason*, translated by N.
K. Smith, New York: St. Martin's Press, A107, p. 136.

6. Cf. Elizabeth Kubler-Ross, *Death the Final State of
Growth*, Englewood Cliffs, New Jersey: Prentice-Hall,
Inc., 1975.

7. See Martin Heidegger's ontological analysis of death in
Being and Time, New York: Harper & Row Publishers, pp.
279-311. According to him, one of the basic structures of
man as a tissue of possibilities is "Being-toward-death."

8. I have used "sense" to indicate this primitive awareness
which is more than a belief.

9. For such arguments see Socrates' argument in the *Phaedo:*
John Haynes Holmes, "Ten Reasons for Believing in
Immortality", *A Modern Introduction to Philosophy*, Paul
Edwards and Arthur Pap, eds., New York: The Free
Press, 1973, pp. 250-259; C. J. Ducasse, "The Empirical
Case for Personal Survival", *Body, Mind and Death*,
edited by Antony Flew, New York: The Macmillan Press,
pp. 221-230; Raymond A. Moody, Jr., *Life After Life;*
New York: Bantam Books, Inc., 1978; Kenneth Ring, *Life
At Death: A Scientific Investigation of Near-Death Expe-*

riences (forthcoming).

10. In describing the complexity of human personality the Ibos distinguish the body *(aho)*, life in general *(ndo)* and the heart *(obi)*. In a special sense, *obi* stands for life, spirit, soul, personality. The soul in the sense of vital principle or essence is "heart-seed" *(mkporo obi)* and it is said to be located within the area of the heart. It is also the spirit *(mmuo)* of man. Breath *(ume)* is a sign of life and is associated with the soul. A man's shadow *(inyu-nyuro)* is a reflection of the soul, or spirit *(mmuo)*. Both breath and shadow are thought to disappear at death. Hence a corpse is thought not to cast a shadow. A sign of ghost is it casts no shadow. The soul *(mmuo)* survives the body at death. See C. K. Meek, *Law and Authority in a Nigerian Tribe,* New York: Barnes and Noble, Inc., 1970, pp. 53-54. Among the Bantu the soul or the departing being is called "the little man" *(muntu)* which lives on in the hereafter, or is reincarnated. For a good discussion of this point see Placide Tempels, *Bantu Philosophy,* (Paris: Presence Africaine), p. 55; John S. Mbiti, *African Religions and Philosophies,* p. 209; Janheinz Jahn, *Muntu* (New York: Grove Press, Inc.) p. 106.

11. The Ibos have a purification ceremony called *iko ihe uwa.*

12. For further discussion of the *Ofo* symbolism, see C. K. Meek, *op. cit.,* pp. 63ff.

13. Some attempts at verifying appearances of ghosts by scientific means have been made. For instance, recordings of a ghost's voice on tape and appearances by photographing have been made. However, the image of the photograph is not well defined; but there is some vague configuration in the photograph that indicates some appearance. This may not be scientifically conclusive evidence but some kind of evidence that is relative to the subject-matter, since ghosts do not have normal human bodies.

14. These material goods also indicate the hope that the deceased person may return (reincarnate) well-to-do or be in a place of abundance.

15. The second burial takes place between two weeks to three years after the interment of the body of the deceased. It is an occasion of feasting and celebration surrounded with

pomp. For further detail see P. A. Talbot, *The Peoples of Southern Nigeria,* Volume III, London: Frank Cass and Company Limited, 1969, p. 520ff.

16.   Joseph Head and S. L. Cranston, ed., *Reincarnation,* New York: Warner Books, Inc., for a treatment of reincarnation from the perspectives of various descriptions. In this book, Dr. Ring, a psychologist in the University of Connecticut headed a study which examined "102 people who survived clinical death, or near-death experiences." The upshot of this investigation is the confirmation of life after physical death or another world beyond this side of the grave.

17.   See my article, "Culture and Technology: A Moral Viewpoint,: *Journal of African Studies,* University of California, Los Angeles, Vol. 7, No. 1, pp. 64-67. Spring, 1980, for a discussion of this problem.

THE AKAN CONCEPT OF A PERSON[1]

Kwame Gyekye

Introduction

A number of scholars, including philosophers, tend to
squirm a little at the mention of "African philosophy," though
they do not do so at the mention of African art, music, history,
anthropology, religion, etc. While the latter cluster of disciplines
is being cultivated or pursued in the various Centres or Insti-
tutes of African Studies in universities round the world, African
philosophy as such is relegated to limbo because it is considered
to be non-existent. Philosophy is thus assumed to be a special
relish of the peoples of the West and the East. To a very great
extent the lack of writing in Africa's historical past, leading in
turn to the absence of a doxographic tradition, that is, a tradition of recorded opinions, has been responsible for the assumption that there is no such thing as African philosophy.

We do not ask the question whether there is European
philosophy or Greek philosophy simply because there are the
classic *Dialogues, Treatises, Essays, Philosophical Investigations,*
which one can immediately delve into if he wants to study European or Greek philosophy. In Africa, traditionally, there has
been a dearth of such philosophical classics. Yet this fact does
not in any way argue the non-existence of African philosophy.
For it is known that Socrates, the celebrated ancient Greek

199

philosopher, did not write anything, although he inherited a written culture; but it is known that he *philosophized*. In India "the Upanishads which are imbued with philosophy ... were not written down for centuries...."[2] An eminent Indian philosopher wrote: "The Vedas were handed down from mouth to mouth from a period of unknown antiquity. ... When the Vedas were composed, there was probably no system of writing prevalent in India."[3] (The Vedas constitute the religious and philosophical classics of India. The Upanishads form the concluding portions of the Vedas.) And I learn that Buddha, the ancient Indian philosopher and religious thinker, "wrote no book, but taught orally."[4] Thus African philosophy is none the worse for the absence, traditionally, of written philosophical literature. To deny to African peoples philosophical thought is to imply that they are unable to make philosophical sense of, or to conceptualize, their experiences; it is in fact to deny them their humanity. For philosophy of some kind is behind the thought and action of every people. It constitutes the intellectual sheet-anchor of their life in its totality.

African philosophic thought not only forms part of the oral literature of the peoples; it is also expressed or reflected in real and vital attitudes. In Africa a great deal of philosophical material is embedded in the proverbs,[5] myths and folk-tales, folk-songs, rituals, beliefs, customs and traditions of the peoples. The interested and careful philosopher can perceive the philosophical relevance of such material and may come across ideas or doctrines or problems that may have some affinity with those of the West or the East, but which originated from the peoples themselves.

After these dialectical preambles, I wish now to turn to a discussion of the Akan[6] concept of a person, in which I shall attempt to interpret, reconstruct, and sort out in a more sophisticated way the elements of the Akan collective thought on the nature of a person, and provide the necessary conceptual or theoretical trimming such as is required by the anthropological and sociological accounts.

I. *Okra* (SOUL)

We are given to understand from anthropological accounts that the Akans hold a tripartite conception of a person, considering a human being to be constituted by three elements: *okra, sunsum,* and *honam* (or *nipadua:* body).

The *okra* is considered to be that which constitutes the very inner self of the individual, the principle of life of that individual, and the embodiment and transmitter of his destiny (fate: *nkrabea*). It is thought to be a spark of God (*Onyame*) in man. It is thus divine and has an ante-mundane existence with God; it derives directly from God. The *okra*, therefore, might be considered as the equivalent of the concept of the soul in other metaphysical systems.

The presence of this divine principle in a human being may have been the basis of the Akan proverb *Nnipa nyinaa ye Onyame mma, obiara nye asase ba* ("All men are the children of God; no one is a child of the Earth").

The conception of the *okra* as the life principle in a person, his vital force, the source of his energy, is linked closely with another concept, namely *honhom*. *Honhom* means "breath"; it is the noun form *home*, to breathe. When a man is dead it is said: *ne honhom ko* ("his breath is gone)" or *ne 'kra afi ne ho* ("his soul has withdrawn from his body"). The two sentences, one with *honhom* as subject and the other with *okra* as the subject, do, in fact, say the same thing; they express the same thought, the death-of-the-person. The departure of the soul from the body means the death of a person, and so does ceasing to breathe. Yet this does not mean that the *honhom* (breath) is the *okra* (soul). The *okra* is that which "causes" the breathing. Thus, the *honhom* is the tangible manisfestation or evidence of the *okra*. (I must say, however, that in some dialects of the Akan language *honhom* has come to be used interchangeably with *sunsum*, so that the phrase *honhom bone* has come to mean the same thing as *sunsum bone*, i. e. evil "spirit." The identification of the *honhom* with the *sunsum* seems to me to be a recent idea and may have resulted from the translation of the Bible into the various Akan dialects: *honhom* must have been used to translate the Greek *pneuma*, breath, spirit. The clarification of the concepts of *okra, honhom* and *sunsum* (spirit) is the burden of this paper.)

II. *SUNSUM* (SPIRIT)

Sunsum is another of the constituent elements of a person. It has usually been rendered in English as "spirit." In some of the literature on Western metaphysics 'spirit' appears to be a generic or comprehensive concept under which are subsumed specific concepts such as soul, mind, self, consciousness--all of which are, however, considered to be identical. But some

Western philosophers distinguish the mind from the soul, for while they are prepared to admit that a human being has a mind (which they would identify with the brain or a brain state), they deny the existence of the soul mainly because of the immortality attribute that has traditionally been claimed for it.[7] In the Akan metaphysics of the person, however, "spirit" is a specific concept. (I shall show in a later publication on Akan ontology that the concept is also used generically in other contexts.) It appears from the anthropological accounts that even when it is used as a specific concept "spirit" (sunsum) is not identical with the soul (okra) as they do not refer to the same thing. However, the anthropological accounts of the sunsum involve some conceptual blunders, as I hope to show presently. As for the mind (when it is not identified with the soul) it might be rendered also by sunsum, judging from the functions that are attributed by the Akans to the latter (see below).

On the surface it might appear that "spirit" is not appropriate rendition for sunsum; but after clearing some misconceptions engendered by some anthropological writings, I shall show that it is an appropriate rendition but that its real nature requires some clarification. Anthropologists and sociologists have held, (i) that the sunsum derives from the father,[8] (ii) that it is not divine,[9] and (iii) that it perishes with the disintegration of the honhom,[10] that is, the material component of a person. It seems to me, however, that all these three characterizations of the sunsum are incorrect.

Let us first take up the third characterization of the sunsum, namely, that it is something that perishes with the perishing of the body. Now, if a body, a physical object, perishes along with the sunsum, then it would follow that the sunsum also is something physical or material. As a matter of fact Danquah in his philosophical analysis concludes that "sunsum is, in fact, the matter or the physical basis of the ultimate ideal of which okra (soul) is the form and the spiritual or mental basis."[11] Elsewhere he speaks of an "interaction of the material mechanism (sunsum) with the soul," and assimilates the sunsum to the "sensible form" of Aristotle's metaphysics of substance and the okra to the "intelligible form."[12] One would conclude from these statements that Danquah also conceived the sunsum as material (although some other statements of his would seem to contradict this). (See below.) The relationship between the honam (body) and the sunsum (supposedly bodily), however, is left unexplained. Thus philosophical, sociological, and anthropological accounts of the nature of a person have given us the impression that the Akans held a triparite conception of a human being:

> *okra* (soul) -- immaterial
> *sunsum* ("spirit") -- material (?)
> *honam* (body) -- material

As we shall see presently, however, this account or analysis of a person, particularly the characterization of the *sunsum* ("spirit") as material, is not satisfactory. I must admit at this point that the real nature of the *sunsum* presents some difficulty for the Akan metaphysics of a person and has been a source of confusion for scholars. The difficulty is not insoluble, however.

There are many things said regarding the functions or activities of the *sunsum* which indicate that it surely is neither material (physical), nor mortal, nor derived from the father. Busia says that the *sunsum* "is what moulds the child's personality and disposition. It is that which determines his character and individuality."[13] Danquah says: "But we now know the notion which corresponds to the Akan 'sunsum', namely, not 'spirit' as such but 'personality' which covers the relation of the 'body' to the 'soul' *(Okra)*."[14] That the *sunsum* constitutes the personality and character of a person is stated by Danquah in several pages of his book.[15] Rattray also observed that the *sunsum* is the basis of character and personality.[16] There are indeed some sentences in the Akan language in which the expression *sunsum* is used in obvious reference to personality (or qualities or traits in a person's character). Thus, for "he has a strong personality" the Akans would say *"ne sunsum ye duru"* (i.e. his *sunsum* is "heavy" or "weighty"). When a man is generous they say that he has a good *sunsum (owo sunsum pa)*. When a man has an impressive or imposing personality they say that he has an over-shadowing *sunsum (ne sunsum hye me so)*. In fact sometimes in describing a dignified person they would simply say, *owo sunsum,* that is, he has a commanding presence. And a man may be said to have a "gentle" *sunsum,* a "forceful" *sunsum,* a "submissive" or "weak" *sunsum.* Thus, the concept of the *sunsum* would correspond in some ways to what is meant by personality, as was observed by some earlier investigators.

Thus, it is now clear that in Akan conceptions the *sunsum* ("spirit") is the basis of a man's personality, his distinctive character and, in the words of Busia, "his ego."[17] Personality, of course, is a word that has been given various definitions by psychologists. But I believe that whatever else that concept may involve, it certainly involves the idea of a set of characteristics as shown in a person's behavior--his thoughts, feelings, actions, etc. (I do not think that it refers exclusively to a person's physical appearance.) Thus, if the *sunsum* is that which embodies a man's personality, it just cannot be a physical thing, for qualities of personality such as courage, generosity, jealousy, gentleness, forcefulness, meekness, dignity are not sensible or physical qualities; they are *psychical.* The jealous man *feels* ill or unhappy because of a possible or actual loss of position, status, expectations, or because of the better fortune of others; a courageous man is able to control *fear* in the face of danger, pain, misfortune, etc.; the ambitious man has strong *desire* to achieve something. The expressions *feel, fear,* and *desire* are of course psychical (psychological), not physicalistic, expressions. (In Akan metaphysics there is no room for materialism, the doctrine held by some philosophers in the West that a person is fundamentally a physical entity and that what is referred to as mind or soul is in fact identifiable with a person's brain, which is a physical organ.) Thus, if in fact personality is the function of the *sunsum,* then the latter cannot conceptually be held to be physical or material; it must surely be something *(ade)* immaterial, i.e. spiritual.

We have already noted certain statements of Danquah which suggest a physicalistic interpretation of the *sunsum.* On the other hand, he also maintains that "it is the *sunsum* that experiences,"[18] and that it is through it that "the *okra* or soul manifests itself in the world of experience."[19] Elsewhere he says of the *sunsum:* "It is the bearer of conscious experience, the unconscious or subliminal self remaining over as the okra or soul."[20] It is not clear what Danquah means by the "bearer" of experience. Perhaps what he means is that the *sunsum* is the subject of experience; that which experiences.

This being so, I would think, at least provisionally, that the subject of experience cannot be physical. If, as he thought,[21] it is the *sunsum* which makes it possible for the destiny *(nkrabea:* fate) of the soul to be "realized" or "carried out" on earth, then, like the *okra* (soul), an aspect of whose function it was going to perform, the *sunsum* also must be considered as something spiritual, not physical. Danquah's position on the concept of the *sunsum* is ambivalent. And so is Busia's. Busia says that one part of a man is "the personality that comes indirectly from the supreme Being,"[22] that is, God. By "personality" Busia must, on his own showing,[23] be referring to the *sunsum* of a man, which must, according to my analysis of that concept, derive directly from God, and not from the father. It must, therefore, be divine and immortal, contrary to what he and others thought.

The explanation the Akans give of the phenomenon of dreaming also indicates that the *sunsum* is something special. For the Akans, as for Sigmund Freud, dreams are not somatic but psychic phenomena. They believe that in a dream it is the person's *sunsum* that is the "actor." In sleep the *sunsum* is said to be released from the fetters of the body. It, as it were, fashions for itself a new world of forms with the materials of its waking experience. Thus, although the person is deeply asleep, his body (*honam*) lying in bed, yet he may "see" himself standing on the top of a mountain or driving a car or fighting with someone. The actor in any of these actions is thought to be the *sunsum,* which thus can leave the body and return to it.

As the basis or determinant of personality traits--which are non-sensible--as a co-performer of the activities or functions of the *okra* (soul), undoubtedly thought to be a spiritual entity, and as the *dramatis persona* of the spiritual or psychical phenomenon of dreaming, the *sunsum* must be something spiritual (immaterial). This is the reason for my earlier assertion that "spirit" might not be an inappropriate translation for *sunsum,* that is to say, the *sensum* is something spiritual.

On my analysis, then, we would have the following picture:

Okra (soul)	)--immaterial (spiritual)
Sunsum (spirit)	)--immaterial (spiritual)
Honam (body)	)--material (physical).

Thus, the Akans hold a dualistic conception of a person: a persons is constituted by two principle substances, one spiritual (immaterial) and the other physical (material).

RELATION OF *OKRA* AND *SUNSUM*

Now having shown that the *sunsum* is in fact something spiritual (and for this reason I shall henceforth use the word "spirit" or "spiritual" in reference to *sunsum* without quotes), we must go on to examine whether the expressions *sunsum* (spirit) and *okra* (soul) denote the same object in Akan metaphysics and philosophical psychology. In the course of my field research I was informed by a number of elderly people I interviewed that the *sunsum, okra,* and *honhom* ("breath") are identical; it is one entity that goes under three names. I have already shown that while there is a close link between the *okra* and the *honhom,* the

205

two cannot, nevertheless, be identified.[24] What about the *sunsum* and the *okra?* Can they be identified?

To say that the two can be identified would logically mean that whatever can be asserted of one can or must be asserted of the other. Yet there are some things the Akans say about the *sunsum* which are not said of the *okra;* the predicates or attributes of the two are different. Thus, the need for a reconstruction of the relation between the *okra* and the *sunsum.* The Akans say:

1) *ne 'kra di awerehow* ("his *kra* is sad": never, "his *sunsum* is sad").
2) *ne 'kra teete* ("his *kra* is worried or disturbed").
3) *ne 'kra adwane* ("his *kra* has run away," an expression they use when someone is scared to death).
4) *ne kra ye* ("his *kra* is good" - a sentence they use when they want to say that a person is lucky or fortunate.
5) *ne kra afi ne ho* ("his *kra* has withdrawn from his body").
6) *ne kara dii n'akyi, anka owui* ("but for his *kra* that followed him, he would have died").
7) *ne kra aniagye* ("his *kra* is happy").

In all such statements, the attributions are made to the *okra* (*kra;* soul), never to the *sunsum.* On the other hand, the Akans say:

1) *owo sunsum* ("he has *sunsum,*" an expression they use when they want to refer to someone as digni- fied and has having a commanding presence. Here they never say *owo (o) kra* ("he has *okra,*" soul, for it is believed that every human being has a soul, the principle of life, but the nature of the *sunsum* differs from person to person; thus they speak of "gentle *sunsum,*" "forceful *sunsum,*" weak or strong *sunsum,*" etc.).
2) *ne sunsum ye duru* ("his *sunsum* is heavy or weighty," i.e. he has a strong personality.
3) *ne sunsum hye* (or *to*) *me so* ("his *sunsum* over- shadows mine").
4) *obi sunsum so kyen obi dee* ("someone's *sunsum* is bigger or greater than another's").
5) *owo sunsum pa* ("he has a good spirit," i.e. he is a generous person).

In all such statements the attributions are made to the *sunsum,* never to the *okra.*

Now, given *x* and *y,* if whatever is asserted of *x* can be asserted of *y,* then *x* can be said to be identical with *y.* If there is at least one predicate, which *x* has but *y* does not have, then *x* and *y* are not identical. On this showing, to the extent that things that are asserted or predicated of the *okra* do not apply to the *sunsum,* the two cannot logically be identified. But while they are logically and functionally distinct, they are not *ontologically* distinct. That is to say, they are not separate existences held together by an external bond. They are a unity in duality, a duality in unity. The distinction is not a relation between two independent entities. And the *sunsum* may, perhaps more accurately, be characterized as *a state* of the *okra* (soul). As mentioned earlier, the *okra* is the principle of life of a person and the embodiment and transmitter of his destiny *(nkrabea).* Personality and character traits of a person are the function of the *sunsum.* The *sunsum* appears to be the source of dynamism of a man, the really active part or force of the psychological system of man. It is said to have extra-sensory powers; it is that which thinks, desires, etc. It is not in any way identical with the brain. Rather it acts upon the brain *(adwen);* it is that which makes the *adwen* (brain) work. In short, it is upon the *sunsum* that man's health, worldly power, influence, position, success, etc. would depend.

Moreover, moral predicates are generally ascribed to the *sunsum.* Lystad is, thus, wrong when he says: "In many respects the *sunsum* or spirit is so identical with the *okra* or soul in its functions that it is difficult to distinguish between them."[25]

In the Akan conception of a person, the soul *(okra)* is held to be a mental or spiritual entity (substance). It is not a bundle of qualities or perceptions, as is held in some western philosophies. The basis for this assertion is the Akan belief in disembodied survival. A bundle theory of substance implies the elimination of the notion of substance, for if a substance is held to be a bundle or collection of qualities or perceptions it would mean that when the qualities or perceptions are removed nothing would be left; there would then be no substance, i.e. no substratum or "owner" of those qualities. Thus, if the soul or mind is held to be a bundle of perceptions, as in Hume, it would be impossible to talk of disembodied survival in the form of a soul or self since the bundle itself is an abstraction. One Akan maxim, expressed epigrammatically, is that "when a man dies he is not (really) dead" *(onipa wu a na onwui).* What they imply by

207

this is that there is something in a human being which is eternal and indestructible, and which continues to exist in the world of spirits (asamandow). An Akan motif expresses the following thought: "Could God die, I will die" (Onyame bewu na m'awu). In Akan metaphysics God is held to be eternal, immortal (Odomankoma), and what is being asserted in the above thought is that since God will not die, a person, that is, his okra (soul), conceived as a spark of God in a person, will not die either. That is to say, the soul of man is immortal. But--and this is the point I want to make--the attributes of immortality and eternity make sense if, and only if, the soul is held to be a substance, and not a bundle of qualities or perceptions.

But where in a human being is this mental or spiritual substance located? Descartes thought that the soul is in the pineal gland. The Akans also seem to hold that the soul (okra) is lodged in the head of a person, although they do not mention any specific part of the head where it is. But although it is in the head "you can not see it with your natural eyes," as they would put it, since it is an immaterial substance.

That the soul is in the head (eti, ti), may be inferred from the following expressions of the Akans: When they want to say that a person is lucky or fortunate they would say ne ti ye ("his head is well") or ne 'kra ye ("his soul is well"). Both sentences express the same thought. And when a person is constantly afflicted with misfortunes he would say "me ti nnye" ("my head is not well") or "me 'kra nnye" ("my soul is not well"). It may be inferred from such expressions that there is some kind of connection between the head and the soul. And although they cannot point to a specific part of the head as the "residence" of the soul, it may be conjectured that it is in the region of the brain (adwen), which, as stated earlier, receives its activism from the sunsum (spirit), a state of the soul (okra). That is, the mind (or, soul) acts on the brain in a specific locality, not that it is itself actually localized.

The Akan conception of a person, as it appears in my analysis, is thoroughly dualistic, not tripartite. A dualistic conception of a person does not necessarily carry with it a belief in a causal relation or interaction between the two parts of the person, soul and body. For instance, some dualistic philosophers in the West maintain a doctrine of psycho-physical parallelism, which completely denies causal interaction between body and soul. Others, also dualists, maintain a doctrine of epiphenomenalism which, while not completely rejecting causal interaction, holds that the causal direction goes in one way only, namely, from body to mind; such a doctrine is thus not an interactionist doctrine. The Akans, however, maintain a thorough interactionist position on the relation between soul and body. They believe that not only does the body have a causal influence on the soul but also the soul has a causal influence on the body *(honam).* What happens to the soul *(okra)* takes effect or reflects on the condition of the body. Similarly, what happens to the body reflects on the condition of the soul.

It is the actual bodily or physical behaviour of a person that gives some idea of the condition of the soul. Thus, if the physical behaviour of a person suggests that he is happy they would say *ne 'kra ani agye* ("his soul is happy"); if unhappy or morose they would say *ne 'kra di awershow* ("his soul is sorrowful"). When the *okra* (soul) is enfeebled or injured by evil spirits ill health results; and the poor conditions of the body also affect the condition of the soul. That is, the condition of the soul depends on the condition of the body. As a matter of fact the belief in psycho-physical causal interaction is the whole basis of spiritual or psychical healing. There are certain diseases which are believed to be "spiritual diseases" *(sunsum yare)* and cannot be healed by the application of physical therapy. In such diseases attention is paid to both physiological and spiritual aspects of the person. Unless the soul is healed the body will not respond to any physical treatment. The removal of a disease of the soul is the activity of the diviners or the "medicine men" *(adunsifo).*

Some similarities have been discovered between the functions and activities of the *sunsum* of the Akan psychology and the ego of Freud. An essential task of the ego is to engage in intercourse with the external world. Like the *sunsum,* it directs the business of everyday living; it is the executive of the personality, that is, the psychological system. It is the representative of the Id in the external world. An aspect of the nature of the *sunsum* is or may be similar to the ego. The *sunsum* of the Akan psyche is not always conscious, and a man does not always know what his *sunsum* wants. It is believed that it is the *sunsum* that the Akan diviner *(okomfo),* believed to possess extra-sensory abilities, communicates with. It tells the diviner what it really wants without the person knowing or being aware of what he wants; thus, the *sunsum* may be unconscious. Freud said: "And it is indeed the case that large portions of the ego and super-ego can remain unconscious and are normally unconscious. That is to say, the individual knows nothing of their contents and it requires an expenditure of effort to make them conscious."[26] It is, I suppose, for these reasons that some scholars[27] have not hesitated to identify the *sunsum* with the ego of Freud, and having done so go on to identify the *okra* with the Id.

But there are dissimilarities which must be stated. Firstly, in Freud the Id is the original system of the psyche, the matrix within which the ego and the super-ego become differentiated. But in the Akan conception both the *okra* and the *sunsum* at once constitute the original system of the psyche. Unlike the Id, the *okra* is not the only component that is present at birth. Secondly, in Freud the ego and the super-ego are formed or developed later. In Akan the *sunsum* is not formed later; it was part and parcel of the original psychical structure, the *okra*, soul. At birth the child possesses a *sunsum*, just as it at that time possesses an *okra*. Freud thought in fact that the mental structure of a man was pretty well formed by the end of the fifth year. Thirdly, the super-ego is the moral dimension of personality; it represents the claims of morality.[28] In the Akan system, as stated earlier, moral attributes are generally attributed to the *sunsum*. Thus the *sunsum* of the Akan seems to perform aspects of the functions of both the ego and the super-ego of Freud.

It seems to me that an interactionist psycho-physical dualism is more realistic than materialism, epiphenomenalism, parallelism, etc. Even apart from the prospects for disembodied survival which this theory of a person holds out, it has had significant pragmatic consequences in Akan communities · as evidenced in the applications of actual psycho-physical therapies. There are countless testimonies of people who have been subjected to physical treatment for months or years in modern hospitals without being cured, but who have actually been healed by traditional "medicine men" applying both physical and psychical (spiritual) methods.

All this seems to underline the facts that a human being is not just a bag of flesh and bones, that he is a complex being who cannot completely be explained by the same laws of physics used to explain inanimate things, and that our world with all its complex and strange phenomena cannot simply be reduced to physics.

FOOTNOTES

1. This article first appeared in The International Philosophi-
    cal Quarterly and is reprinted here by permission. *Inter-
    national Philosophical Quarterly.* 18 (1978): 277-287.

2. G. Parrinder, *Religion in Africa* (London, 1969), p. 25.

3. S. Dasgupta, *A History of Indian Philosophy* (Cambridge,
    1963), I. 10.

4. P. T. Raju: *The Philosophical Traditions of India*
    (London, 1971), p. 114.

5. See my "The Philosophical Relevance of Akan Proverbs,"
    Second Order, An African Journal of Philosophy, July
    1975.

6. The Akans constitute about two-thirds of the peoples of
    Ghana.

7. See, e.g. Jenny Teichman, *The Mind and the Soul*
    (London, 1974), p. 3f.

8. K. A. Busia, "The Ashanti of the Gold Coast," in D.
    Forde, *African Worlds* (Oxford, 1954), pp. 197 and 200;
    M. Fortes, *Kingship and the Social Order* (Chicago, 1969),
    pp. 199, note 14; R. A. Lystad, *The Ashanti: A Proud
    People* (New Brunswick, 1958), p. 155; Rev. Peter Kwasi
    Sarpong, *Ghana in Retrospect: Some Aspects of the
    Ghanian Culture* (Ghana Publishing Corporation, 1974), p.
    37.

9. Busia, *loc. cit;* Lystad, *loc. cit;* S. L. R. Meyerowith:
    The Sacred State of the Akan (London, 1949), p. 86;
    "Concepts of the Soul in Akan," *Africa* (1951), p. 26.

10. Busia, *loc. cit;* Lystad, *loc. cit;* P. A. Twumasi, *Medical
    Systems in Ghana: A Study in Medical Sociology,* (Ghana
    Publishing Corporation, 1975), p. 22.

11. J. B. Danquah, *The Akan Doctrine of God* (London, 1944), p. 115.

12. Ibid., p. 116.

13. Busia, *op cit.*, p. 197.

14. J. B. Danquah, *op. cit.*, p. 66.

15. E. g., pp. 67, 75, 83, 205.

16. R. S. Rattray, *Ashanti* (Oxford, 1923), p. 46.

17. Busia, *op. cit.*, p. 197.

18. Danquah, *op. cit.*, p. 67.

19. *Loc. cit.*

20. Danquah, *op. cit.*, p. 112.

21. Ibid., pp. 66-67, 115.

22. Busia, *op. cit.*, p. 200.

23. *Loc. cit.* in note 16.

24. See above.

25. Lystad, *op. cit.*, p. 158.

26. Sigmund Freud, *New Introductory Lectures on Psycho-a-nalysis* (Penguin, 1973), pp. 101-102.

27. See for instance, E. L. R. Meyerowitz, *The Sacred State of the Akan,* p. 84; "Concepts of the Soul in Akan," *Africa,* (1951), p. 26; Rev. H. Debrunner, *Witchcraft in Ghana* (Kumasi, 1959), p. 15.

28. Freud, *op. cit.*, p. 92.

AFRICAN AND WESTERN PHILOSOPHY:
A COMPARATIVE STUDY

Benjamin Ewuku Oguah

The very concept of African philosophy is apt to cause scornful or, at least, sceptical laughter in certain quarters in the west. As far as the east is from the west, so far is Africa removed from philosophy. The west is the home of civilization and philosophy; Africa is the home of wild trees, wild animals, wild people and wild cultures.

Prejudice dies hard and western anti-African prejudice dies even harder. Nevertheless, I shall make an attempt to show in this paper that this image of Africa is a prejudice; that philosophy is a universal discipline. My object is to compare African philosophy with western philosophy. Many of the doctrines of western philosophy can be seen expressed in African thought as well, not in documents but in the proverbs, ritual songs, folktales and customs of the people. We shall also see, especially when we come to consider ethical and political problems, how African philosophy differs from western philosophy. In this paper, I shall consider one African language group, the Fantis of Ghana. The philosophical ideas of the Fantis are reflected in the philosophies of many other African societies.

BENJAMIN EWUKU OGUAH

Metaphysics

Persons

What is a person? To this question Rene Descartes, the
father of modern western philosophy answers that a person
consists of two logically distinct, though causally related, entities: a mind or soul and a body. This dualistic conception of
man is found in Fanti thought as well. For the Fanti, a man is
made up of two entities: *okra* (soul) and *honam* (body). The
okra and the *honam* are, like Descarte's soul and body, logically
distinct. For the two can exist independently of each other.
Thus at death the *okra* is separated from the *honam* but the
separation does not mean the end of the *okra*. The *okra* continues to live as a *saman* (ghost) in *samanadze* (the place of the
dead). Like Descarte's soul and body, the *okra* and *honam* are,
while they are together, causally related. Not only does the
body act on the soul but also the soul acts on the body. What
happens to the *okra* takes effect in the *honam*. If the *okra* of
person A is attacked by evil forces, the effect of the spiritual
attack appears in the body of A in the form of, perhaps, illness.
To heal the body, it is not sufficient to apply physical remedies
to the body. Unless the soul is healed the body will not respond
to any physical treatment. The curing of the *okra* is one by
eninsifo (spiritual healers) who perform certain spiritual rites--
-the slaughtering of a sheep, incantations, etc.--to pacify the
attacking spirit. It is after the spiritual healing rites that the
physical treatment of the body begins. Physical events are said
to have spiritual causes. Thus if a person suffers bodily injuries
in an accident, if he is bitten by a snake, if he is struck down
by lightning, if he drowns, the cause is attributed to some
condition of the *okra*; his soul has done something wrong *(ne kra
afom)*, his soul is 'weak' *(ne kra ye har)*, his soul is grieving
(ne kra ridzi yaw), his soul requests something *(ne kra pe
biribi)*, etc. Finding the spiritual cause of physical events is the
special office of the *akomfo* (seers). We thus see in Fanti philosophy a version of Cartesian dualism and body-soul interactionism.
Man consists of a body and a soul which, though logically
distinct, act on each other.

Other Minds

The *okra*, like the Cartesian soul, is not spatially identifiable. It does not exist in space. It is an immaterial
substance. But if so a problem arises as to the existence of
others' souls or minds. Descartes considers that he cannot doubt
the existence of his own mind. He has to think in order to

doubt. But there can be no thinking without a thinker or a mind. *Cogito, ergo sum,* he concludes. He thus has no doubt about the existence of his own mind. But what about the minds of other people? If I have no access to the minds of others how do I know that they have minds? According to the argument from analogy I can tell that others have minds from their external bodily behavior because in my own case I notice a certain correlation between similar bodily behavior and my mental states. When I feel internally happy I bare my teeth and laugh. When I feel depressed tears stream down my face. Therefore when tears stream down my neighbor's face I can be sure that he his depressed. When my neighbor bares his teeth and laughs I can be sure that he is happy. I therefore attribute consciousness to others on the basis of their overt behavior by analogy with my own case.

This argument, however, philosophical scepticism will not countenance for the following reasons. Firstly, it is an inductive argument and therefore suffers the fate of all such arguments: its conclusion is merely probable. But the sceptic has little patience with mere probability. Secondly, even if we accept inductive reasoning as valid this particular kind of inductive reasoning is especially poor. For the analogical argument arrives at the conclusion that the existence of other minds is not doubtful by examining merely one case. By examining myself along and finding a correlation between certain mental and bodily states, I conclude that in the case of others also the same correlation holds. Reasoning from only one case to a conclusion about a multitude of cases is the worst kind of inductive reasoning, which itself, even at its best, does not satisfy the sceptic. Thirdly, the fact that it is theoretically possible for a robot to imitate human bodily behavior in all its complexity shows that bodily behavior is no infallible criterion on the basis of which to ascribe consciousness to others. Hence arises one of the perennial problems of western philosophy, the problem of our knowledge of the existence of other people's minds.

But the problem of other minds is not confined to western philosophy. We find the same problem expressed in Fanti philosophy thus: *Obi nnyim obi ne tsirmu asem* (No one knows what goes on in the head of another).

Philosophical Theology

(a) The ontological argument. In the appellations of God in the Fanti language one can see the very same idea that leads Anselm to formulate the ontological argument for the existence of God. In Fanti thought God is considered as the Highest being conceivable. Thus God is likened to the elephant: *Oson kese a w'ekyir nnyi abowa* (Thou mighty elephant: there is no animal mightier than you). The elephant has no superior among the animals of the forest. It is the largest of them all. He is the Highest conceivable being. He is called *Bubur-a-obur-adze-do* (He who is infinitely greater than all). From the conception of God as the Highest conceivable being Anselm argues that God must exist. If He did not exist necessarily He would not be the Highest conceivable being since we can conceive of a being who exists necessarily. If, therefore, God's existence is merely contingent He would not be the Highest being conceivable. This argument is, of course, unsound and the Fanti philosopher does not argue that way. But we see in Fanti philosophy at least that conception of God from which Anselm works out his proof.

(b) The Cosmological argument. One of the arguments for the existence of God in Fanti philosophical theology is the cosmological argument. God is described as *Boadze* (The creator of the world). A justification for regarding God as the creator of the world in western philosophy is the principle of universal causation, the principle that whatever exists must have a cause. The principle of universal causation is expressed in Fanti in the proverb *'se biribi annkeka mpapa a, nkye mpapa annye kredede'* (If nothing had touched the palm branch, the palm branch would not have emitted a sound.) If every event has a cause the world must also have a cause.

One of the objections to the cosmological argument is that if the principle of universal causation is true then God must also have a cause. It is, however, not only the western philosopher who has raised this objection. Many an African child has received a smack from the Sunday School teacher for asking *'Woana boo Nyame?'* (Who created God?)

To this question Aristotle's followers answer that God has no creator: God is the 'unmoved mover.' Whether satisfactory or not this answer finds expression in Fanti philosophical theology as well. God is described as *Obianyewo* (The uncreated one), *Onnyiahyese-Onnyiewie:* (He who has no beginning or end), *Daadaa Nyankopon* (The God who has always been).

(c) The teleological argument. The Fanti mind is impressed by the enormous manifestations of order, art and design in the world. Even the maggots, which seem to be in utter disarray, have each a definite path which they follow *(Nsambaa nyakanyaka wonan hon akwan do)*. This order, this

216

plan must have a cause because *Se biribi annkeka mpapa a nkye mpapa annye kredede* (If nothing had touched the palm branch, the palm branch would not have emitted a sound). Everything has a cause. The cause of the plan evident in the universe is *Opamfo Wawanyi* (The Wonderful Planner)--which is one of the appellations of God in Fanti. He is the wonderful planner who planned the universe. Thus we see in Fanti philosophical theology another of the arguments advanced by western theologians in proof of the existence of God, the teleological argument. We are not here concerned with its validity but only to show how it appears in Fanti philosophy.

(d) The problem of Evil. The Fanti recognizes the presence of evil, at least in the present world. Thus many lorries in Ghana carry the inscription *'Wiase ye yaw'* (The world is tragic). Given the fact of evil, how can it be said that the world was created by an omnibenevolent, omniscient and omnipotent God? This is what is called in western philosophical texts the problem of evil. We can also see in Fanti theology these very three attributes of God which generate this problem.

The Fanti believes in divine omnibenevolence. God is compared to a nursing mother: *Obaatan kese a wo do wonsusu* (Thou mighty nursing mother whose love is immeasurable). *'Nyame ye do'* (God is love) can be read on many lorries in Ghana. God is described as the Father of orphans and the Husband of widows *(Nganka hon Egya, ekunafo hon kun)*. God stops the tears of orphans *(Oma ngyanka gyae su)*. God does not discriminate *(Ompa mu nyi):* He feeds both the good and the evil; *onyen aboronoma, onyen nanka* (He feeds both the dove and the panther). He feeds both great and small. *Se oma oson edziban a ne wire mmfir mpatakowaa* (When He gives food to the elephant He does not forget the ant). God is called *Nyankopon* (The Mighty Friend).

But God is not only all-loving. He is also all-knowing. Divine omniscience is expressed in the appellation *Huntanhunii* (He who sees the hidden). God is able to count the footsteps of a deer on the driest rock *(Okan otwe n'anamon wo obotan sakoo do)*. The deer is a light-footed animal. It hardly leaves traces of its footsteps even on ordinary ground. But God can, in His omniscience, trace and count the footsteps of a deer on the driest rock. In addition to being all-loving and all-knowing God is all-powerful. His omnipotence is expressed in Fanti thus: *Otumfo* (the Powerful); *Oso-kor-otsee-apem* (The one ear which hears and discriminates the voices of thousands at the same time); *Ehunabobrim* (All tremble when they see Him); *Mbonsamsuro* (The Terror

217

of the devils); *Biribiara nnso Nyame ye* (Nothing is beyond the power of God).

(e) <u>Immortality</u>. The Fanti answer to the problem of evil may, perhaps, be seen in the doctrine of immortality. The Fantis believe that when a person dies the *okra* continues to live. It departs to *samanadze* (the place of the dead) where it answers for its deed on earth. The righteous *okra* may have seen a lot of suffering in this present world, but in the next world this injustice is righted. The righteous are rewarded with happiness in the life after death. The wicked are there punished with misery, and justice is done. The problem of evil arises only when we take the present world for all that there is. But if we see the picture in its entirety, if we see the universe as consisting not only of the present world but also of the next, there is no problem of evil. For the present injustices are only temporary. In the end justice will prevail. For the Fanti it is the end that matters: *'Ahyese nnhia de ewiei'* (The beginning is not as important as the end). That all will reap the consequences of their deeds is expressed in the thought *'Ibu dzea idua'* (you reap what you sow). The same idea is expressed in the saying *'Obi nhuhu na obi nkeka'* (No one prepares the food for another to eat it).

But if God is all-good, why does He allow evil at all in the present world? Why does He not make the universe uniformly good? Why does He not, for example, prevent the criminal from committing murder but instead allows him to do so and then punishes him in the after life? To this question western philosophical theologians have given various answers. Augustine's lay in the doctrine of free will. Man is a free agent. If God were, therefore, to interface in this way He would be divesting man of his freedom to choose between good and evil, of his free will.

Fantis do not defend the fact of evil in the present world this way. But what I want us to note here is that the western doctrine of the freedom of the will is also a Fanti doctrine. We have already seen that the principle of universal causation--the principle of determinism--is accepted by Fantis. But there is another school in Fanti philosophy which believes in the doctrine that men are free agents. The doctrine of free will is expressed in the saying, *'Obra nyi woara abo'* (Life is as you make it). We are the authors of our destiny. We are responsible for our actions. No one is to blame for our actions but we ourselves. We are free beings.

Epistemology

Rationalism and Empiricism

On the issue between rationalism and empiricism as to the origin of human knowledge, Fanti philosophy takes sides with rationalism. The Fanti believes in innate ideas. Thus there is the saying *'Obi nnkyere abofra Nyame'* (No one teaches a child about God). A child does not acquire knowledge of God from experience or teaching. He is born with that knowledge. It is not only the idea of God which is innately given to man. The Fantis believe that certain individuals are born with certain abilities, abilities which are not acquired from, though developed through, experience. Thus some herbalists are said to possess their knowledge of the use of herbs not from experience but innately. Some spiritual experts are supposed to possess their knowledge of spiritual matters innately.

Extra-Sensory Perception

Some of these 'special' abilities are also supposed to be acquired through extra-sensory perception. There is a wide belief among Fantis in extra-sensory perception. *Akomfo* (seers), *Eninsifo* (healers) and *Abayifo* (witches) are widely believed to possess the faculty of extra-sensory perception. It is through this that they are able to perceive spirits and receive messages from them for communication to those who visit them for spiritual inquiries *(ebisa)*. There is, however, an equally wide disbelief among Fantis in these supernatural phenomena. Many believe that these 'special' people are tricksters. Thus there is the sceptical saying *'Nananom mpow nyimpa na woyee'* (The mysteries surrounding the grove of the dead fathers were created by men). A brief word needs to be said about the origin of this saying. There was on the outskirts of Mankessim, one of the big towns in the Fanti areas of Ghana, a grove which for a long time served as a cemetery. As time went on it fell into disuse. Then a group of cunning people decided to use it as a means of gain. At night they would take their places in the grove, pretend to be the spirits of the dead fathers, make loud frightful noises, demand sacrifices in the form of money, sheep and fowls, and threaten to destroy the city if their demands were ignored. The money was to be deposited in the grove, and the sheep and fowls were not to be slaughtered but to be tied to some of the trees in the grove. The next morning the mayor of the town and his councilors would collect from the citizens the things that the 'spirits of the fathers' demanded and take them to the grove. The night after, the tricksters would enter the grove and take everything away to a safe place for their use. The next day the mayor and his councilors would visit the grove to see if their sacrifices had been accepted; there was no money, sheep and fowls to be seen where they were left. This practice went on for a long time and reduced the citizens to considerable misery. A group of men became suspicious and decided to make investigations. One evening they went where the grove was and hid themselves near it. Then, when night fell, they saw to their great astonishment some thoroughly familiar faces, living citizens of Mankessim, entering the grove with the instruments with which they made the noise! Quietly the men who had gone to investigate returned to the town and announced their discovery. The whole town was alerted. At midnight the tricksters began their noise. The mayor and the whole town rushed to the grove. Lo and behold! There were respectable citizens of Mankessim ruining the town through treachery! They were apprehended and punished and the mystery surrounding the grove of the dead fathers ended. This is how the saying *'Nananom mpow nyimpa na woyee'* (The mysteries surrounding the grove of the dead fathers were the work of ordinary human beings) began. It expresses a widespread Fanti scepticism with regard to anything mysterious or supernatural. The saying serves as a precept urging people to exercise a healthy scepticism about whatever appears mysterious, never to give up the search for a naturalistic explanation of such things, and not to yield readily to superstition. Extra-sensory perception is widely accepted but also widely denied among the Fantis.

Ethics

The Repudiation of Egoism

The Fanti system of ethics is essentially anti-egoistic. Egoism, the theory that each individual should seek his own good and not the good of his neighbor or his community, is frowned upon by the Fanti moralist. For the Fanti the good of the individual is a function of the good of society. The *summum bonum* of Fanti moral philosophy is the welfare of the society. For the individual cannot prosper unless the society prospers. A great emphasis is placed on social ethics as opposed to the ethics of the self, the kind of ethics which the west, with its maxim of 'Each one for himself and God for us all', practices. Here the west may learn something from Africa. It is no exaggeration to say that the practice of competitive personal accumulation is one of the main factors that generate violence in western society. What you compete to gain you must compete to guard. For others will compete to take from you what you compete to take from them. Competition leads to suspicion and suspicion to violence and tragedy. One of the things that must strike the visitor who comes to the United States is the omnipresence of the police officer carrying a pistol. This potential death dealer is seen patrolling university premises, patrolling grocery stores, patrolling streets and highways. This show of militarism is, without doubt, ultimately attributable to the individualistic ethics practiced in the society. For if it is impressed on the individual not to seek his own good first but that of the community, there will be less of that savage competition which leads to violence and consequently there will be less need for this death dealer. The individual cannot expect to enjoy his wealth in safety surrounded by a world of need. If you do not ensure that the world around you has something you cannot have everything. *Se amma wo nyenko eentwa akron a wo so irrentwa du* (If you do not make it possible for your neighbor to have nine you will not have ten). Each is his brother's keeper. Each has a right and an obligation to expect help from, and give help to, his neighbor. In this way the phenomenon of concentration of wealth in the hands of a few surrounded by poverty-stricken neighbors is avoided. The doctrine of the interdependence of human beings, the doctrine of social ethics is what accounts for many of the institutions that one comes across in Africa. Thus the extended family system whereby a man's obligation extends beyond his own wife and children to his other relations, is meant to ensure that there be no haves and have-nots.

The Fantis have a way of giving moral instructions to their children. This is often done through folk tales. There are many Fanti folk tales whose object is to impress upon the hearer this doctrine of social ethics. Thus many of the stories about the cunning egoist, Kewku Ananse (The Wednesday-born Spider), are meant as attacks on egoistic ethics. The stories themselves are often simple, but it is the theory behind the story that matters to the story teller. Thus the Fanti expert story teller adds at the end of his tale, in tones of thunderous conviction: Seek the good of the community, and you seek your own good. Seek your own good, and you seek your own destruction. Mutual aid is a moral obligation.

Theory of Punishment

Why should a person be punished for wrongdoing? To this question western philosophers have given various answers. According to one school the purpose of punishment is to deter others from committing the crime for which the offender is

221

punished. According to another school, the retributivist school, punishment ensures that the offender is paid back in his own coin. An eye must be taken for an eye, and a tooth for a tooth. Both of these theories of punishment appear in the Fanti penal system; but there is a third theory which is more dominant in the system. For the Fanti punishment is not only a deterrent or a means of exacting restitution but also a means of reforming, 'purifying' the offender. The offender, in committing adultery, for example, not only wrongs his neighbor but also brings upon himself and his own a curse, *mbusu*. To punish him he is not only made to pay damages to the offended but also he is asked to bring a sheep to be slaughtered in the court, which consists of the chief and his councilors, the offended party, a traditional priest and the inquisitive citizen. The priest performs certain rituals with the blood of the sheep to remove the curse from the offender, thereby purifying him. This ritual practice serves as a psychological therapy, freeing the offender of the feeling of guilt. The western judge pronounces the offender guilty, but does not have a means for ridding the offender of the guilt-feeling, which modern psychiatry shows is responsible for many nervous conditions that psychiatrists have to treat. The ritual is not only psychologically therapeutic but also its very solemnity is often enough to reform the offender.

Political Philosophy

Socialism

Fanti political philosophy rejects both socialism and capitalism. The German Jew, Karl Marx, the chief priest of the socialist faith, sees society as a battleground where the forces of the rich and those of the poor are eternally pitched against each other. The rich, by their wealth, dominate the politics of the community and arrange all other matters to suit themselves, and oppress the poor. Marx therefore urges the poor to seize political power. How? By voting? Marx was scornful of the ballot box as a means of effecting social change. In his day the majority of the poor did not have voting rights. But even if the working classes could vote, the rich had the means for ensuring their success at elections; they had the money to bribe their way to success. But if, *per impossible*, elections could be fair, the poor could not afford the money needed for a thorough election campaign. For Marx the poor could come into power only through force, only through revolution. But--

"The same arts that did gain
A power, must it maintain."

Having come into power the poor are urged to establish a dictatorship of the proletariat. Why? The reason is that if they do not, the overthrown classes will attempt to return to power through the very means by which the working class came to power. Thus having once come into power the proletariat finds itself in an eternal contract with force. Force must be used to destroy the might of their former oppressors lest they should return to power. As time goes on, however, not only the former rich oppressors but also some members of the proletariat who dare to dissent from the decisions of the new leaders become victims of the new dictatorship. Fanti philosophy, with its doctrine of the citizen as *odehye* (free-born), repudiates the concept of government by the sword, which is what socialism is both in theory and in practice. For the Fanti, the citizen is born free (*Amamba ye adehye mba*) and he cannot, whether rich or poor, be maltreated without just cause. Dictatorship, whether it be that of the proletariat or of the rich classes, is not countenanced in Fanti political philosophy.

Though the chief is not elected by popular vote he has to govern in accordance with the popular will. For the people retain the right to destool their chief at any time. When he is appointed to lead the community he becomes a leader for life but only insofar as he remains an *ohen pa* (a good chief). The moment he begins to exhibit dictatorial tendencies the people initiate a destoolment suit against him. What shames the Fanti ruler most is to hear the expression *'Woetu no egua do'* (He has been removed from the stool). Thus the fact that the Fanti ruler holds his appointment for life does not mean that he is licensed to dictate for life.

For the Fanti chief's rule is not an autocracy but a consultative system of government. He has to consult his councilors on all decisions affecting the society. Indeed, while in council he does not speak. It is his first minister (*Okyeame* or State Linguist) who does all his speaking. If there is a major disagreement between him and his councilors on any decision of his, the decision cannot be put into effect.

His council usually consists of the elders of the society. For the Fantis tend to equate maturity with age and experience, as the saying *'Opanyin ne tu wo kotokorba'* shows. (This does not admit of literal translation. What it means is that an old man's word cannot be safely set at nought). The elders are not

223

appointed as councilors because of their wealth but because of their maturity. Thus rich and poor both find themselves on the council. There are usually representatives of the various language groups of the community on the council. It might be thought that because the councilors are not elected by popular vote Fanti society is undemocratic. The inference does not at all follow. The reason why the councilors are not elected is that there is no need for them to be elected. For all adult members of the society have a right to be present at the meetings of the council, participate in the eloquent debates, and to vote by exclaiming approval or disapproval. In practice only the inquisitive few attend the meetings of the councilors. But when there is a controversial issue hundreds of citizens turn up at the meetings to ensure that the will of the people prevails. If a democratic government is defined, not as one elected by the people but, as one which does the will of the people, then the Fanti system of government is democratic.

Traditional Fanti libertarianism is inconsonant with socialism. The socialist conceives of society as a parallelogram of antagonistic forces. The socialist ruler therefore sees himself as perenially fighting the 'enemy'. But 'enemy' is a variable which takes for its value, at the initial stages of the revolution, the rich, and, later, the poor. Thus the Fanti saying comes true: *'Abaa no a wodze boo Takyi no, wodze bobo Baah so'* (The very rod which was used to beat Mr. Taky will eventually be used to beat Mr. Baah, the beater's own ally). Eventually not only the rich but also the poor, who dare to refuse to dot the i's and cross the t's of the regent, become objects of official persecution; they too are denied employment, imprisoned without trial, tortured to make confessions, murdered, and have their houses burned down. Fantis value human life too much to allow the politician to make it his plaything.

Capitalism

But neither is Fanti society capitalistic. Behind the western capitalist philosophy is the doctrine of *laissez-faire,* Adam Smith's doctrine of free individual enterprise. It is interesting to note, in reading western political philosophers, Hobbes, Locke, Rousseau, etc., that the function of government is seen as being primarily legal: government exists not to create wealth for society but to provide legal protection for the citizens. The greatness of Karl Marx as a political philosopher lies in part in his widening of the function of government to cover the economic. For the capitalist the economic activities in the state are the prerogative of the individual. The individual should be free to undertake

224

economic enterprises. The state should interfere as little as possible with the individual's economic ventures. Now, since the individual's aim is to make a success of his venture, he employs every means to ensure success. One of the means he uses to maximize his profits is to pay his employees as little as is convenient. This system eventually leads to the maximization of the gap between the rich and the poor. But wealth offends the eye of the poor and absolute wealth offends absolutely; and so friction is begotten.

Libertarian Basicalism

Fanti political philosophy rejects the doctrine of *laissez-faire*. The purpose of government, for the Fanti, is not only to give legal protection to society but also to ensure, as far as possible, that all have and none is in need. Government is both the legal and economic custodian of society. For unless there is economic justice, legal justice becomes a chronic problem. *Se amma wo nyenko eentwa akron a wo so irrentwa du* (If you do not make it possible for your neighbor to have nine, you will not have ten either). People can have true legal freedom to enjoy their property only if their neighbors are not hungry. *At least the basic necessities of life must be provided freely for all in a free society.* For the sake of a label we might call this doctrine Libertarian Basicalism. This is the political philosophy of the Fantis, as also of many other African societies.

The world today is on the brink of self-destruction because of idealogical conflicts, because of wrong philosophies, capitalism and socialism. The capitalist cries: Wealth for the wealthy, poverty for the poor! The socialist cries: A pint of blood for a loaf of bread! The world is asked to choose between the scylla of capitalism and the charybdis of socialism. But might their not be a third? The Fanti political philosopher answers: Yes, Libertarian Basicalism.

PHILOSOPHICAL JUSTIFICATIONS
FOR CONTEMPORARY AFRICAN
SOCIAL AND POLITICAL
VALUES AND STRATEGIES

Diana E. Axelsen

Introduction

It is often assumed that western philosophy began with Socrates; but as Henry Olela has documented, the western philosophical tradition has its roots in Ethiopian and Egyptian thought.[1] In a similarly culture-bound way, reference to "philosophical systems" usually calls to mind Plato, Aristotle, Kant, Mill, Sartre, Russell--all of them thinkers who attempted to develop a systematic normative position on the basis of an ontology and an epistemology. However, such systematic attempts can also be found in the African tradition, and deserve considerably more attention than they have received. Though world views in traditional African societies have been analyzed, and though the positions of African political leaders have been extensively studied by western and non-western historians and political scientists, insufficient attention has been given to the way in which such leaders have grounded their strategies of social change in systematically developed world views. In this essay, I want to suggest that the works of Kwame Nkrumah, Julius Nyerere, Amilcar Cabral, and Frantz Fanon represent a major contribution to the effort to ground their strategies for social change in a world view coupled with empirical analysis of concrete situations. These positions, I would argue, represent four of the most significant challenges to the philosophies of Plato, Marx, and Sartre, all of whom have made similar attempts to ground their plans for social change and their commitment to specific moral values in an underlying ontological and general normative commitment. My descriptions are of a tentative and exploratory nature. My aim is not to present definitive classifications of these philosophical theorists and activists. Rather, I want to suggest some reasons for a preliminary classification, with the hope that these persons will be studied more widely from a philosophical standpoint as well as from a political one.

Definition of 'World View'

The argument in this essay will rely heavily on the concept of 'world view,' which is closely analogous to the western analytical notion of conceptual scheme. However, as a minimum, a world view as I interpret it will include (a) a position concerning the nature of ultimate reality (ontology); (b) a statement concerning the nature of knowledge and what constitutes personhood (e.g., Are persons substances or processes? Are they individuals or manifestations of a single cosmic process or both? What is the relation between physical and psychological properties of persons, if both are acknowledged to exist?); (d) a view about the nature of human history; (e) an identification of the fundamental values which individuals ought to pursue; and (f) an identification of cultural norms and a specification of their relationship to individual norms.

Summary of Central Themes

The saying "The best gift you can give your children is the combination of roots and wings," is one which embodies one of the most central themes in African social and political thought. The inclusion of elements of traditional African ontology is particularly emphasized in the justification of the broad moral values supported by Nkrumah, Cabral and Nyerere. Among the themes of particular importance in this essay are:

A. The importance of African culture in the development of a contemporary value system for the African continent;

B. Egalitarianism;

228

C. Self-determination (including both a clear sense of self-identity and of group identity as the basis for acts of self-determination);

D. The significance of community, specifically, the communal experience;

E. The need to justify violence as a means to liberation, together with an insistence on the need for empirical analysis of the oppressive forces one is struggling against;

F. A vision of a humanistic world community; and

G. An emphasis on grounding one's social, political, economic, military, and educational programs in a value system which is justified by appeal to broad normative principles, and, in some cases, to an explicit ontological position.

Nkrumah's Ontology and Its Relationship to His Social and Political Philosophy

In *Consciencism,* Nkrumah expounds a type of materialism which stresses that all reality is ultimately a homogeneous physical substance. Nkrumah sees his materialism as the correct alternative to both rationalist and empiricist idealism. However, it is probably a mistake to classify Nkrumah's materialism as similar to a western view of material *substance* as primary; for Nkrumah says:

> The minimum assertion of materialism is the absolute and independent existence of matter. Matter, however, is also a plenum of forces which are in antithesis to one another. [2]

Nkrumah, moreover, not only stresses the dialectical and process elements in his materialism; he is also at pains to emphasize that he does not deny the existence of spirit or mind. His doctrine of "categorial conversion" is an attempt to reconcile his commitment to materialism with his acknowledgement of spirit or mind, or more specifically, of persons. However, he makes it clear (much as Strawson does in *Individuals*) that the logically primary category is matter:

229

DIANA E. AXELSEN

> ...If one says that matter is the primary
> category, then spirit must, to the extent
> that it is recognized as a category, be a
> derivative category. And in order that
> propositions about spirit should make
> sense, there must be matter. Secondly,
> even when propositions about spirit make
> sense, in order that they be true, certain
> propositions about matter need to be
> true.[3]

What, then, is the place of categorial conversion in Nkrumah's
ontology? He notes,

> When materialism becomes dialectical, the
> world is not regarded as a world of
> states, but as a world of process; a
> world not of things, but of facts. The
> endurance of the world consists in
> process...when materialism becomes
> dialectical it ensures the material basis of
> categorial conversion.[4]

By categorial conversion, Nkrumah is referring to the process
whereby a material of physical process takes on psychological or
mentalistic properties (properties which belong to the category of
mind rather than the category of body). This "conversion" is
possible, he argues, because matter as process possesses the
property of self-motion. The models for categorial conversion
used by Nkrumah, however, are drawn from the physical world,
and may thus seem not wholly satisfactory to the philosopher of
mind. He says:

> For philosophy's model of categorial
> conversion, it turns to science. Matter
> and energy are two distinct, but, as
> science has shown, not unconnected or
> irreducible, categories. The inter-reduc-
> ibility of matter and energy offers a
> model for categorial conversion. And
> another model is given in the distinction
> between physical and chemical change, for
> in chemical change physical quantities
> give rise to emergent qualities.[5]

However, in Chapter 4 of *Consciencism* Nkrumah makes it clear
that the sort of self-motion which he regards as particularly

significant from the moral standpoint is the capacity for being self-conscious, for perceiving, for having purposes, and finally for choosing intentionally. Nkrumah utilizes a theory of types to suggest that matter itself is of one logical type; (material or physical) properties of matter belong to a higher logical type; and out of the tension between these material properties arises the category of mind, or psychological properties of the material properties of matter itself. While Nkrumah seems satisfied with analogies to physical transformations in explaining how self-motion allows bodies to acquire psychological properties, some speculation may be in order concerning how his analysis makes use of dialectical reason. For example, one might argue that while both animals and persons have the physical capacity either passively to adapt to their environments or actively to transform them, it is only with persons that these alternatives are experienced fully as a tension; hence, in persons these physical capacities give rise to conflict and to purpose, as persons struggle to reconcile such tendencies as activity and passivity. Similarly, we might suggest that while in principle we can distinguish among the atomic particles making up a tree, and the tree itself, or we can distinguish the trees making up a forest from the forest itself, only in persons do we find an awareness of the potential *tension* between identity as part of a whole: hence, only in persons do we find the self-conscious attempt to *resolve* this tension. While I am not sure these are the sorts of examples Nkrumah would accept, it seems to me that they are compatible with his analysis and also give us a way of relating the somewhat abstract doctrine of categorial conversion to the actual emergence of psychological properties of persons. However, the need for viewing mental properties as third-level seems unnecessary; we could say (again with Strawson) that persons are bodies (a) which have both physical and psychological properties, and (b) whose psychological properties are dependent on their physical ones. At any rate, it is clear that for Nkrumah the doctrines of dialectical materialism and of categorial conversion are the two fundamental ontological principles on which he wishes to construct a value system. In Chapter 3, Nkrumah emphasizes that in his analysis, idealism is the world view appropriate to a society embodying class structure, while some form of materialism is a necessary though not sufficient ontological base for an egalitarian society. Nkrumah's ontology, as outlined above, constitutes what he would call a descriptive or "general theoretical base" for specific moral values.

How does Nkrumah make this connection? First, he points to the fundamental homogeneity of all existence as a justification for rejecting class structure and for adopting equality among persons as a fundamental value. Second, his principle of categorial conversion leads him to stress the importance of human autonomy, or of the Kantian principle of treating persons as ends, not merely as means. At the same time, he does not see this principle as incompatible with the advocacy of armed struggle for African liberation; for the doctrine of categorial conversion with its suggestion of the special status of persons must always be seen as dependent upon his materialism. Beginning with a class analysis similar to Marx's, Nkrumah then analyzes the impact of racism on the struggle for the ideal society--for him, the liberation of Africa as a Black nation, which in turn will pave the way for world communism. In *Class Struggle in Africa*, themes of class struggle and Pan-Africanism are interwoven, but his vision extends to the human community:

> The total liberation and the unification of Africa under an all-African socialist government must be the primary objective of all Black revolutionaries throughout the world. It is an objective which when achieved, will bring about fulfillment of the aspirations of Africans and people of African descent everywhere. It will at the same time advance the triumph of the international socialist revolution, and the onward progress toward world communism, under which, every society is ordered on the principle of--from each according to his ability, to each according to his needs. [6]

It should be noted, however, that the emphasis on class struggle in the Marxian sense becomes particularly significant in Nkrumah's work after Ghana was granted political independence by the British. A question worth examining is the extent to which Nkrumah's theory of class struggle reflects a Marxian view of history, as opposed to being a more pragmatic response to neo-colonial class divisions and tribal conflicts which had to be confronted after independence.

Because I shall want to argue that Nkrumah sees a need for continuity between the African past and present, Nkrumah's position with respect to religion is particularly significant. On first examination, it may seem that his insistence that modern Africa must be secular constitutes a rejection of the earlier traditional African culture in which religion played so central a role. However, Nkrumah has several replies to this point. First, he emphasizes that in his view the fundamental principles underlying African society were humanist, and that a humanist ideology can thereby contain not only the pre-colonial African culture, but also the "new society enlarged by Islamic and Euro-Christian influences."[7] Moreover, Nkrumah notes,

> The traditional face of Africa includes an attitude towards man which can only be described, in its social manifestation, as being socialist. This arises from the fact that man is regarded in Africa as primarily a spiritual being, a being endowed originally with certain inward dignity, integrity, and value. It stands refreshingly opposed to the Christian idea of the original sin and degradation of man.[8]

Finally, Nkrumah notes that his opposition to religion is based on its social use as an instrument of oppression. He suggests that prior to colonialism, African societies may have been on the road to an approach to religion that would have avoided the evils to which Marx pointed; this development in attitude, however, was not allowed to emerge naturally. Thus Nkrumah feels that it is essential to emphasize the need for modern Africa to take account of this interruption of the natural evolution of African thought and to insist on a secular world view. In describing the earlier development of thought, he notes:

> Many African societies in fact forestalled this kind of perversion [the use of religion as an instrument of exploitation]. The dialectical contradiction between 'inside' and 'outside' was reduced by making the visible world continuous with the invisible world. For them heaven was not outside the world but inside it. These African societies did not accept transcendentalism, and may indeed be regarded as having attempted to synthesize the dialectical opposites 'outside' and 'inside' by making them continuous, that is, by abolishing them.[9]

In summary, then, we find Nkrumah emphasizing the socialist ideals of equality and human integrity, on the basis of his dialectical materialism and his doctrine of categorial conversion. His application of dialectical materialism leads him, too, to

DIANA E. AXELSEN

a Marxist treatment of class struggle, but with a profound difference; he acknowledges the centrality of racial and national liberation, and thus develops the doctrine of Pan-Africanism, as
described in more detail in his own works.

Julius Nyerere's Defense of His Social
and Political Philosophy

Nyerere's ontology is less clearly articulated than Nkrumah's; however, his emphasis on the value of community in traditional African life, together with his emphasis on the value of
commitment to some of the humanistic elements of Christianity,
suggest that he would be likely to regard ultimate reality as that
of process rather than of substance. Nyerere begins the explicit
articulation of his world view with a theory of personhood.
Certainly he acknowledges the existence of psychological states;
moreover, despite his stress on implementing the policy of *ujamaa*
through economic, social, and political changes at the national
level, he also emphasizes that the state exists for individual
persons.[10] His emphasis, too, on self-reliance suggests that he
would agree with Nkrumah that autonomy and human freedom are
essential to the full realization of one's humanity. However,
because he also stresses so heavily the human need to interact in
a communal context, there is a suggestion that he sees persons as
"becoming" rather than as "being," and further, as elements in
an all-pervasive universe of dynamic forces. Superficially, this
may seem closer to the traditional African ontology, and to western existentialism and process philosophy, than to Nkrumah's
dialectical materialism. But as I have tried to suggest above,
Nkrumah's own commitment to materialism takes a unique form
which does not rule out some such view of a universe of forces,
though for Nkrumah such forces would, admittedly, depend for
their existence on the existence of material forces.

The argument Nyerere gives to support the central
values of equality and community seems to lie in his psychological
analysis of the nature of persons. In his recognition of the
human need for security, he points to what he regards as an
essential feature of being a person; then, adding the implicit
assumption that this is a need which *ought* to be met, he
concludes that society ought to be constructed in a way that
allows for the meeting of these needs, yet also allows for individual initiative and national development to meet human material
needs. Such a society, of course, will preserve many of the
values of the traditional African community, though the institutions in which they are embodied will reflect radically different

234

material conditions. Finally, like Nkrumah, Nyerere focuses his attention on the African continent; indeed, much of his analysis applies primarily to the situation after colonialism which existed in Tanganyika. However, he too has a vision which extends not only to the African continent as a whole but to the entire human community:

> To the extent that we in Tanzania succeed in the struggle to which we have committed ourselves, so we shall be taking our place in the march of humanity toward peace and human dignity... By thinking out our own problems on the basis of those principles which have universal validity Tanzania will make its contributions to the development of mankind. [11]

In addressing himself to the need to revitalize institutions so as to fully realize the principles of *ujamaa* (or "African socialism," as some have termed it), Nyerere identified two areas in which traditional society had problems to be solved. First, the inequality of women was accepted; second, poverty led to a level of material existence that did not guarantee the meeting of basic human needs. [12]

Nyerere does not insist, however, that there is a clear-cut ontological and materialistic basis for these humanistic values. Certainly there is no doubt about his commitment to these values; however, he seems committed to the view that individuals should be free to define the ontological basis for these values in their own ways. He says:

> Socialism is concerned with man's life in *this* society. A man's relationship with his God is a personal matter for him and him alone; his beliefs about the here-after are his own affair. These things have nothing to do with anyone else as long as he does not indulge in practices which adversely affect the similar private rights of other members of the society.... But a religion which involved human sacrifice, or demanded the exploitation of human beings, could not be allowed to carry out these practices. [13]

DIANA E. AXELSEN

He continues,

> Socialism's concern about the
> organization of life on earth does not
> involve any supposition about life else-
> where, or about man's soul, or the
> procedures for fulfilling the will of God
> or Gods. Socialism is secular. It has
> nothing to say about whether there is a
> God. Certainly it rests on the assump-
> tion of the equality of man, but people
> can reach this conclusion by many routes.
> People can accept the equality of man
> because they believe that all men were
> created by God, they can believe it
> because scientific evidence supports such
> a conclusion [presumably Nkrumah's posi-
> tion], or they can accept it simply
> because they believe it is the only basis
> on which life in society can be organized
> without injustice. It does not matter why
> people accept the equality of man as the
> basis of social organization; all that
> matters is that they do accept it. [14]

Here, I would argue, we encounter a clearcut difference
between Nkrumah and Nyerere. For Nkrumah, it *does* matter why
persons accept their equality; they ought to accent it on the
basis of a scientific or "objective" analysis of their shared common
material being. Nyerere's statement, moreover, should not be
regarded as exhausted of the reasons why persons accept human
equality (nor do I mean to imply that it is meant to be exhaustive). Another important reason why persons accept their equality is an existential one: they experience themselves as fellow
creatures in the universe in which they find themselves. Some
such existential experience may well be regarded by some as
religious; and, I would argue, it is such an experience that is
the ontological ground for the egalitarianism found not only in the
many traditional African societies, but also in some native American cultures, as well as religious cultures based on experience
rather than on authority. In his attitude toward the religious
foundation for *ujamaa,* Nyerere could be interpreted as departing
from an apparently central aspect of traditional African culture;
but his maintenance of the values deriving from that equality
provides the link which places him in the African tradition.

Another theme in Nyerere's social and political philosophy which deserves careful attention is that of violence. Nyerere, in his criticism of the use of violence as a means to liberation, does not categorically oppose violent struggle; however, he
does see violence as inevitably dehumanizing, even to those who
overthrow oppressive forces through violence. Fanon's concept of
violence as a cleansing force is absent; Nyerere says rather:

> ....violence is a short cut only to the
> destruction of institutions and power
> groups of the old society; they are not a
> short cut to the building of the new....
> The necessity for violent revolution
> brings its own problems to the building of
> socialism; they may be different from
> those experienced by the states which are
> fortunate enough to be able to move
> peacefully from one kind of social system
> to another, but they are nonetheless real.
>
> In fact those who talk as if violence must
> always and everywhere precede socialism,
> and who judge a country to be developing
> only if violence has occurred, are almost
> certainly not socialist in their own atti-
> tudes. For violence cannot be welcomed
> by those who care about people. [15]

Nyerere seems to have two concerns in this passage,
which also are expressed in his essay "Ujamaa-the Basis of African Socialism," which was originally published as a TANU
pamphlet in April, 1962. First, he wants to reject any straightforward imposition of Marxist doctrines onto the African situation;
on this point the other persons we are considering would
certainly agree. But he wants also to reject the general concept
of violent struggle between opposing groups as an inevitable part
of historical development; and his reasons seem to me to be not
pragmatic but profoundly moral. It is important, I think to have
someone of Nyerere's stature forcing us always to examine
violence and to recognize the human price it exacts. At the same
time, Nyerere's position on this particular issue--unlike his stand
on many others--seems to ignore the need for empirical analysis
of oppression. Where *are* the states which have moved peacefully
to socialism? Tanganyika, it is true, attained independence relatively peacefully from the British; but it was the *violent* coup on
Zanzibar engineered by Okello which eliminated Arab control and
made possible the subsequent union of Zanzibar and Tanganyika

to form Tanzania. And even within continental Tanzania, many would argue that ultimately violence will be required to overcome deeply entrenched and locally powerful capitalist elements.[16] Thus, while there is a moral ideal and sensitivity embodied in Nyerere's position on violence, our assessment of it should be tempered by an awareness that all moves toward socialism now take place in a highly charged international situation in which both internal and external threats to the new nation must be examined.[17]

However, as noted above, in general Nyerere does give careful attention to the empirical situation, in planning for new institutions to embody traditional values. For example, in his essay "Education for Self-Reliance,"[18] he is careful to combine agricultural training with the academic curriculum, and he includes many safeguards against encouraging the development of a national elite. His concern with this problem is also reflected in the concrete proposals of Part Five of the Arusha Declaration, which are designed to separate political power from economic power.[19]

In general, then, especially in his educational and economic programs, Nyerere re-affirms the importance of basing social change on an over-arching value system (for him, *ujamaa,*) together with a through-going empirical analysis of one's own situation.

The Work of Amilcar Cabral

The themes mentioned above in the discussion of Nkrumah can be found running throughout Cabral's work, but I shall not undertake here any systematic analysis of his ontology and its expression. Cabral gave careful attention to the role of women in revolutionary struggle and in a liberated society; he also elaborated on the need for an international perspective, in ways which made the potentially unifying effect of class struggle particularly clear. However, he never neglected the importance of the African experience, nor did he fail to stress the need for adapting strategy to problem; thus, for example, we find his careful argument in "Brief Analysis of the Social Structure in Guinea," which appears in condensed form in *Revolution in Guinea.*[20] However, one theme which Cabral stressed in his address to the first Tricontinental Conference of the Peoples of Asia, Africa, and Latin America, in Havana in January, 1966, places in very sharp focus one of the themes of this essay: the great social and political leaders of liberation movements in Africa have not been merely strategists, nor have they stopped with advocating a socialist value system; they have gone beyond this to root their positions in a total philosophical system. Cabral's commitment to such an endeavor is reflected clearly in this address, called "The Weapon of Theory":

> ...if national liberation is essentially a political problem, the conditions for its development give it certain characteristics which belong to the sphere of morals.[21]

and

> ...national liberation is the phenomenon in which a given socio-economic whole rejects the negation of its historical process. In other words, the national liberation of a people is the regaining of the historical personality of that people, its return to history through the destruction of the imperialist domination to which it was subjected.[22]

In this speech, Cabral's emphasis on the historical dimension of one's world view is seen very clearly; and he argues at length for the importance of basing revolutionary practice on a world view which includes a dialectical conception of history.

Philosophical Justification in Frantz Fanon's Thought

My comments here will be brief; but surely no discussion of significant philosopher/activists can fail to include Fanon. One of Fanon's greatest philosophical contributions, it seems to me, lies in his systematic defense of a value system and of a strategy for liberation using a phenomenological analysis of oppression and liberation.[23] Fanon's work does not fit easily into the analytic framework of this essay. This is not only because he makes the categories of oppressor and oppressed central, but also because his philosophical method includes the specific insights of phenomenology, combined with psychoanalysis. However, it is clear that *Black Skin, White Masks* and *Wretched of the Earth* form a powerful statement of two different world views, that of the oppressor and that of the oppressed. Through his psychological descriptions of particular persons embodying in their selfhood these two world views, he vividly and powerfully defends the claim that it is the oppressor who ought to be

239

eliminated, by means of organized and responsible violent struggle.

Moreover, unlike Nyerere, Fanon argues that responsible violence can be a cleansing force, and can create among those who struggle together the very socialist attitudes which Nyerere is convinced can emerge only later, after further struggle in a new and different setting. A question worth exploring here is whether actual involvement in organizing at the grass roots level, and the sharing of revolutionary responsibilities in life and death situations, have an effect on one's ability to emerge as a consistent socialist leader. One might study the effects, for example, of the involvement of Cabral, Fidel Castro, Mao Tse-Tung, Che Guevara, and Samora Machel, on their political attitudes; and these might be compared to the attitudes, and actions, of leaders such as Sekou Toure or Jomo Kenyatta.

Although his underlying world view reflects his focus on the concept of consciousness as primary, Fanon, like the other African leaders discussed, has constructed a philosophical system which is perhaps the sharpest non-western challenge to Marxist analysis. In particular, he shows how the universal categories of oppressor and oppressed must be understood, and applied to a concrete situation (e.g., Algeria), in order to identify the most significant forms of oppression at a particular time and place, for a particular person or group. For example, he expresses his own existential experience as an oppressed person through the development of the categories of colonizer and colonized. Yet he leaves us to explore the myriad other ways in which oppression may manifest itself, never limiting the application of his theory to the obvious categories of race, class, and sex.

The world views of Nkrumah, Cabral, and Nyerere embody a concept of history as moving toward a state of world communism whose structures can be envisioned in at least rough detail. Fanon's view of the future, like his view of persons, has an openness which sets him apart from the other three. Certainly, he shares the commitment to equality, self-determination, and community which we have noted above. But he would perhaps formulate the human ideal differently from Nkrumah, Nyerere, or Cabral. Nyerere, for example, seems to believe that not only physical security but also psychological security are desirable and attainable human goals. Fanon leaves us with a question as to whether such security ought to be pursued at the psychological level; one senses that it is a kind of existential authenticity and autonomy which he seeks most of all as a reality for all persons. As he says at the end of *Black Skin, White*

Masks: "Make of me always a man who questions!"

Conclusion

At any rate, it is in a spirit of openness to criticism and elaboration that I offer these speculations concerning the foundations for contemporary African social and political philosophy. I am not confident that I have accurately described the justifications which these four leaders would offer; but I hope to have established, at least, that there is a complex and challenging philosophical system to be identified in the work of these and other African leaders; and I hope that others will further analyze the connection between world views, values, and strategies for social change, so that we can have a fuller appreciation of the scope and importance of philosophical systems in the thought of ancient and modern Africa. Only with this appreciation can we approach with responsibility the question of the nature of philosophy generally.

The study of philosophical justifications for African models of social change could also profit from an explicitly interdisciplinary approach to issues such as:

A. The effect of achieving independence with and without violent struggle;
B. The relevance to the independent nation of the national source of colonization; and,
C. The impact of differing religions on the development of socialist attitudes of equality.

In conclusion, I want to emphasize the theme of social commitment which runs through the work of all four men. We should note, too, that they directed their philosophical activity toward the goal of meeting urgent human needs. Each seems vitally concerned with the world in which their children, and all our children, will live. They recognize the historical significance of the African past; at the same time, they force us toward realistic approaches to the present and the future.

DIANA E. AXELSEN

FOOTNOTES

1. I am very grateful to Mrs. Quincy Tillman for her invalua-
    ble help in preparing this manuscript. I also want to
    thank Professor Jesse McDade for many helpful insights
    into Fanon's work. Finally, I am deeply indebted to my
    friend and colleague, Professor Henry Olela, both for
    many probing conversations on African philosophy and for
    his helpful and detailed criticisms of this essay. I have
    profited, too, from a reading of the manuscript of
    Professor Olela's book, *An Introduction to the History of
    Philosophy: From Ancient Africa to Ancient Greece*
    (forthcoming).

2. Kwame Nkrumah, *Consciencism,* rev. ed. (New York:
    Monthly Review Press, 1970), p. 79.

3. Ibid., p. 22.

4. Ibid., p. 25.

5. Ibid., p. 21.

6. Kwame Nkrumah, *Class Struggle in Africa* (New York:
    International Publishing Co., 1970), p. 88.

7. Nkrumah, *Consciencism,* p. 70.

8. Ibid., p. 68.

9. Ibid., p. 12.

10. Julius Nyerere, "The Purpose is Man," in *Freedom and
    Socialism (Uhuru na Ujamaa)* (New York: Oxford Univer-
    sity Press, 1971), p. 316.

11. Ibid., p. 32.

12. Ibid., p. 339-340.

13. Ibid., p. 12.

14. Ibid., p. 12-13.

15. Ibid., p. 24.

16. See, for example, Robert Ouko, "An Analysis of a Rural Village in Tanzania: Ujamaa Policy and Socialist Development," (unpublished manuscript); also, see John Iliffe, "The Age of Improvement and Differentiation (1907-45)," in *A History of Tanzania,* ed. I.N. Kimambo and A.J. Temu (Nairobi, Kenya: East African Publishing House, 1969), pp. 123-160.

17. One of the most significant cases here is that of Chile. After Salvador Allende was elected through constitutional democracy to the presidency of Chile, both internal and external capitalist and imperialist elements combined forces to engineer a violent overthrow of a peacefully established socialist state.

18. Julius Nyerere, "Education for Self-Reliance," in *Freedom and Socialism,* pp. 267-290.

19. "Arusha Declaration," in *Freedom and Socialism,* pp. 231-250.

20. Amilcar Cabral, *Revolution in Guinea* (New York: Monthly Review Press, 1969), pp. 56-75.

21. Ibid., p. 110.

22. Ibid., p. 102.

23. There are many aspects of Fanon's philosophical thought which deserve study; among the most interesting is the theory of responsibility which underlies his case studies in *The Wretched of the Earth.* See, for example, the footnote on p. 253 in "Colonial War and Mental Disorders," in the first Evergreen Black Cat Edition, 1968 (paperback).

A COMPARATIVE ANALYSIS
OF PAN-AFRICANISM[1]

Benyamin Neuberger

Some scholars may argue that pan-Africanism is a form
of multi-nationalism, or internationalism, but certainly no nationalism. We do not accept this view. It is true that no pan-African nation exists; but in the same way, there is no Nigerian,
Kenyan or Zairos nation, if 'nation' is kept separate from the
concept of the state and defined as a popular emotional-psycho-
logical solidarity and a rational-conscious consensus. There
exists a Kenyan, Nigerian or Zairois nationalism--the aspiration to
build a nation to be found among the 'national' elite--but such
nationalism is a 'nationalism without nations'. The same holds for
pan-Africanism. Pan-African nationalism and a pan-African 'pro-
jected nation' may exist without the existence of a pan-African
nation. What makes a Nigerian nation a less-remote projection is
the fact that a Nigerian state is already there and, if the consoli-
dation of the state contributes to nation-building, then a Nigerian
nation is easier to achieve than a pan-African nation. The aspiration to build a political pan-Africa constitutes pan-African
nationalism, and a politically united Africa would encourage
nation-building within the confines of the state as any other state
does. We do not accept that per definitionen large empires or
continental states are supra-national, that they are not able to
further the growth of nationhood. There certainly exists an
American nation and perhaps an incipient Soviet nation. Even in
the medieval past, insofar as Christian or Moslem empires rested

245

BENYAMIN NEUBERGER

on popular identification, solidarity and political 'we-feeling', a phenomenon of nationhood clearly existed. On this issue we wholly agree with Lemberg:

> Der Universalismus umfassender Weltreiche hat sich bei naherer Betrachtung als einer Art Nationalismus erwiesen, gagen eine fremde, barbarische, heidnische Welt ausserhalb ihrer Grenzen gerichtet. [2]

As Znaniecki defined nationalism, four cardinal features are part and parcel of any nationalist ideology. These are national independence, national progress, national mission and national unity. [3] All of these elements figure in the territorial concepts of nationhood, whether Tanzanian, Senegalese or Congolese. They are also characteristic of revisionist, secessionist and irredentist nationalism, whether Biafran, Somali, Eritrean or Southern Sudanese. They all equally fit the description of pan-Africanism, where the factor of unity is particularly stressed. The elements of independence, progress and mission are also not lacking in pan-African nationalism, and we will demonstrate this fact in the following analysis.

The element of independence characterizes not only nationalism under foreign rule (or anticolonial nationalism, as we call it in Africa). The ideal of independence reappears in the nationalism of independent peoples in the form of a wish to shake off foreign pressure and influence, to achieve economic independence in addition to political sovereignty, and to emancipate the indigenous national culture by 'purification' and a 'return to the roots'. Any nationalism accumulates power to make independence 'real', 'true' and 'meaningful'.

The danger that a disunited or 'balkanized' Africa will lose its independence is a common theme in pan-African nationalism. According to Kwame Nkrumah, neocolonialism or foreign economic control will destroy African independence if a united pan-Africa is not achieved:

> Small units are not viable in the modern world, either politically or economically. [4]

> African states must unite or sell themselves out to imperialist or colonialist exploiters for a mess of pottage. [5]

Julius Nyerere's view is in its essence not different. According

246

to his opinion, an Africa split into many states will fall prey to imperialist machinations and lose its independence. He sees the present states of Africa as too weak and small to withstand the divide and rule strategy of the imperialist powers.[6] Thus to Nyerere, the national independence ideal demands pan-African unity:

> The weak and divided can never hope to maintain a dignified independence however much they may proclaim their desire to be strong and united.[7]

> As long as there remain separate nations there will remain too a danger that other states will exploit our differences for their own purposes. Only with unity can we ensure that Africa really governs Africa. Only with unity can we be sure that African resources will be used for the benefit of Africa.[8]

Sikou Toure, Diallo Telli, Modibo Keita and other leaders concur with these views, which are representative of the radical leaders of Africa's first independent decade:[9]

> We are convinced that the states of Africa will never be independent in the full sense of the word if they remain small states.[10]

> The African states have to pool their resources in order to consolidate their independence and safeguard their territorial integrity and to achieve the liquidation of imperialism and colonialism.[11]

It is noteworthy that the necessity of pan-African unity in order to remain independent and escape the status of nominal independence is absent from the writings of the more conservative African leaders. They explain their pan-African aspirations in different terms. The reasons for this difference between the Nkrumahs and the Toures, and the Ahidjos and Senghors is all too obvious. The very concept of 'nominal independence' is a radical critique of the conservative states which have maintained close links with the former colonial power or with other Western states and economic corporations. It is only logical that those who are not hostile to capitalism and who reject the identification

BENYAMIN NEUBERGER

of foreign investment with neocolonialism, will not agree that the present-day African states are only nominally independent because of neocolonial economic domination.

The conservative argument is that unity will enhance the power and prestige of Africa, but this will be an addition to existing independence and not the creation of independence. Tom Mboya, for example, wanted pan-African unity to achieve a "stronger Africa,"[12] an Africa which would have a say in world affairs:

> Africa's influence could only be felt in unity...it is the only way of being able to make a real impact on international affairs.[13]

Jomo Kenyatta talks in a similar manner. His objective is to achieve "a united Africa without which the peoples of this continent can never gain their rightful place in world affairs."[14] Haile Selassie also urges unity, not in order to become independent but in order to be strong, for "in unity there is strength."[15] The radical leaders will not disagree with this 'power ideal' which Znaniecki mentioned as a necessary element in any nationalist ideology and which, in fact, is omnipresent in modern nationalism. While Nyerere disdains great power ambitions and envisages unity only as a means to overcome the current weakness, Nkrumah openly concedes that his vision is of an African which will be among the greatest powers of the world.[16] Thus we may say that almost all African leaders espouse the power ideal; but while the radical leaders combine the independence and power ideals, the conversations substitute the power ideal for the independence ideal because they consider independence to be real and not nominal.

Another frequent theme in pan-African nationalism is the vision of prestige and greatness which we may ascribe to both Znaniecki's mission and power ideals. Radical and conservative African nationalists are in agreement that one aim of pan-African unity is to enhance respect for Africa in the world. Nkrumah wants a prestigious "African personality in international affairs"[17] and "respect from a world that has regard only for size and influence."[18] His vision is one of "the African race united under one federal government ... and being a Great Power whose greatness is indestructible."[19] The conservative nationalists talk in almost identical terms, for to both groups the 'power ideal' is common. Nnamdi Azikiwe asserts that unity "will raise the prestige of African states in the councils of the world."[20] He even

248

goes so far as to claim that unity "will revive the stature of man by guaranteeing to African citizens the fundamental rights of man."[21] Others, like the conservtive Mboya or the radical Toure, voice similar sentiments about the desirability of a "bigger Africa"[22] or a "big community"[23] which will enhance and develop the "African personality."[24]

Znaniecki mentions that in all unification nationalisms, the element of external threat and military security figured prominently. Again we are able to show that this element exists in pan-African nationalism in the same way that it has existed in European unification nationalisms, including the current Western European unification idea. Nkrumah's argument is that only a pan-African Union will assure the security of Africa.[25] Nyerere follows him when he says that there is no security for any single African state.[26] On this issue there is a consensus along the radical-conservative spectrum. While, according to Azikiwe, pan-African unity "will protect the people of Africa...from external aggression."[27] Toure reminds that "the safety and survival of the independent countries of Africa are tied to the social, economic, cultural and political unity of Africa."[28] A frequent theme in Nkrumah's pan-African nationalism is also that only a united Africa will secure the liberation of the whole continent.[29] It is of interest to note that this argument does not appear in the writings and speeches of any other African leader.

The Royal Institute study on nationalism states that "political unity is in fact never sought as an end in itself; it is sought either as a means to some social advantage, or, more usually as a means to power whether for purposes of aggression or of mutual defense against it.[30] We have seen the motive of defense in the thought of almost all leaders, while the offensive motive, "the liberation of the whole of Africa," is particularly strong in Nkrumah's case.

A further element in unification nationalism is Znaniecki's 'progress ideal', or what the Royal Institute study calls the "social advantage variable."[31] The most common aspect of the 'progress ideal' is the expectation of economic gain, which Deutsch also regards as a *conditio sine qua non* of any unification ideal.[32] Deutsch demonstrated his point with the examples of the Italian and German unification nationalisms and with the case of the English-Scottish union.[33] The same expectation of economic benefits characterizes pan-African nationalism. In Nkrumah's thought, the economic rationale is omnipresent. Nkrumah views only the whole united continent and not the existing states as "an optimum area of development,"[34] for it is suited for "a rational division of labour, exploitation of resources and the provision of a market."[35] According to Nkrumah, effective accumulation of capital, rational planning, prevention of destructive competition, and realization of the potential for industrialization can be accomplished only in a united Africa.[36] The strength of Nkrumah's belief in the economic benefits of pan-African unity can be seen from his statement that continental economic planning within a pan-African Union will do away with economic imbalances and modernization gaps between relatively prosperous and poor areas.[37] Coming from a leader of a relatively well-to-do country which will have to sacrifice in such a planned continental levelling scheme, this statement testifies to a powerful pan-African zeal. Nkrumah's frequent resort to economic explanation, argumentation and rationalization certainly stems partially from his proximity to socialist thought. In his last years, Nkrumah went even so far as to accept the Leninist-Stalinist material criterion of a common market for the constitution of a pan-African nation:

> The community of economic life is the major feature within a nation and it is the economy which holds together the people living in a territory. It is on this basis that the new Africans recognize as potentially one nation, whose dominion is the entire African continent.[38]

A closer analysis reveals Nkrumah's thought to be more pan-African nationalism than supranational Marxism. Marxism postulates that the economic substructure of the market will make the super-structure of a nation. What Nkrumah says is wholly different. His nationalism calls for the creation of a market in order to be a nation; thus, the nationalist motivation remains dominant although the objective is to achieve nationhood along Marxist definitions.

Nyerere's thought is very similar. According to him, only African unity will enable economic planning, joint research, a rational distribution of resources and rapid economic growth.[39] Toure holds that the "arbitrary borders" and "the markets of the size of Gabon" are responsible for Africa's slow economic growth.[40] Other leaders, whether the radical Telli,[41] the middle-of-the-road Mboya[42] or the conservative Ronald Ngala,[43] say the same things in other words. They all confirm Deutsch's point that expected economic gain is a vital element in any unification ideal.[44] Not one leader seems to have any doubts in this regard, although Deutsch's historical-empirical study reveals that there is no correlation between the size of the country and the

250

market and the rate of growth of the economy.[45]

All the radical leaders--Nkrumah, Nyerere, Toure, Telli--add another quasi-materialist argument for pan-Africanism, an argument which combines economic and political motivations to enhance the power of Africa. All of them mention the indisputable fact that at present the African states with their "National micro-economies"[46] are in a weak bargaining position vis-a-vis the developed states and the international economic corporations.[47] Their position is weak because they are disunited and conduct a zero-sum game in the fields of export of primary products, import of technical assistance and attraction of foreign capital.[48] All the radical leaders agree that pan-African unity may provide the answer. Again it is striking that the issue of bargaining power in the international economic market is notably absent in the writings and speeches of the more conservative and pro-Western leaders.

In the history of unification nationalism--as we call the nationalist ideologies aimed at uniting parts of what they regarded as one whole--the motive to put an end to conflicts and wars between the parts was always present. The way to 'pacify' the parts is seen to be by their strict subordination to one political roof. The pan-Africanism of Nkrumah, Toure and Nyerere contains this 'pacific' element. For them, a pan-African Union will solve the problem of divided tribes,[49] do away with the explosive potential of arbitrary borders[50] and prevent wars "as in Europe".[51]

The 'pacific' motive also reappears in another disguise---more ambitious, missionary and utopian. The unity of Africa is declared as a necessary step to assure world peace. Thus Nkrumah declared that

> ...a united Africa would become one of the greatest forces for the good of the world;[52]

> ...only a united Africa...can be truly...a force for peace;[53]

> ...Africa united would be another bulwark for world peace.[54]

In a joint statement Nkrumah and Toure declared that a united Africa will "contribute more easily to safeguarding the peace of the world."[55] The same universalist-utopian element also appears

251

in the Sanniquellie Declaration of Nkrumah, Toure and Tubman,[56] and in Telli's[57] and Nyerere's[58] writings. The theme is particularly stressed by Quaison-Sackey, Nkrumah's Minister of Foreign Affairs:

> ...the preservation of world peace becomes an impossibility in the long run if unity is not achieved;[59]
>
> war and division are by nature allied just as peace is connected with unity;[60]
>
> African unity...spells African peace.[61]

As Nkrumah draws analogies from European history on the issue of border conflicts, so Nyerere's thought is also influenced by European history or its image in Africa. He wants unity and peace in order to not follow the "negative example" of Europe, an example of disunity and wars among small nation-states.[62]

The 'peace ideal', the idea that pan-African nationalism will bring peace to the world, confirms Kohn's observation that every nationalism believes in a mission it has to fulfill for the good of the world.[63] Usually nationalism perceives its function to be as much universalist as particularist. Some may regard the universalist ingredient as a cloak or a myth; but there can hardly be any doubt that many people sincerely believe in the complementarity symbolized by the universalist function of particularist nationalism.

In Mickiewicz's Polish nationalism, Poland was the Christ to suffer for all oppressed peoples; in Mazzini's thought, Italy will be a 'Third Rome'--a center for liberation of nations and world peace; in pan-Slavism, Russia will save the world from Western decadence; in German nationalism, German culture serves as the model culture of the world; in British nationalism, we discern Kipling's 'white man's burden'; and in Jewish Zionism is the idea of *'Or-Lagoyim'*--light to the people.[64] Thus the idea of peace for the world through pan-African unity falls within the 'mission ideals' of all known nationalisms--a confirmation of the view that nationalism must be understood as a universal phenomenon with particularist varieties.[65]

Any attempt to do the impossible and define what a 'nation' is, will have to concede the conclusion of a subjective dimension as a necessary ingredient of any nationhood. While Emerson's statement that pan-Africanism exists as an "emotional fact"[66] may be a little exaggerated with regard to the bulk of Africa's peoples, there is certainly a good part of emotion and affect in pan-African nationalism in addition to the subjective, rational-intellectual part of pan-Africanism.

One leader who very much emphasizes the sentimental dimension of pan-Africanism is Nyerere:

> Colonization had one significant result. A sentiment was created on the African continent--a sentiment of oneness.[67]

> There now exists a strong feeling of unity on the continent. It is an emotion which has...grown out of the struggle for freedom;[68]

> In the struggle against colonialism, the fundamental unity of the people of Africa is evident and deeply felt.[69]

Nyerere's "sentiment of Africanness" and "emotional unity"[70] is, in a way, a reaction to white prejudice and sentiments. In an interview with *Jeune Afrique,* Nyerere explained that white Europeans "in Paris or Moscow" would regard him as African and not as Zanaki or Tanzanian.[71] His reaction is to feel strongly African. This is an example of the importance of the 'they' and their pressures, repressions and images to the constitution of a subjective 'we'. It is also a good example of the strength of the racial under-current in African nationalism even in the thought of leaders who are well known for their racial tolerance. There can be hardly any question that what causes the identification as 'African' in "Paris or Moscow" is the colour of the skin. The emotional ingredient is much weaker in the pan-Africanism of the other African leaders. However, this does not mean that other irrational elements do not exist in pan-African nationalism.

One such irrational and even mythical element in pan-African thought is the 'discovery' of a common history and culture, which objectively hardly exists. With regard to history, it could be argued that colonialism is a common historical experience of almost all African peoples. All African leaders emphasize this common colonial and anti-colonial period, the *"similitude de notre situation d'ancienne colonisee."*[72] In Asia and Latin America, pan-feelings are much weaker, and Scott explains the weakness of pan-Americo-Latinism by the absence of a common recent colonial past.[73] The weakness of pan-Asianism may also be rooted

253

BENYAMIN NEUBERGER

in the fact that large parts of Asia - Turkey, Arabia, Persia, China, Japan, Thailand - did not become colonies, as did almost the whole of Africa. In Africa we had some varieties of colonial rule, but all colonial systems had many common features. Thus Nkrumah's "common experience under colonialism"[74] and Nyerere's "common colonial repression"[75] are certainly important ingredients of any pan-African consciousness.

The irrational aspect of the pan-African historical identity comes to the fore in the current myths about a precolonial common pan-African history. Nyerere talks, for example, about a "feeling of unity" rooted in "pre-European history."[76] Kenyatta speaks about a "pan-African community" with a common heritage and tradition;[77] Toure mentions ancient Africa which was "one country," and calls for "reunification";[78] Nkrumah has hardly any doubts that Africa had a common traditional past.[79] In order to argue for pan-Africanism and against territorial nationalism, Nkrumah states:

> The African 'nations' of today created
> artificially by foreigners for their own
> purposes do not originate from ancient
> African civilizations...[80]

Nkrumah implies that pan-Africa, in contrast to the artificial "'African nations' of today," is well rooted in pan-African "ancient civilization," an implication substantiated by other references to traditional history made by Nkrumah.

The phenomenon of 'discovering' a mythical historical past is nothing uniquely African. Again we face the specific African expression of a well-known general phenomenon which recurs in all nationalisms.

A variation of the same theme is the myth about the cultural unity of Africa, a myth which was effectively propagated by Cheikh Anta Diop's *L'Unite Culturelle de l'Afrique Noire.*[81] It is less known, but no less true, that Africa's political leaders who believe in pan-Africanism and who seem to be influenced by the cultural element in European nationalism also regard it as a necessity to 'create' a common all-African culture. Thus Toure talks about the common cultural fond of all African states[82] Leopold Senghor frequently mentions *"cette communaute culturelle que j'appelle africanite."*[83] He also writes about the Arab-African "convergences" in thought and arts which are rooted in "prehistoire."[84] Quaison-Sackey attempts to give to Nkrumah's 'African Personality' a cultural identity and definition when he

254

says that "the African Personality is the...cultural expression of what is common to all peoples whose home is on the continent of Africa."[85]

Like any other nationalism, pan-Africanism does not lack the irrational and mythical theses about the "inevitability" of African unity[86] and the declaration of Africa as "by nature one."[87] Nkrumah frequently talks about the "destiny" of Africa to be one, about the "march of history" which cannot be halted.[88] Africa is to Nkrumah "one and indivisible,"[89] a statement which reminds one of French Jacobine nationalism in its peak periods. Nyerere also regards African unity as a "natural thing."[90] The same is true for Quaison-Sackey, for whom "Africa is by nature one,"[91] and Telli, who discerns a "natural movement toward unity."[92] For Ahmadu Ahidjo, African unity is "holy,"[93] while for Ako Adjei, it is also "inevitable."[94] The greatest density of irrational and mythical statements we find in Toure's writings. That confirms Shafer's observation about the mythical ingredient of any nationalism.[95] The more radical the nationalism, the more irrationality and myths it may contain. That explains why the secular-socialist Toure so often resorts to irrational myths. Thus, Toure talks about *"les etapes historiques"* which *"fait de chaque africain un complement naturel des autres."*[96] To him, Africa is one organic body which cannot be cut or divided.[97] A repetition of 'organic nationalism' well known to the students of the German Romantik. Repeatedly, Toure mentions the *"communaute de destin,"* the *"solidarite naturelle,"* the pan-African *"personnalite,"* the "indivisibility" and "historic necessity" of pan-African unity.[98]

Deutsch, the student of unification nationalisms, mentions as one of their features the belief in "natural" tendencies toward unity and the "inevitability" of amalgamation.[99] As an empirical social scientist, Deutsch attempts to check the truth content of these belief systems. Deutsch's findings deny the existence of a "natural" trend toward larger units. On the contrary, Deutsch contends that in the last centuries there was a shift from large political systems to smaller units.[100] Nevertheless, belief in "natural" and "inevitable" unity will continue to be a part of pan-Africanism, and of any other unification nationalism, for that matter.

Pan-Africanism should be compared to other pan-movements, for the comparative perspective will lead us to understand things as they are and not only as they appear. All pan-movements were motivated by the aspiration to accumulate power, to assure security and to accelerate socio-economic development.

255

This aspiration includes the wish to be truly independent in both politics and economics, a disdain for small and weak states and the striving for prestige and grandeur. These basic drives are common to pan-Slavism, pan-Americanism, pan-Turanism, pan-Arabism and pan-Africanism. Nevertheless, there are also important differences. The racial element is strong in pan-Turanism[101] and pan-Slavism,[102] and much weaker in continental pan-Africanism. Still, the racial origin of continental Africanism and the racial connotation of the word 'African' do not enable pan-Africanism to be devoid of racial connotations, although it embraces both Black Africans and non-Black Arabs. In contrast to pan-Slavism, pan-Latino-Americanism, pan-Turanism, pan-Arabism and pan-Germanism, the linguistic or religious factors in pan-Africanism are almost non-existent. There is relatively little stress on culture compared to the emphasis on political, diplomatic, economic and military variables, although there is some attempt to 'create' a pan-African culture. The same applies to the historic dimension, which is objectively better grounded in the other pan-movements; but as any other nationalism would do, pan-Africanism 'produces' the common history.

Pan-Africanism may come closest to resembling pan-Europeanism with its emphasis on defense, economics, power and prestige, and with its geographic-continental rather than ethnic-cultural dimension. On the other hand, pan-Europeanism (like pan-Arabism) conflicts with territorial state-nationalisms, while pan-Africanism (like pan-Latin-Americanism and pan-Slavism) often complements rather than collides with territorial nationalism.[103]

FOOTNOTES

1. This paper was originally written for the first edition of this book, but appeared just in the *Canadian Review of Studies in Nationalism.* It is used here by permission of the author and the editor of *Canadian Review of Studies in Nationalism.*

2. E. Lemberg, *Nationalismus II--Soziologie und Politische Padagogik* (Hanmburg: Rowohlt, 1964), p. 82.

3. F. Znaniecki, *Modern Nationalities--A Sociological Study* (Urbana: University of Illinois Press, 1952), p. 35.

4. K. Nkrumah, *Ghana Today* (Accra) July 29, 1964.

5. K. Nkrumah, "Handbook of Revolutionary Warfare : in *Dark Days in Ghana,* (New York: International Publishers, 1969), p. 35.

6. *The Nationalist* (Dar-es-Salaam) February 26, 1968; J. Nyerere, "The Politics and Purposes of Pan-Africanism," *Review of International Affairs* 14, No. 313 (1963):1.

7. J. Nyerere, quoted in C. Legum, *Pan-Africanism--A Short Political Guide* (New York: Praeger, 1965), p. 74.

8. J. Nyerere "A United States of Africa," *Journal of Modern African Studies* 1, No. 1 (Spring 1963):2-3.

9. D. Telli, "The Organization of African Unity in Historical Perspective," *African Forum* 1, No. 2 (Fall 1965): 18; For Toure and Keita, see quotations nos. 9 and 10.

10. M. Keita, quoted in *Pan-Africanism*, p. 64.

11. "Declaration of the United African States," ibid., p. 66.

12. T. Mboya, in *Politics of Integration--An East African Documentary,* ed. D. Rothschild (Nairobi: East African

Publishing House, 1968), p. 82.

13. T. Mboya, "African Unity and the OAU," *East Africa Journal* 1, 10 (October 1964): 21.

14. J. Kenyatta, *Harambee--The Prime Minister of Kenya's Speeches 1963-1964* (Nairobi: Oxford University Press, 1964), p. 35.

15. H. Selassie, "Towards African Unity," *Journal of Modern African Studies* 1, No. 3 (Fall 1963), 283.

16. *Ghana Today* (Accra), August 31, 1960.

17. K. Nkrumah, *I Speak for Freedom* (New York: Praeger, 1961), p. 125.

18. Ibid., p. xii (preface).

19. Ibid.

20. N. Azikiwe, "Pan-Africanism," in *The Political Awakening of Africa,* ed. R. Emerson and M. Kilson (Englewood Cliffs: Prentice Hall, 1965), p. 153.

21. Ibid.

22. T. Mboya, in Rothschild, *Politics of Integration,* p. 82.

23. S. Toure, on Radio Conakry (April 30, 1968).

24. R. Ngala, "Uhuru na Federation," *Spearhead* 2, No. 2 (February 1962):16.

25. *Jeune Afrique* (Paris), June 3, 1963.

26. *The Nationalist* (Dar-es-Salaam), February 26, 1968.

27. N. Azikiwe, "Pan Africanism," p. 153.

28. S. Toure, "Africa's Destiny," in *Africa Speaks,* ed. J. Duffy and R. Manners (Princeton: Van Nostrand, 1961), p. 38.

29. *Jeune Afrique* (Paris), June 3, 1963; *Ghana Today* (Accra), June 5, 1963; K. Nkrumah, "Angola," *Presence Africaine,* No. 42 (1962):39.

30. *Nationalism--* A Report by a Study Group of Members of the Royal Institute of International Affairs (New York: Kelley, 1968, p. 1.

31. Ibid.

32. K. Deutsch, *Nationalism and Its Alternatives* (New York: A. Knopf, 1969), pp. 115-120.

33. K. Deutsch, *Political Community in the North Atlantic Area* (Princeton: Princeton University Press, 1968), pp. 46-50.

34. K. Nkrumah, *Ghana Today* (Accra), May 19, 1965.

35. Ibid.

36. *Ghana Today* (Accra), June 5, 1963; July 29, 1964; April 26, 1961; K. Nkrumah, "Handbook of Revolutionary Warfare," in *Dark Days in Ghana*, p. 26; C. Welch, *Dream of Unity--Pan Africanism and Political Unification in West Africa* (Ithaca: Cornell University Press, 1966).

37. *Ghana Today* (Accra), June 5, 1963.

38. K. Nkrumah, *Class Struggle in Africa* (New York: International Publishers, 1970).

39. J. Nyerere, *Freedom and Unity* (Dar-es-Salaam: Oxford University Press, 1966), pp. 85-98, 214; idem *The Nationalist* (Dar-es-Salaam), February 26, 1968; C. Legum, *Pan-Africanism*, p. 74; idem, "The Policies and Purposes of Pan-Africanism," *Review of International Affairs* 14, No. 313 (1963):2.

40. S. Toure, *Doctrine of Methods of the Democratic Party of Guinea* (No place, no publisher, no date), pp. 68, 272: idem, *The Nationalist* (Dar-es-Salaam), April 1, 1968.

41. According to Telli, only a united Africa will win the war for development. See Telli, "Organization of African Unity" p. 18.

42. T. Mboya supports African unity in order "to be able to act effectively in dealing with the problems of economic reconstruction at home." (T. Mboya, "African Unity and the OAU," *East Africa Journal* 1, No. 10 (October 1964):21.) The choice of the word 'reconstruction' is

interesting because, as with 'reunification' of Africa, it contains the common nationalist reference to a past golden age which one aspires to 'reconstruct'. Mboya also calls for continental planning and division of labour in order to achieve a "more effective Africa." *See Also* T. Mboya, *Challenge of Nationhood* (London: Heinemann, 1970), p. 156; "An Escape from Stagnation," *African Report* 12, No. 3 (March 1967); 14-20, 37-39; Rothschild, *Politics of Integration*, p. 82.

43.　Ngala, "Uhuru no Federation," p. 16.

44.　Deutsch, *Political Community,* pp. 46-50.

45.　Deutsch, *Nationalism,* pp. 115, 120.

46.　S. Toure, "Africa's Future and the World," *Foreign Affairs,* 41, No. 1 (October 1962):150.

47.　Ibid; Nkrumah, *Ghana Today* (Accra) June 5, 1963; Telli, "Organization of African Unity," p. 18; Nyerere, *Freedom and Unity,* p. 213; *The Nationalist* (Dar-es-Salaam) February 29, 1968; and "The Policies and Purposes of Pan-Africanism," *Review of International Affairs* 14, no. 313 (1963):2.

48.　Ibid.

49.　Nyerere, *Freedom and Unity,* pp. 41, 85-88.

50.　Radio Conakry, April 30, 1968.

51.　*Ghana Today* (Accra), June 5, 1963.

52.　Nkrumah, *I Speak for Freedom,* p. x (preface).

53.　Nkrumah, *Ghana Today* (Accra), March 10, 1965.

54.　Ibid., September 13, 1961.

55.　C. Legum, *Pan-Africanism,* p. 202.

56.　Ibid., p. 180.

57.　D. Telli, "Organization of African Unity," p. 18.

58.　J. Nyerere, "L'Unite Africaine," *Presence Africaine,* No.

39 (1961):10; "Scramble for Africa," *Spearhead*, 2, No. 2 (February 1962): 15-16.

59.   A. Quaison-Sackey, "Africa and the United Nations: (Observations of a Ghanaian Diplomat," *Africa Forum* 1, No. 1 (Summer 1965):62.

60.   Ibid.

61.   Ibid.

62.   Nyerere, "Scramble for Africa," pp. 15-16.

63.   H. Kohn, *The Idea of Nationalism--A Study in its Origins and Background* (New York: Collier, 1967), p. 36.

64.   Znaniecki, *Modern Nationalities*, p. 41.

65.   Ibid., p. 35.

66.   R. Emerson, "The Problem of Identity, Selfhood and Image in New Nations: The Situation in Africa," *Comparative Politics* 1, No. 3 (April 1969):310.

67.   J. Nyerere, quoted in A. Mazrui, "On the Concept 'We are all Africans'," *American Political Science Review* 57, No. 1 (March 1963):89-90.

68.   Nyerere, *Freedom and Unity*, p. 153.

69.   Ibid., p. 39.

70.   Nyerere, "A United States of Africa," p. 1.

71.   *Jeune Afrique* (Paris), March 16, 1971.

72.   L. Senghor, in an interview with *Jeune Afrique* (Paris), October 30, 1966.

73.   R. E. Scott, "Nationbuilding in Latin America," in *Nation-building*, ed. K. Deutsch and N. Foltz (New York:Atherton Press, 1966), pp. 73-83.

74.   Nkrumah, *Class Struggle in Africa*, p. 9.

75.   Nyerere, "A United States of Africa," p. 1.

76. Nyerere, *Freedom and Unity*, p. 153.

77. J. Kenyatta, "African Socialism and African Unity," *Africa Forum* 1, No. 1 (Summer 1965):24.

78. S. Toure, *Guinean Revolution and Social Progress* (Cairo: Societe Orinetale de Publicite, 1963), p. 400; idem, *Jeune Afrique* (Paris), June 3, 1963; idem, "The Party and Democracy," *Spearhead* 1, No. 11 (November 1961):11.

79. Nkrumah, *Class Struggle in Africa*, p. 9; idem, *I Speak for Freedom*, p. ix (preface); *Ghana Today* (Accra), July 29, 1964.

80. Nkrumah, "Handbook for Revolutionary Warfare," p. 25.

81. C. A. Diop, *L'Unite Culturelle de l'Afrique Noire* (Paris: Presence Africaine, 1959), *passim.*

82. Toure, *Doctrine and Methods*, p. 272.

83. L. Senghor in *Jeune Afrique* (Paris), June 3, 1963.

84. L. Senghor in an interview with *Jeune Afrique* (Paris), October 30, 1966.

85. A. Quaison-Sackey, *Africa Unbound--Reflections of an African Statesman* (New York: Praeger, 1963), p. 36.

86. Ako Adjei, in C. Legum, *Pan-Africanism*, p. 188.

87. Quaison-Sackey, "Africa and the United Nations," p. 62.

88. On Nkrumah's terminology, see K. Grundy, "The Political Ideology of K. Nkrumah," in *African Political Thought-- -Lumumba, Nkrumah, Toure*, ed. W. Skurnik (Denver: Monography Series in World Affairs 1964, V, No. 3/4 - 1967/1968), 69; see also *Ghana Today* (Accra) July 29, 1964.

89. K. Nkrumah, *Ghana Today* (Accra), June 20, 1962.

90. Nyerere, "A United States of Africa," p. 2.

91. Quaison-Sackey, "Africa and the United Nations," p. 62.

92. D. Telli, "Organization of African Unity," p. 14.

93.   A. Ahidjo in an interview with *Etudes Congolaises* (Kinshasa) 2, No. 3 (July/August/September 1968):112-116.

94.   A. Adjei, in C. Legum, *Pan-Africanism,* p. 188.

95.   B. Shafer, *Nationalism - Myth and Reality* (London: Gollancz, 1955), *passim.*

96.   S. Toure, *Experiment Guineen et Unite Africaine,* p. 127.

97.   S. Toure, *Guinean Revolution,* p. 119; idem, "Africa's Future and the World,; *Foreign Affairs* 41, No. 1 (October 1962):150.

98.   S. Toure in *Jeune Afrique* (Paris) June 3, 1963; idem, *Guinean Revolution,* p. 400; idem, *Doctrine and Methods,* pp. 70-170; idem, *The International Policy of the Democratic Party of Guinea* (no place, no publisher, no date), p. 104; idem, "Africa's Destiny," p. 55.

99.   K. Deutsch, *Political Community,* pp. 22-24.

100.   Ibid.

101.   K. Minogue, *Nationalism* (London: Batsford, 1967), p. 14.

102.   H. Kohn, *Pan-Slavism - Its History and Ideology* (New York: Random House, 1960), *passim.*

103.   C. Legum, "Nationalism's Impact on Pan-Africanism," *East Africa Journal* 1, No. 4 (April 1965):5.

BIBLIOGRAPHY
of African Philosophy

Compiled by
Richard A. Wright

The following bibliography was compiled on the basis of research, with each item having been examined by myself or another researcher. Each item included was judged to have some interest to a person studying African Philosophy, even though not all might judge it as 'pure' philosophy. Rather, the included items fall roughly into three categories: (1) 'pure' African Philosophy; (2) African Philosophy from a non-African perspective; and (3) ethnologically relevant works from which one might glean philosophical insights.

Preparation of this bibliography has been an ongoing project, with its production the result of many people's efforts. The basic work was done under a research grant from the University of Toledo, and preparation of the index was accomplished using the University computer system. I also received assistance from Richard Lineback and the Philosophy Documentation Center of Bowling Green State University, as well as from Kwame Gyekye, A.J. Smet, B. J. van der Walt, and Eugene Maier. I am particularly indebted to the library staff of the African Studies libraries at Michigan State University, Boston University, and the Library of Congress for their patience and assistance.

Additions to the bibliography are most welcome, and should be sent to me, along with suggestions for indexing, or an abstract, c/o the Department of Philosophy, University of Toledo, Toledo, Ohio, 43606.

1. Abiola, Irele. "Negritude - Philosophy of African Being." *Nigeria Magazine* 122/123 (1977):1-3.

2. Abimbola, W. & Ayorinde, J.A. "Ifa as a Body of Knowledge and as an Academic Discipline." *Lagos Notes* 2 (1968):30-40 and (1969):63-68.

3. Abraham, W. E. *The Mind of Africa.* Chicago: University of Chicago Press, 1962.

4. Abrahams, R.G. "Occasional Papers in African Traditional Religion and Philosophy." *International Journal of African Historical Studies* 7, no.1 (1974):131.

5. Abrahamsson, H. *The Origin of Death. Studies in African Mythology.* Uppsala,Sweden: Studia Ethnographica Uppsaliensia, 1951.

6. Ackah, Christian A. "An Ethical Study of the Akan Tribes of Ghana." Ph.D. Dissertation, London School of Economics, 1959.

Adalberto de Postioma. See Postioma, Adalberto de

7. Adelaja, Kola "Social Philosophy and African Emancipation: Some Preliminary Notes on E.W.Blyden." *Quarterly Journal of Administration* (Ibadan) 7, no.4 (1973):411-420.,

8. _____. "Sources in African Political Thought." *Presence Africaine* Part I -- 70 (1969):7-26; Part. II -- 80 (1971):49-72.

9. Adesanya, A. "Yoruba Metaphysical Thinking." *Odu* 5 (1958):36-41.

10. Agblemahnan, F. "L'afrique noire; la metaphysique, l'ethique, l'evolution actuelle." *Comprendre* 21/22 (1960):74-82.

11. _____. "Du 'temps' dans la culture Ewe." *Presence Africaine* 14/15 (1957):222-232.

12. Agudze-Vioka, Bernard. "De la conception de la vie et la mort chez les Ewe." *Bull.ensign.sup.benin* (Rome) 6 (1968):121-28.

13. Ajay'i, D.D. "Taboos and Clinical Research in West Africa." *Journal of Medical Ethics* 6 (1980):61-63.

14. Aguesse, Honorat. "Concerning Traditional African Religion as a Source of Civilization Values." *Presence Africaine* 74 (1970):94-97.

15. _____. "Tradition orale et structure de pensee; essai de methodologie." *Cahiers D'Histoire Mondiale* 14 (1972):269-297.

16. *Akten des XIV International Kongress fur Philosophie.* Vienna: Universitat Wien, 1968.

17. Albert, E. "African Conceptual Systems." In Paden and Soja (1970)

18. Albert, Ethel M. " 'Rhetoric', 'Logic', and 'Poetics' in Burundi: Culture Patterning of Speech Behavior." *American Anthropologist* Special Issue (1964-65):197-215.

19. _____. "Woman of Burundi: a Study of Social Values." In Paule (1963):35-54.

20. _____. "Une etude de valeurs en Urundi." *Cahiers d'Etudes Africaines* 2 (1960):148-160.

Alberto de Postioma. See Postioma, Adalberto de

21. Allen, S.W. "Muntu." *Presence Africaine* 2 (1960):148-160.

22. Allier, R. *The Mind of the Savage.* Translated by F. Rothwell London: G. Bell and Sons, 1929.

23. Amadl, Elechi. *Ethics in Nigerian Culture.* Exeter, N.H.: Heinemann Educational Books, Inc., 1982.

24. Anciaux, L. "Philosophous un rien." *Bulletin Militaire* 72 (1955):409-423.

25. Anderson, E. "The Concept of Justice and Morality Among the Bakuta in the Congo-Brazzaville." *Ethnos* 37 (1972).

26. Ankunde, L. "Philosophie et developpement." *Presence Africaine* (1972):3-17.

27. Antonini, A.R. "Les fondements metaphysique de la morale chez les Kirdis du Tchad et du Cameroun." *Bulletin et Memorie Soc. Anthro.* (Paris) 11, no. 6 (1966):367-376.

28. Apostel, Leo. *African Philosophy: Myth Or Reality?* Gent, Belgium: Scientific Publishers, E. Story-Scientia, 1981.

29. Ardener, Edwin. "Belief and the Problem of Woman (Bakweri)." In Lafontaine (1971):135-158

30. _____. "Conversations with Ogotommelli." *Man* n.s.1, no.3 (1966):515.

31. Armstrong, Robert G. "Prolegomena To the Study of the Idoma Concept of God." *African Notes* 4, no.1 (1966):11-17.

32. Armstrong, Robert P. *Wellspring: on the Myth and Source of Culture.* Berkeley: University of California Press, 1975.

33. Arnott, K. *African Myths and Legends.* 2nd ed. London: Oxford University Press, 1965.

34. Arewa, Ojo. "Zande Ultimate Reality and Meaning." *Ultimate Reality and Meaning* 1 (1978):240-250.

35. Ataragaboine, G. "The Concept of the Supreme Being Among the Batoro." Paper #204 in Byaruhanga, Vol. 19.

36. Auge, Marc, et. al. *La Construction du Monde: Religion Representation, Ideologie.* Paris: Francois Maspero, 1974.

37. Avery, W.L. "Concepts of God in Africa." *Journal of the American Academy of Religion* 39, no.3 (1971):391.

38. Awolalu, J. Omosade. "Aiyelala; a Guardian of Social Morality." *Ibadan Journal of Religious Studies* 2 (1968):79-89.

39. _____. "The Yoruba Philosophy of Life." *Presence Africaine* 73 (1970):20-38.

40. Awooner, Kofi. *The Breast of the Earth: a Survey of the History, Culture, and Literature of Africa South of the Sahara.* Garden City, N.Y.: Anchor Press, 1975.

41. Ayandele, E.A. *African Exploration and Human Under-standing.* Edinburgh: Center For African Studies, University of Edinburgh, 1972.

42. Ayoade, John A.A. "Death in Yoruba Life." Mimeograph, Department of African Studies, University of Ibadan, Nigeria, 1977.

43. _____. "Time in Yoruba Thought." In Wright (1984)

44. Axelsen, Diana. "Philosophical Justifications For Contempo-rary African Social and Political Values and Strategies." In Wright (1984).

*** B ***

45. Ba, A.H. "La notion de personne en Afrique noire." In Centre National (1973):181-192.

46. Babalolo, S.A. *The Content and Form of Yoruba Ijala.* Oxford: Clarendon Press, 1966.

47. Bachelard, G. "Temoignage sur la philosophie bantoue du P. Tempels." *Presence Africaine* 7 (1949): (Whole Issue).

48. Bahoken, Jean-Calvin. *Clairieres Metaphysiques Afri-caines. Essai sur la Philosophie et la Religion Chez Les Bantu du Sud-Cameroun.* Paris: Presence Africaine, (1967).

49. Bakabulindi, J. "The Traditional Wisdom of the Bagauda Concerning Moral Behavior." Paper #184 in Byaruhanga, Vol.17.

50. Balandier, Georges. *Ambiguous Africa: Cultures in Collision.* Translated by H. Weaver. New York: Patheon Books, 1966.

51. Balandier, G. & Maquet, J. *Dictionary of African Civil-izations.* Paris: F. Hozan, 1968.

52. Balongun, Ola. "Ethnology and Its Ideologies." *Conse-quence* 1 (1974):109-125, 126-144.

53. Barone, O.R. "Lega Culture - Art, Initiation and Moral Philosophy Among a Central African People." *Social Education* 39, no.2 (1975):114.

54. Barrett, D.B. "African Religions and Philosophy." *Journal for the Scientific Study of Religion* 9, no.2 (1970):179.

55. Bascom, W.O. "Yoruba Concepts of Soul." In Wallace, Fifth International (1960):401-410.

56. _____. "Yoruba Religion and Morality." In Religions Africaines :50-63.

57. Baziota, A.F. "Analogie et symbolisme du proverbe." *Pour Servir* 1, no.6 (1957):13-15.

58. Beattie, J.H.M. "On the Nyoro Concept of 'mahano'." *African Studies* 19 (1960):145-150.

59. Beidelman, T.O. "Myth, Legend and Oral History; a Jaguru Traditional Text." *Anthropos* 65, no. 23, (1970):74-97.

60. _____. "Social Theory and the Study of Christian Missions in Africa." *Africa (London)* 44, no.3 (1974):235-49.

61. Beier, Ulli. *The Origin of Life and Death: African Creation Myths.* African Writers Series no. 23. London: Heineman, 1966.

62. Biebuyck, D. *Lega Culture: Art, Initiation, and Moral Philosophy Among a Central African People.* Berkeley: University of California Press, 1973.

63. Blacking, J. "The Social Value of Venda Riddles." *African Studies* 20 (1961):1-32.

64. Blakeley, Thomas J. "The Bantu-African Contribution To Dialoue." In Acten des XIV (1969):184-188.

65. _____. "The Categories of Mtu and the Categories of Aristotle." In Wright (1984).

66. Bock, Paul. "Exploring African Morality." *Cross Currents* 27 (1978/79):462-467.

67. Bodenstein, W. & Raum, O.F. "A Present Day Zulu Philosopher." *Africa* 30, no.2 (1960):166-81.

68. Bodunrin, P.O. "The Question of African Philosophy." *Philosophy* 56 (1881):161-179. Also in Wright (1984).

69. ____. "Which Kind of Philosophy for Africa?" In Diemer (1981):8-22.

70. ____. "Witchcraft, Magic and ESP: a Defence of Scientific and Philosophical Scepticism." *Second Order* 7, no.1/2 (1978):36-51.

71. Bohannan, P.J. "Concepts of Time Among the Tiv of Nigeria." *Southwestern Journal of Anthropology* 9 (1953):251-262.

72. ____. *Justice and Judgement Among the Tiv.* New York: Oxford University Press, 1957.

73. Bolle, Jacques. "Zur Frage de Bantu-philosophie." *Institute Afrika Forum* (Munich) 1, no.3 (1965):35-37.

74. Booth, N.S. "African Religions and Philosophy." *International Philosophical Quarterly* 11, no.2 (1971):266.

75. ____. "Time and Change in Traditional African Thought." *Religion in Africa* 7, no.2 (1975):81-91.

76. Botolo, Magoza. "La philosophie en Afrique; pour un renouvellement de la question." *Afrique* (Zaire) 85 (1974):261-273. Also in Dubois & Dewijngaert (1973).

77. Boubou, Hama. *Le Retard de l'Afrique: Essai Philosophique.* Paris: Presence Africaine, 1972.

Boulaga, F.E. See Eboussi-Boulaga, F.

78. Bourgi, A.C. & Williams J.C. "La pensee politique de Frantz Fanon." *Presence Africaine* 88 (1973):139-162.

79. Brelsford, V. "The Philosophy of the Savage." *Nada* 15 (1938):62-68.

80. ____. *Primitive Philosophy.* London: John Bale Sons and Danileson, 1935.

81. Brentjes, B. "Amo, A. W. 1st African Philosopher in European Universities." *Current Anthropology* 16, no.3 (1975):443-444.

82. Brinker, P.H. "Suppositionen Uber die Etymologisch-mythologische Bedeutung Der Nominum Fur 'leben', 'seele', 'geist', und 'tod' in Der Lingua-Bantu." *Zeitung Fur Africana und Oceanische Sprachen* 1 (1895):164-168.

83. Brokensha, D. & Crowder, M., Eds. *Africa in the Wider World*. New York: Pergaon Press, 1967.

84. Bucumi, Jean. "Imana; Some Names of God in the Kirundi Language." *International Philosophical Quarterly* 4 (1964):394-418.

85. Bujo, Benezet. "Christologischen Grundlagen einer Afrikanischen Ethik." *Frei Zeitung fur Philosophischen Theology* 29 (1982):223-238.

86. Burton, John W. "The Divination of Atot Philosophy." *Journal of Religion in Africa* 13, no.1 (1982):1-10.

87. Busia, A.K. "African World View." *Presence Africaine* 4 (1965):16-23.

88. Byaruhanga-Akiiki, A.B. *Occasional Papers in African Traditional Religion and Philosophy*. Kampala: Makerere University Press, 1971 on.

*** C ***

89. Carothers, J.C. "Further Thoughts on the African Mind." *East African Medical Journal* (Nairobi) 37 (1960):458-463.

90. Centre Nationale de la Recherche Scientifique. *La Notion de Personne en Afrique Noire*. Paris: Centre National de la Recherche Scientifique, 1973.

91. Cesaire, Aime. "La pensee politique Sekou Toure." *Presence Africaine* 29 (1959-60):65-73.

92. Chalasinski, J. "Narodzigny Afrykanskiej Mysli Humanistyczne." ("The Study of African Humanism.") *Przeglad Socjologiczny* 21 (1967):8-12.

93. Charevskara, B. "Le general et le particulier dan les religions autochtones de l'Afrique au sud du Sahara." In Korostovstev (1966):62-71.

94. Chiri, Mujynya. "La theorie du "ntu' ou la theorie de la nature intime des etres. Les lois de l'universe." In Smet (1974).

95. Chukwukere, B. "Individualism in an Aspect of Igbo Religion." *Kroniek Von Afrika* (Leiden) 2 (1971):106-112.

96. Colle, P. "La notion de Dieu chez les Bashi." *Congo* 2 (1925):37-42.

97. Conradie, Anna-Louize. "Africa." In *Handbook of World Philosophy*. John Barr, ed. Westport: Greenwood Press, 1980:409-419.

98. Considine, John J. *Africa, World of New Man*. New York: Dodd, 1954.

99. Cotte, R.P. "Concepts religieux, moraux, et sociaux des Bakka." *Trait D'Union* 2 (1950):17-20.

100. Courlander, H. *Tales of Yoruba Gods and Heroes*. New York: Crown, 1973.

101. Crahay, Franz. "Conceptual Take-off Conditions for a Bantu Philosophy." *Diogenes* 52 (1965):61-84.

102. Crowley, D. "Lega Culture - Art, Intiation and Moral Philosophy Among a Central African People." *Journal of American Folklore* 88 (1975):435-443.

103. Culwick, A.T. *Good Out of Africa; a Study of the Relativity of Morals*. Livingstone, N. Rhodesia: Rhodes-Livingstone Institute, 1943.

*** *D* ***

104. Danquah, J.B. *The Akan Doctrine of God; a Fragment of Gold Coast Ethics and Religion*. London: Lutterworth Press, 1944. 2nd Ed. London: Frank Cass & Co., 1968.

105. Davidson, Basil. *The African Genius; an Introduction To African Cultural and Social History*. Boston: Little-Brown and Co., 1970.

106. Debauyne, E. "Katteekeningen Bij de Bantu-philosophie." *Knogo-Overzee* 10/11, no.4/5 (1944-1945):255-260.

107. Debeas Herrero, Jose Luis. "Le Natural y lo Sobernatural en Algunos Pueblos Yorubas y Bantues." *Africa* (Madrid) 24 no.365 (1972):177-180.

108. Decliene, N. "A propos de la philosophie Bantoue." *Inst. Royal Colon. Belge, Bull. Seances* 17, no.2 (1946):489-509.

109. Deheusch, Luc. "Le sorcier, le Pere Tempels et les jumeaux mal venus." In Centre National (1973):231-242.

110. Demahieu, W. "Mythe, science, philosophie et religion." *Afrique* (Congo) 29 (1968):457-465.

de Postioma, Adalberto. See Postioma, Adalberto de

111. Devaux, V. "La philosophie Bantoue." *Bull. des Juridictions Indg. et du Droit Contumier Congolais* 14, no.8 (1946):225-230.

112. Diaz, Mendez E. "El problema del nal en la filosofia Bantu." *Revista de Filosofia* (Madrid) 27 (1968):247-278.

113. Dickenson, Kwasi and P. Ellingworth, eds. *Pour une Theologie Africaine: Recontre des Theologiens Africains, Ibadan, 1966.* Paris: Yaounde, Editions Cle, 1969.

114. Diemer, Alwin, Ed. *Philosophy in the Present Situation of Africa.* Weisbaden, Germany: Franz Steiner Erlagh, GMBH, 1981.

115. Dieterlen, Germaine. "L'image du corps et les composantes de la personne chez les Dogon." In Centre National (1973):205-229.

116. _____. "The Mande Creation Myth." *Africa* 27 (1957):124-138.

117. _____. "La personne chez les Bambara." Journal de Psychologie Normale et Pathologique (Jan-Mar 1947):45-53.

118. _____, ed. *Textes Sacres d'Afrique Noire.* UNESCO Series Africaine. Paris: Gallimard, 1965.

Dieterlen, G. & Fortes, D. See Fortes, D.

Dieterlen, G. & Griaule, M. See Griaule, M.

119. Dirven, E. "La polygamie admise par la philosophie?" *Revue du Clerge Africaine* 27 (1972):49-73.

120. Dixon, V.J. "African Oriented and Euro-American Oriented World Views." *Review of Black Political Economy* 7 (1977):119-156.

121. Done, C.M. "Lamba Ideas of Cosmogony." *South African Geological Journal* 11 (1928):18-21.

122. Donne, J.B. "African Art as Philosophy." *Man* 10, no.4 (1975):659.

123. Dougall, J.W.C. "Characteristics of African Thought." *Africa* 5 (1932):249-265.

124. Douglas, Mary. *Implicit Meanings: Essays in Anthropology*. Boston: Routledge & Kegan Paul, 1975.

125. _____. *Natural Symbols: Explorations in Cosmology*. 2nd ed. New York: Vintage Books, 1973.

126. _____, ed. *Witchcraft, Confessions and Accusations*. London: Tavestock, 1970.

127. Dourelou, Albert. "Note sur le troisieme seminaire international Africain." *Zaire* 14, no.5/6 (19):549-554.

128. Dubb, Allie, ed. *The Myth in Modern Africa*. Lusaka: Rhodes-Livingstone Institute, 1960.

129. Dube, W.M. "African Religions and Philosophy." *Canadian Journal of African Studies* 5, no.1 (1971):123.

130. Dubois, J. & Van Dewijngaert, L. *Initiation Philosophique*. 2nd ed. Kinshasa: Okapi,1973.

131. Dutoit, B.M. "Some Aspects of the Soul-concept Among the Bantu-speaking Nguni Tribes of South Africa." *Authors Quarterly* 33 (1960):134-142.

*** E ***

132. Eboussi-Boulaga, F. "Le bantou problematique." *Presence Africaine* 66 (1968):4-40.

133. _____. "Muntu Chrisis, African Authenticity, and Philosophy."

134. Echero, M.J.C. "Nnamdi Azikiwe and Nineteenth Century Nigerian Thought." *Journal of Modern African Studies* (London) 12, no.2 (1974):245-263.

135. Edel,A. "Anthropology and Ethics in Common Focus." *Journal of the Royal Anthropological Institute* 92 (1962):55-72.

136. Emmet, D. "Haunted Universes." *Second Order* 1
(1972):34-42.

137. Elungu. E.P. "La philosophie, condition du developpment
en Afrique aujord'hui." *Presence Africaine* 103
(1977):3-18.

138. _____. "Religions africaines et philosophie." *Cahiers
Religions Africaines* 11, no.21/22 (1977):91-103.

139. Erassov, Boris. "Concepts of 'Cultural Personality' in the
Ideologies of the Third World." *Diogenes* 78
(1972):123-40.

140. Erny, Pierre. "La perception de l'espace et du temps dans
l'Afrique noire traditionelle." *Revue Psychologie Peuples*
25, no.1 (1979):67-74.

141. Esmail, A. "The Task of Philosophy in Africa." *Thought
and Practice* 1, N.2 (1974):17-26.

142. Espane, P.L. "Quelques aspects metaphysiques du 'boniti
mitshogo'." *Afrique* (Geneva) 7 (1968):53-57.

143. Evans-Pritchard, E.E. *The Nuer.* Oxford: Clarendon
Press, 1968.

144. _____. "The Nuer Conception of Spirit in its Relation to
Social Order." *American Anthropologist* 55 (1953):201-214.

145. _____. *Theories of Primitive Religion.* Oxford: Clarendon
Press, 1965.

146. _____. "Zande Notions About Death, Soul and Ghost."
Sudan Notes (Khartoum) 50 (1969):41-52.

Evans-Pritchard, E.E. & Fortes, D. See Fortes, D.

147. Ezzanya, S.N. "Dieu, les espirits, et le monde de espirits." In Dickenson (1966).

*** F ***

148. Fabian, Johannes. *Anthropology and Interpretation;
Essays on the Thought of the Jamaa Movement.* Chicago:
Northwestern University Press, 1972.

149. _____. "Language, History and Anthropology." *Journal For the Philosophy of the Social Sciences* 1 (1971):19-47.

150. _____. *Philosophie Bantoue; Placide Tempels et son Oeuvre vus dans une Perspective Historique.* Brussels: Centre des Rechesrches et d'Information Sociopolitiques, 1970.

151. Fanon, Frantz. "Fondement reciproque de la culture nationale et des luttes de liberation." *Presence Africaine* 24/25 (1959):82-89.

152. _____. *Peau Noire, Masques Blancs.* Paris: Editions du Seuil, 1952.

153. _____. *Wretched of the Earth.* New York: Grove Press, 1963.

154. Faublee, Jacques. "Espace et temps dans la tradition malgache." *Revue de Synthese* (Paris) 55/56 (1969):297-327.

155. *Filosofia, Religione, Religioni.* Torino: Societa Editrice Internazionale, 1966

156. Finazza, G. "Una filosofia africana?" *Africa* (Rome) 29 (1974):11-120.

157. Finnegan, Ruth. "How To Do Things With Words: Performative Utterances Among the Limba of Sierra Leone." *Man* n.s.4, no.1 (1969):537-551.

158. Forde, Cyril D. ed. *African Worlds: Ideas and Social Values of African Peoples.* New York: Oxford University Press, 1968.

159. Fortes, Meyer. *Oedipus and Job in West African Religion.* Cambridge: University Press, 1959.

160. _____. "On the Concept of the Person Among Tallensi." In Centre National (1973):283-320.

161. Fortes, M. & Evans-Pritchard, E.E., eds. *African Political Systems.* London: Oxford University Press, 1958.

162. Fortes, M. & Dieterlen, G., eds. *African Systems of Thought.* New York: Oxford University Press, 1965.

163. Fote, H. Memel. "L'idee du monde dans les cultures negro-africaines." *Presence Africaine* 73 (1970).

164. Fouba, B.J. *La Philosophie Negro-africaine de l'Existence.* Lille: Faculte des Lettres, 1967.

165. Fraser, Douglas. *African Art as Philosophy.* New York: Interbook, Inc., 1974.

166. Froelich, J.C. *Animismes: Les Religions Paiennes de l'Afrique de l'Ouest.* Editions de l'Orante, 1964.

*** G ***

167. Gaba, Christian R. "An African People's (Anlo) Concept of the soul." *Ghana Bulletin of Theology* (Legon) 3, no.10 (1971):1-8.

168. ____. "The Idea of a Supreme Being Among the Anlo People of Ghana." *Journal of Religion in Africa* 2 (1969):64-79.

169. Garvey, Marcus. *Philosophy and Opinions of Marcus Garvey; or, Africa For the Africans.* Compiled by Amy Jacques Garvey. London: F. Cass, 1967.

170. Gelfand, Michael. "The Normal Man; a New Concept of Shona Philosophy." *Nada* 9 (1965):78-93.

171. George, K. "The Civilized West Looks At Primitive Africa: 1400-1800." *Isis* 49 (1958):62-72.

172. Gillies, Francis. "The Bantu Concept of Time." *Religion* (London) 10 (1980):16-30.

173. Ginsberg, M. "On the Diversity of Morals." *Journal of the Royal Anthropological Institute* 83, no.2 (1953).

174. Gjertsvn, D. "Closed and Open Belief Systems." *Second Order* 7, no. 1/2 (1978):51-69.

175. Gluckman, M.,ed. *The Allocation of Responsibility.* New York: Humanities Press, 1972.

176. Gluckman, M. "Moral Crises; Magical and Secular Solutions." In Gluckman (1972):1-50

177. Griaule, Marcel. *Conversations With Ogotemmeli: an Intro-duction To Dogon Religions Ideas.* London: Oxford University Press, 1965.

178. _____. "The Idea of Person Among the Dogon." *Culture* (1960):265-371.

179. _____. "L'image du monde au Soudan." *Journal de la Societe de Africainistes* 19,no.1 (1949):81-88.

180. _____. "Mythe de l'organization du monde chez les Dogon du Soudan." *Psyche* (Paris) 2, no.6 (1947):43-453.

181. _____. "Novelles recherches sur la notion de personne chez les Dogon." *Journal de Psychologie Normale et Pathologi-que* 40, no.4 (1947):425-431.

182. _____. "La personnalite cez les Dogon." *Journal de Psychologie Normale et Pathologique* 37, no.9-12 (1940-1941):468-475.

183. _____. "Philosophie et Religion des Noirs." *Presence Afri-caine* 8/9 (1964):307-322.

184. Griaule, M. & Dieterlen, G. "La conception du monde et de la Matiere au Soudan." *Atomes* 47 (1950):50-52.

185. _____. "The Dogon." In Forde (1968):83-110.

186. Gurr, A. & Zirma, P. eds. *Black Aesthetics; Papers From A Colloquium Held At the University of Nairobi, June 1971.* Nairobi: East African Literary Bureau, 1973.

187. Gusimana, Bartholeme. "L'homme et l'unite de la race humanie selon la philosophie pendee basee sur la legende de Gawigan Zanza." *Revue du Clerge Africain* (1971).

188. _____. "L'homme selon la philosophie Pende." *Cahiers des Religions Africaines* (Louvain-Kinshasa) 2 (1968):65-72.

189. _____. "Nzambi selon la philosophie Pende." *Cahiers des Religions Africaines* 4, no.7 (1970):31-40.

190. Gyekye, Kwame. "African Religions and Philosophy." *Second Order* 1 (1975):86-89.

191. _____. "The Akan Concept of a Person." *International Philosophical Quarterly* 18 (1978):277-287. Also in Wright (1984).

192. _____. "Akan Language and the Materialist Thesis: A Short Essay on the Relation Between Philosophy and Language." *Studies in Language* 1, no.2 (1977):237-234.

193. _____. "Philosophical Relevance of Akan Proverbs." *Second Order* 2 (1973):45-53.

*** H ***

194. Hagan, G.P. "Some Aspects of Akan Philosophy." M.A. thesis, Institute of African Studies, University of Ghana, 1964.

195. Hallen, Barry. "Phenomenology and the Exposition of African Traditional Thought." *Second Order* 5, no.2 (1976):45-65.

196. _____. "A Philosopher's Approach To Traditional Culture." *Theoria To Theory* 9, no.4 (1975).

197. _____. "Robin Hortin on Critical Philosophy and Traditional Thought. *Second Order* 6, no.1 (1977).

198. Hart, W.A. "The Philosopher's Interest in African Thought." *Cahiers Philosophiques Africains* 1 (1972):61-73.

199. _____. "The Philosopher's Interest in African Thought; a synopsis." *Second Order* 1 (1972):43-52.

200. Heritier-Izard, Francoise. "Univers feminin et destin individuel chez les Samo." In Notion de Personne (1973):243-254.

201. Herskovits, Melville J. *The Human Factor in Changing Africa.* New York: Knopf, 1965.

202. Holas, Bohumil T. *Les Dieux de l'Afrique Noire.* Paris: Guethner, 1968.

203. _____. "Mythologies des origine en Afrique noire." *Diogene* 48 (1964):102-118.

204. _____. *La Pensee Africaine; Textes Choisis 1949-1969* Paris: Guethner, 1972.

205. _____. "La pensee spirituelle africaine et l'evolution." In Holas (1968):493-495.

206. Horton, Robin. "African Traditional Thought and Western Science." *Africa* 37 (1967) Part I:50-71, Part II:155-187.

207. _____. "Destiny and the Unconscious in West Africa." *Africa* 31, no.2:110-117.

208. _____. "The Kalabari World-view; an Outline and interpretation." *Africa* 32, no.3 (1962):197-220.

209. _____. "Philosophy and African Studies." In Brokensha & Crowder (1967).

210. _____. "Spiritual Beings and Elementary Particles." *Second Order* 1 (1972):21-33.

211. _____. "Traditional Thought and the Emerging African Philosophy Department: A Comment on the Current Debate." *Second Order* 6 (1977):64-80.

212. _____. "Understanding Traditional Religion: a Reply To Professor Beattie." *Second Order* 5, no.1 (1976):3-29.

213. Horton,R. & Finnegan A., eds. *Modes of Thought.* New York: Humanities Press, 1974.

214. Hountondji, P.J. "African Philosopher in 18th Century Germany--A.G. Amo." *Etudes Philosophiques* 1 (1970):25.

215. _____. "African Philosophy; Myth and Reality." *Thought and Practice* 1, no.2 (1974):1-16.

216. _____. "African Wisdom and Modern Philosophy." In African Humanism (1970):183-193.

217. _____. "Comments on Contemporary African Philosophy." *Diogenes* 71 (1970):109-130.

218. _____. "The Myth of Spontaneous Philosophy." *Consequence* 1 (1974):11-37.

219. _____. "Le mythe de la philosophie spontannee." *Cahiers Philosophiques Africains* 1 (1972):107-142.

220. _____. "La philosophie et ses revolutions." *Cahiers Philosophiques Africains* 3/4 (973):27-40.

221. _____. "Philosophy and Development." In Diemer (1981).

222. _____. "Le probleme actuel de la philosophie africaine." In Klibansky, Vol.IV, (1971):613-621.

223. _____. "The Scandal." *Cahiers Philosophiques Africains* 1 (1972):1-4.

224. _____. *Sur la Philosophie Africaine: Critique de l'Ethnophilosophie.* Paris: Francois Maspero, 1980.

225. _____. " What Can Philosophy Do?" *Magyor Filozof Szemle* (1981):181-130.

226. Hunnings, G. "African Traditions and Scientific Creativity." In Oruka (forthcoming).

227. Hunnings, W. "Philosophy At African Universities." In Oruka (forthcoming).

*** / ***

228. Idowu, E. Bolaji. *African Traditional Religion.* Maryknoll, N.Y.: Orbis Books, 1973.

229. _____. "Dieu." In Dickenson (1966):23-67.

230. _____. *Olodumare: God in Yoruba Belief.* New York: Praeger, 1963.

231. _____. "The Study of Religion With Special Reference To African Traditional Religion." *Hibbert Journal* 66 (1968):89-94.

232. Ikenda-Metuh, Ememie. "Religious Concepts in West African Cosmogenies." *Journal of Religion in Africa* 13, no.1 (1982).

233. Irele, Abiola. "Negritude Revisited." *Odu* (Ibadan) 5 (1971):3-26.

234. Irving, T'shitambal'z Malang. "L'impact de la philosophie sur le development de l'Afrique." *Prob. Soc.* (Zarois) 118/119 (1977):161-169.

235. Ita, J.M. "Frobenius, Senghor and the Image of Africa." In Horton & Finnegan (1973):306-336.

*** J ***

236. Jahn, Janheinz. "Kunyu: l'impossibilite de la metamorphose du style." *Presence Africaine* 22 (1958):10-28.

237. _____. *Muntu; an Outline of the New African Culture.* New York: Grove Press, 1961.

238. _____. "Wervorstellungen in Afrikanischen Denken." *Institute Auslansbeziehungen Mitt.* 16, no.4 (1966):249-252.

239. Jahoda, Gustov. "Supernatural Beliefs and Changing Cognitive Structures Among Ghanaian University Students." *Journal of Cross Cultural Psychology* 1, no.2 (1970):115-130.

240. Jeffreys, M.D.W. "A Triad of Gods in Africa." *Anthropos* (Fribourg) 67, no.5/6 (1972):723-735.

241. Jensen, A.E., ed. *Mythe, Mensch Und Umwelt; Beitrage zur Religion, Mythologie und Kulturgeschichte.* Bamberg: Bamberger Verlagshaus Meisenbach, 1950.

242. Jinadu, L. Adele. "Some Aspects of the Political Philosophy of Frantz Fanon." *African Studies Review* 16, no.2 (1973):255-289.

243. July, Robert W. *The Origins of Modern African Thought.* New York: F.A. Praeger, 1968.

244. Junod, H.P. "Essai sur les notions fondamentales de la pensee Africaine-bantoue." *Afrique* (Geneva) 7, no.2 (1968):83-90.

*** K ***

245. Kabamba. A. "Individualitie africaine et determinisme traditionnel et colonial." *Problems Sociaux Congolais* 87 (1969):131-161.

246. Kagame, Alexis. "L'ethno-philosophie des Bantu." In Kilbansky, Vol. IV, (1971):589-612. Also in Smet (1974).

283

247. _____. "Le fondement ultime de la morale Bantu." *Au Coeur de l'Afrique* (Bujumbura, Burundi) 5 (1969):231-236.

248. _____. *La Philosophie Banturwandaise de l'Etre.* Memoire in 8 de l'Academie Royale des Sc. D'outre-mer (Arsom) Nouvelle Serie, Tome xii,1, Brussels, 1956.

249. _____. "La place de Dieu et de l'homme dans la religion des Bantu." *Cahiers des Religions Africaines* (Univ. Louvanium Kinshasa) 2 (1968).

250. _____. "Mes premiers contacts avec la civilization." *Institut Royal Colon. Belge Seances* 24, no.3 (1953):851-862.

251. Kalu, Ogbu U., Ed. *African Cultural Development: Readings in African Humanities.* Enugu: Forth Dimension, 1978.

252. _____. Precarious Vision: the African's Perception of His World." In Kalu (1978):37-44.

253. Kandeke, Timothy K. "Towards Praxis Humanism." *The Journal of Africa* 1, no.4/5 (1968):7-11.

254. Kane, Abdoulaya. "L'espace-temps dans les representations africaines precoloniales: clause de finabilitie du "modele communautaire"." *Annual Letters of the Faculty of Science and Humanities* (Dakar) 8 (1978):49-69.

255. Karioki, James. *The Philosophy and Politics of Julius K. Nyerere.* Ann Arbor, Mich.: University Microfilms, 1970.

256. Karp, I. and C. Bird, eds. *Explorations in African Systems of Thought.* Bloomington, In: Indiana University Press, 1980.

257. Katedza, Jano. "O significado filosofico dos costumes Bantos." *Portugal en Africa* 22, no.127 (1965):51-64.

258. Katshi. *Muntu et sa Pensee (Philosophie Bantu).* Kinshasa, Zaire: Presses Universitaires du Zaire, 1974.

259. Katuambi, Kapinga. "De l'ennui ou du "mal d'exister"." *Afrique et Philosophie* 2 (1978).

260. Keita, Lancinay. "African Philosophical Systems: A Rational Reconstruction." *Philosophical Forum* 9 (1978):169-189.

261. ____. "The African Philosophical Tradition." In Wright (1984).

262. Kews, A. et.al., eds. *Biblical Revelation and African Beliefs.* London: Lutterworth Press, 1969.

263. Kiambi, Abbe B. "L'etre chez les Bantu." *Revue du Clerge Africain* (Mayidi, Congo-Kinshasa) 21 (1966):428-435.

264. Kilson, Marion. "Taxonomy and Form in Ga Ritual." *Journal of Religion in Africa* (Leiden) 3 (1970):45-66.

265. Kimilu, D.N. "The Akamba Concept of God," Paper #7 in Byaruhanga, Vol.1.

266. ____. "Essai sur la foundation epistemologique d'une philosophie hermeneutique en Afrique: la cas de la discursivite." *Presence Afriacines* 109 (1979):11-28.

267. Kinyongo, J. "Philosophie en Afrique: conscience d'etre." *Cahiers Philosophiques Africains* 3/4 (1970):13-26.

268. ____. "Philosophy in Africa; an Existence." *Cahiers Philosophiques Africains* 3/4 (1973):205-211.

269. Kirk-Green, Anthony H. *Mutumin Kirkii; the Concept of the Good Man in Hausa.* Bloomington, Ind.: African Studies Program, Indiana University, 1974.

270. Kitchen, H., ed. *Africa and the United States; Images and Realities.* 1961.

271. Klibansky, Raymond, ed. *Contemporary Philosophy; a Survey,* 4 Vols. Firenze, Italy: La Nouva Italia Editrice, 1971.

272. Knappert, Jan. "Social and Moral Concepts in Swahili Islamic Literature." *Africa* 40 (1970):125-136.

273. Korostovtsev, M.A., ed. *Essays on African Culture.* Translated by L.M. Ozerooa, et.al. Moscow: Nauka Pub. House, Central Dept. of Oriental Literature, 1966.

274. Kruks, S. "African Philosophy: an Introduction To the Main Philosophical Trends in Contemporary Africa." *Africa* 52, no.4 (1982):103.

275. Kudadjie, J.N. "Does Religion Determine Morality in African Society? -- a Viewpoint." *Ghana Bulletin of Theology*
4 (1973):30-49.

276. Kunene, Mazisi. "The Relevance of African Cosmological
Systems To African Literature Today." *African Literature
Today (London)* 11 (1980):190-205.

277. Kuper, L. and Smith, M.G., eds. *Pluralism in Africa.*
Berkeley, Ca.: University of California Press, 1969.

*** L ***

278. Lafontaine, J.S., ed. *The Interpretation of Ritual;
Essays in Honor of I.A. Richards.* London: Tavis-
tock,1971.

279. Lagneau-Kesteloot, Lilyan. *Intellectual Origins of the
African Revolution.* Washington D.C.: Black Orpheus
Press, 1972.

280. Laleye, Issiaha P. "De la Recherche En Philosophie; le Cas
de l'Afrique." *Cahiers Philosophiques Africains* 1
(1972):15-40.

281. ____. *La Conception de la Personne Dans la Pensee
Traditionelle Yoruba.* Publications Universitaires Europe-
ennes, serie 20: Philosophie, 3. Beren: Herbert Lang,
1970.

282. ____. "Le mythe: creation ou recreation in monde?
Contribution a d'elucidation de la problematique de la
philosophie en Afrique." *Presence Africaine* 99/100
(1976):41-59.

283. ____. "La Philosophie? Porquoi En Afrique?" *Cahiers
Philosophiques Africains* 3/4 (1973):77-114.

284. Lambert, R.E. "Problem With Problems in African Philosophy." *Worldview* 18, no.12 (1975):2.

285. LeBeuf, J.P. "Systeme du Monde et Ecriture En Afrique
Noire," *Presence Africaine* 53, no.1 (1965):129-135.

286. Lebzella, V.D. "Energetische Weltbild de Primitiven."
Jahrbuch de Osterreich Leo-ges. (1934):117-130.

287. Leenhardt, Maurice. "La propriete et la personne dans les societes archaiques." *Journal de Psychologie Normale et Pathologique* 45, no.3 (1952):278-292.

288. Legesse, Asmarom. "Human Rights in African Political Culture." In Thompson (1980):109-122.

289. Lepapp, M. "Analyse de Quelques Etudes sur le Temps." *Cahiers O.R.S.T.O.M. Series Scientific/Humanistic* 5, no.3 (1968):77-89.

290. Levi-Strauss, Claude. *La Pensee Sauvage.* Paris: Plon, 1962.

291. _____. *The Savage Mind.* London: Weidengeld & Nicelson, 1966.

292. Lienhardt, Godfrey. *Divinity and Experience: the Religion of the Dinka.* Oxford: Clarendon Press, 1961.

293. _____. "The Situation of Death; an Aspect of Anuak Philosophy." In Douglas (1970).

294. Little, Kenneth. "Values in Primitive Society." *Listner* (London) 14 (1950):335-336.

295. Luchende, C. ed. "An Interview With Mazisi Kunene on African Philosophy." *Ufahanu* (Los Angeles) 7, no.2 (1977):3-27.

296. Lufuluabo, F.M. *La Notion Luba-bantoue de l'etre.* Tournai; Casterman, 1969. Exerpts in Smet (   )

297. Lundback, Torben, ed. *African Humanism-Scandinavian Culture: a Dialogue.* Copenhagen:1970.

298. Luvai, A.I. "Negritude; a Redefinition." *Bursara* (Nairobi) 6, no.2 (1974):79-90.

299. Lystad, Robert A. "Tentative Thoughts on Basic African Values." In Kitchen (1961):177-190.

*** M ***

300. Mabona, Antonio. "The Depths of African Philosophy." *Personnalite Africaine et Catholicisme.* Paris: Presence Africaine, 1963.

301. _____. "Philosophie Africaine." *Presence Africaine* 30 (1960). Also in Smet (1974).

302. _____. "Towards an African Philosophy." *Africa* (Rome) 22, no.1 (1967):3-14.

303. Macbeath, A. "The Study of Tribal Ethics." *Human Problems* 24 (1958):38-50.

304. Mafema, C. "Philosophie et la conception de l'art africain." *Documents Pour l'Action* 2, no.7 (1962):19-23.

305. Maglaugbayou, Shawna. *Garvey, Lumumba and Malcolm; Black National Separatists.* Chicago: Third World Press, 1972.

306. Mainberger, Gonsalv. "Africanisch Philosophie." *Civitas* 16, no. 4 (1960):82-86.

307. Maquet, J.J. "Connaissance des religions traditionelles; commentaires epistemologiques." In Religions Africaines (1965).

308. Martins-Vaz, Jose. *Filosofia Tradicional Dos Cabindas, I-II.* Lisbon: Agencia-General Do Ultramar, 1970.

309. Masolo, D. "Some Aspects and Perspectives of African Philosophy Today." *Africa* (Rome) 31, no.3/4 (1980):414-448.

310. Mativo, K. "Ideology in African Philosophy and Literature." *Ufahamu* (Los Angeles) 8, no.1 (1977):67-94.

311. Maurier, Henri. "Avons-nons Une Philosophie Africaine?" *Revue du Clerge Africaine* 25 (1970):365-377.

312. _____. "Do We Have an African Philosophy?" In Wright (1984).

313. _____. "Methodologie de la Philosophie Africaine." *Culture et Developpement* 6, no.1 (1974):85-107.

314. _____. *The Other Covenant; a Theology of Paganism.* Translated by C. Mcgrath. Glen Rock, N.J.: Newman Press, 1968.

315. _____. *Philosophie de l'Afrique Noire.* Bonn: St. Augustin, 1976.

316. Maurier, H. and Rodegem, F. "Les dies de nos peres -- essai de methodologie critique pour l'etude des conceptions traditionelles de dies en Afrique noire." *Cultures et Developpement* 7, nos. 3-4 (1975):663-680.

317. Mazrui Ali Al'amin. *Violence and Thought; Essays on Social Tensions in Africa.* Harlow: Longmans, 1969.

318. Mbiti, John S. *African Religions and Philosophies.* New York: Doubleday, 1970.

319. _____. "African Theology." *Worldview* 16, no.8 (1973):33.

320. _____. "An African Views American Black Theology." *Worldview* 17, no. 8 (1974):41.

321. _____. "Les Africains et la Notion du Temps." *Afrika* (Bonn) 8, no.2 (1967):33-38; 41.

322. _____. *Concepts of God in Africa.* New York: Praeger, 1970.

323. _____. "Harmony, Happiness and Morality in African Religion." *Drew Gateway* (Madison, N.J.) 43. no.2 (1973):108-115.

324. McKenzie-Rennie, Rhoda. *Nkrumah: Greatest of Modern Philosophers.* N.Y.: Vantage Press, 1977

325. McVeigh, M.J. *God in Africa; Conceptions of God in African Traditional Religion and Christianity.* Cape Cod, Mass.: Claude Stark, 1974.

326. _____. "Investigating African Traditional Religions in Kenya Today." *Thought and Practice (Kenya)* 2, no.1 (1975):39-48.

327. Meebelo, H.S. *Main Currents of Zambian Humanist Thought.* Lusaka: Oxford University Press, 1973.

328. Menkiti, Ifeanyi. "Person and Community in African Traditional Thought." In Wright (1984).

329. _____. "Philosophy in an African Culture." *Harvard Educational Review* 51, no.1 (1981):185-187.

330. Mercier, P. "The Fon of Dohomey." In Forde (1968).

331. Metuge, W.M. "The African Concept of Man."
      Pan-Africanist (Evanston, III.) 4 (1972):36-42.

332. Meyerowitz, Eva L.R. *The Akan of Ghana; Their Ancient
      Beliefs.* New York: Faber, 1958.

333. _____. "Concepts of the Soul Among the Akan of the Gold
      Coast." *Africa* 21, no.1:24-31.

334. Mezy, Sebastian O., ed. *The Philosophy of Pan-African-
      ism; A Collection of Papers on the Theory and Practice of
      the African Unity Movement.* Washington D.C.: George-
      town University Press, 1965.

335. Middleton, John. "The Concept of the Person Among the
      Lugbara of Uganda." In Centre National (1973):491-506.

336. _____. *Myth and Cosmos: readings in Mythology and
      Symbolism.* Austin, Tx.: University of Texas Press,
      1976.

337. Migeod, F.W.H. "The Basis of African Religion." *JRAS*
      19, no.73 (1919).

338. Minkus, Helaine K. "Causal Theory in Akwapim Akan
      Philosophy." In Wright (1984).

339. _____. "The Concept of Spirit in Akwapim Akan Philo-
      sophy." *Africa* 50, no.2 (1980):182-192.

340. _____. "The Philosphy of the Akwapim Akan of southern
      Ghana." Ph.D. Dissertation, Northwestern University,
      1975.

341. _____. "Scepticism in Akwapim Akan Philosophy," Paper
      Presented To the Central States Anthropological Society,
      1977. Mimeo, Department of Sociology, University of
      Wisconsin-Eau Claire.

342. Misenga-Nkongolo. "La philosophie comme lumiere qui luit
      dans les Tenebres." *Cahiers Philosophiques Africains* 3/4
      (1973):115-124.

343. Monfonga, J., at. al. "Reflections ethnopsychiatriques sur
      la'organisation temps espace de la personne." In Centre
      Nationale (1973):507-518.

344. Morton-Williams, Peter. "An Outline of the Cosmology and
      Cult Organization of the Oyo Yoruba." *Africa* (London)
      34, no.3 (1964):243-260.

345. Mosley, Albert. "The Metaphysics of Magic: Practical and Philosophical Implications." *Second Order,* 7, no.1/2 (1978):3-20.

346. M'phahlele, E. *The African Image.* Rev. Ed. London: Faber and Faber, 1974.

347. Mudimbe, V.Y. "Des philosophes africaines en mal de developpement." *Zaire-Afrique* 108 (1976):453-458.

348. Mugambi, J.N.K. "The African Experience of God." *Thought and Practice* (Nairobi) 1, no.1 (1974):49-58.

349. Mujynya, E. "Le mal et le fondement dernier de la morale chez les Bantu interlacustres." *Cahiers des Religions Africaines* 3, no.5 (1969):55-78.

350. _____. "Le mystere de la mort dans le monde Bantou." ,bd Cahiers des Religions Africaines. 3, no.6 (1969): 199-208.

351. Mukendi, Nkonko. "La philosophie africaine face aux exigences de developpement." *Afrique et Philosophie* 2 (1978):90-101.

352. Mulago, Abbe V. "La conception de Dieu dans la tradition bantoue." *Revue du Clerge Africain* 22 (1967):272-299.

353. _____. "Dialectique existentielle des Bantou." *Recherches et Debats, Centre Catholique Intellectuel Francais* 24 (1958):146-171.

354. _____. "Le dieu des Bantu." *Cahiers des Religions Africaines* 3 (1968):23-64.

355. Murungi, John. "Toward an African Conception of Time." *International Philosophical Quarterly* 20 (1980):407-416.

356. Musa, Mubutairu. "A Philosophy of Education For Midwestern Nigeria." B.A. Thesis, Nsukka, 1965.

357. Musey, Matheen. "Quelques remarque sur la philosophie africaine contemporaire." *Geneve-Afrique* 19, no.2 (1981):136-143.

358. Musharhamina, Mulage. "Eubache philosophique." In Smet (1974).

359. Mveng, E. *L'Art d'Afrique Noire: Liturgie Cosmique et Langage Religieux.* Mame,1964.

360. Mwaigoga, C. "An Ethical Evaluation of Commercial Advertisements in a (sic) Selected Kenya Newspspers Namely: *E(ast) A(frican) Standard, Tiafa Leo,* and *Drum Magazine,"* Paper #146 in Byaruhanga, Vol.13.

*** N ***

361. Ndaw, Alassane. "Pense africaine et developpement." *Annual Letters of the Faculty in Science and Humanities* (Dakar) 3 (1973):7-19.

362. _____. "Prolegomenes a une etude de la philosophie africaine *Annual Letters of the Faculty in Science and Humanities* (Dakar) 8 (1978):9-27.

363. _____. "Traditions and Philosophy in Africa."In Diemer (1981)

364. Nduka, Otonti. "African Traditional Systems of Thought And Their Implication For Nigerian Education." *Second Order* 3, no.1 (1974).

365. Nellis, John R. *A Theory of Ideology; the Tanzanian Example.* London: Oxford University Press, 1972.

366. Neuberger, Benyamin. "A Comparative Analysis of Pan-Africanism." In Wright (1984).

367. Ngoma, Binda. "Pour une orientation authentique de la philosophie en Afrique: l'hermeneutique." *Zaire-Afrique* 17, no.113 (1977):143-158.

368. Nicolas, Guy. "Essai sur les structures fondamentales de l'espace dans la cosmologie Hausa." *Journal de la Societe des Africanistes* 36, no.1 (1966):65-108.

369. _____. "Un systeme numeriqe symbolique; le quartre le trois et le sept dans la cosmologie d'une societe Hause." *Cahiers d'Etudes Africaines* 8, no.4 (1968):566-616.

370. Njoh-Moulle, Ebenezer. *Jalons II. Recherche d'une Mentalite Neuve: l'Africanisme Aujourd'hui.* Yaounde: Editions Cle, 1975.

371. _____. Les taches de la philosophie aujord'hui en Afrique."
Abbia 22 (1969):41-56.

✶ 372. Njoroge, R.J. "The Meaning of Life in the African Social
Context." *Dialectic Humanism* 8 (1981):115-124.

373. Nkrumah, Kwame. "African Socialism Revisited." *African
Forum* 1, no.3 (1966):3-9.

374. _____. *L'Afrique Doit S'unir.* Paris: Payot, 1963.

375. _____. *Axioms of Kwame Nkrumah.* London: Nelson,
1967.

376. _____. *Consciencism: Philosophy and Ideology.* New
York: Monthly Review Press, 1970.

377. _____. *Ghana; Autobiographie.* Paris: Presence Africaine, 1960.

378. Nordenstam, Tore. *Sudanese Ethics.* Uppsala: Scandinavian Institute of African Studies, 1968.

379. Norro, M. "Humanisme, base et critere de l'action politique
et economique." *Presence Universitaaire Kinshasa* 11th
Annee, no.30 (1969):7-17.

380. Nothomb, Dominique. *Un Humanisme Africain; Baleurs et
Pierres d'Attente.* Preface by A. Kagame. Tradition et
Renouveau, 2. Brussels: Editions Lumen Vitae, 1965.

381. Ntumba, Tshiamalenge. "Acculturation linguistique et
confusion des languages en Afrique: la cas de "philosophies africaines"." *Afrique et Philosophie* 2 (1978):81-89.

382. _____. "La vision ntu de l'homme: essai de philosophie
linguistique et anthropologique." *Cahiers Religions
Africaines*

383. Nyere, Julius K. *Man and Development.* Dar Es Salaam:
Oxford University Press, 1974.

*** O ***

384. Ocayalakiti, D. "Towards an African Philosophy of Education." *Prospects* 10, no.1 (1980):13-25

385. Ocholla-Ayayo, A.B.C. *Traditional Ideology and Ethics Among the Southern Luo.* Uppsala: Scandinavian Institute of African Studies, 1976.

386. Odepa, H. "The Meaning of Liberty." *Cahiers Philosophique Africains* 1 (1972):144-171.

Odera, H. See Oruka, H. Odera

387. Ogieiriaixi, E. "In Defence of Metaphysics." In Proceedings of the Staff Seminars, University of Lagos (Nigeria), School of African and Asian Studies (1968-1969):115-126.

388. Ofori, Patrick E. *Black African Traditional Religions and Philosophy.* (Bibliographic Survey of Sources from Early Times to 1974) Nendeln, Liechtenstein: KTO Press, 1974.

389. Oguah, Benjamin. "African and Western Philosophy: a Comparative study." In Wright (1984)

390. Ojuka, A. "African Thought and the Concept of Essence." *Thought and Practice* (Nairobi) 1, no.1 (1974):19-26.

391. Okafor, Stephen O. "Bantu Philosophy: Placide Tempels Revisited." *Journal of Religion in Africa* 13, no.2 (1982).

392. Okeke, C. "African Concept of Time." *Cahiers Religions Africaines* 7, no.14 (1973):297-302.

393. Okolo, Chukwudum B. *Racism: A Philosophical Probe.* Jerico, N.Y.: Exposition Press, 1974.

394. Okoye, Mokwugo. *Points of Discord; Studies in Tension and Conflict.* London: F. Muller, 1973.

395. Okpewho, I. "Diop, Anta - The Search for a Philosophy of African Culture." *Cahiers d'Etudes Africaines* 21, no.4 (1981):587-602.

396. Olela, Henry. "The African Foundations of Greek Philosophy." In Wright (1984)

397. _____. *An Introduction To the History of Philosophy; from Ancient Africa To Ancient Greece.* Atlanta, Ga: Select Publishing Co., 1980.

398. Olivier de Sardan, J.P. "Personnalite et Structures Sociales." In Centre National (1973):421-446.

294

399. Oluwole, Sophie B. "On the Existence of Witches." *Second Order* 7, no.1/2 (1978):20-36.

400. Omijeh, M.E.A. "Ehi -- Some Notes on the Paradox of Self-predestination in Bini Religion." *Nigeria Magazine* 110/112 (1974):101-104.

401. Onwuanibe, Richard. "Culture and Technology: A Moral Viewpoint." *Journal of African Studies* 7, no.1 (1980):64-67.

402. _____. "The Human Person and Immortality in Ibo (African) Metaphysics." In Wright (1984).

403. _____. The Philosophy of African Medical Practices." *Quarterly Journal of Africanist Opinion* 9, no.3 (1979):25-28.

404. _____. *Frantz Fanon: A Critique of Revolutionary Humanism.* St. Louis, Mo: Warren Green, Inc., 1981.

405. Onyewuenyi, I.C. "Is There an African Philosophy?" *Journal of African Studies* (Los Angeles) 3, no.4 (1976):513-528.

406. _____. "Philosophical Reappraisal of African Beliefs in Reincarnation." *Internatinal Philosophical Quarterly* 22, no.3 (1982):157-168.

407. _____. "Towards an African Philosophy." In Kalu (1978):242-254.

408. Oruka, H. Odera. "The Fundamental Principles in the Question of African Philosophy." *Second Order* 4 (1975):44-55.

409. _____. "Mythologies in African Philosophy." *East African Journal* 9, N.10 (1972).

410. _____. "Mythologies et philosophie africaine: une confusion." *Consequence* 1 (1974):38-55.

411. _____. "On Philosophy and Humanism." *Philosophy* 5 (1979):7-13.

412. _____. "Four Trends in African Philosophy." In Diemer (1981)

413. Oruka, H. Odera, and Kwasi Wiredu, eds. *Philosophy in Africa; Contemporary Academic Standpoints.* (forthcoming).

414. Osei, Gabriel K. *The African Philosophy of Life.* London: The African Publication Society, 1971.

415. Ottenberg, Simon. *Double Descent in an African Society; the Afikpo Village Group.* Seattle: University of Washington Press, 1970.

416. _____. *Leadership and Authority in an African Society; the Afikpo Village Group.* Seattle: University of Washington Press, 1971.

417. _____. *Masked Rituals of Afikpo; the Context of an African Art.* Seattle: University of Washington Press, 1975.

*** P - Q ***

418. Paden, J. & Soja, E. *The African Experience.* Evanston: Northwestern University Press, 1970.

419. Paques, Vivian. "Unite de la pensee africaine." *Revue de l'Institute Sociologique* (Brussels) 3 (1966):501-518.

420. Parish, S. " A Rationale For an African Social Philosophy." *Thought and Practice* (Nirobi) 1 (1974):1-9.

421. Parrinder, E.G. "Monotheism and Pantheism in Africa." *Journal of Religion in Africa* 3 (1970):81-88.

422. _____. "Philosophy and Cosmology." In Parrinder (1970).

423. _____. *Religion in Africa.* London: Pall Mall, 1970.

424. Patri, Aime. "Ya-t-il une philosophis bantoue?" *Presence Africaine* 2 (1948):203-208.

425. Philip, Edward P. "Can Ancient Egyptian Thought Be Regarded As the Basis of African Philosophy?" *Second Order* 3 (1974).

426. Philip, Horace R.A. *God and the African in Kenya.* London: Marsall, Morgan and Scott, 1935.

427. Postioma, Adalberto De. "Elementi constitutivi per una filosofia africana." *Filosofia e Vita* (Rome) 5, no.3 (1964):68-77.

428. _____. "Esiste una filosofia africana?" *Filosofia e Vita* 10 (1969):64-74. Also in *Itinerarium* 18 (1972):219-231.

429. _____. *Filosofia Africana.* Milan: Editiones Missioni Estere Coppussini, 1967.

430. _____. "Idee religiose e idee filosofiche nell 'africa di oggi." In Filosofia, Religione, Religioni (1966):305-356.

431. _____. "La fondamenti del socialismo africano." *Filosofia e Vita* 6, no.3 (1965):50-59.

432. _____. "Per una filosofia africana." *Filosofia e Vita* 4, no.3 (1963):79-85.

433. _____. "Premesse filosofiche africane e cristianesimo." *Filosofia e Vita* 10, no.2 (1969):63-71.

434. _____. "Presenza africana nella filosofia universale." *Filosofia e Vita* 5, no.1 (1964):68-76. Also in *Contenti* 51, no.2 (1965):30-32.

435. "Pourquoi la philosophie en Afrique?" *Cahiers Philosophiques Africains* 3/4 (Special Issue 1973).

436. Pratt, Vernon. "Science and Traditional African Religion." *Second Order* 1 (1972):7-20.

*** R ***

437. Rachel, Christian. "Philosophische Aspekte Der Ideologischen Konzeption Kwame Nkrumahs." *Deutsche Zeitschrift fur Philosophie* 13 (1965):436-455.

438. Rattray, R. Sutherland. *Ashanti.* New York: Oxford University Press, 1923.

439. _____. *Ashanti Proverbs; the Primitive Ethics of a Savage People.* Oxford: Clarendon Press, 1969. (Reprint of the 1916 Edition)

440. _____. "What the African Believes as Revealed by His Literature." *West African Review* 6, no.88 (1935):13-15.

441. Ravoajanahary, Charles. "La notion de liberte chez les Malgaches." *Annales de l'universite de Madagascar* (Tananarive) 7 (1967):45-61.

442. Ray, Benjamin C. *African Religions: Symbol, Ritual and Community.* Englewood Cliffs, N.J.: Prentice Hall, 1976.

443. Ray, B. " 'Performative Utterances' in African Rituals." *History of Religions* (Chicago) 13, NO.1 (1973):16-35.

444. _____. "The Story of Kintu: Myth, Death and Ontology in Buganda." In Karp and Bird (1980):60-79.

445. *Religions (les) Africaines Comme Source de Valeurs de Civilisation.* Colloque de Contonou, August 16-22,1970. Paris: Presence Africaine, 1972.

446. *Religions (les) Africaines Traditionnelles.* Paris: Editions du Seuil, 1965.

447. Richards, Audrey I. "African Systems of Thought: an Anglo-French Dialogue." *Man* (London) 2, N.2 (1967):286-298.

448. Robbe, Martin. "Tendenzen in Der Geistigen Auseinandersetzung Zwischen Socislismus Und Imperialismus in Jungen Nationalstaaten Asiens Und Afrikas." *Deutsche Zeitschrift fur Philosophie* 17 (1969):1029-1053.

449. _____. "Nationalismus und Sozialismus im Befreiungskampf der Volker Asiens Und Afrikas." *Deutsche Zeitschrift fur Philosophie* 16 (1968):719-729.

450. Roberts, J.D. "African Religions and Philosophies." *Philosophy East and West* 22 (1972):339.

451. _____. "Black Theological Ethics; a Bibliographic Essay." *Journal of Religious Ethics* 3, no.1 (1975):69-109.

452. Rodegem, F.M. "Rundi's Ideas on Ultimate Reality and Meaning." *Ultimate Reality and Meaning* 4 (1981):260-271.

453. Roumeguere-Eberhardt, Jacqueline. *Pensee et Societe Africaines; Essais sur une Dialectique de Complementarite Antagoniste chez les Bantoues du Sud-Est.* Paris-the Hague: Mouton, 1963.

454. Rousseau, Madeleine. "La Philosophie des Negres." *Misee Vivant* (Paris) 12, no.36/37 (1948):9-12.

455. Ruch, E.A. "African Attitudes to Knowledge." *Mohlomi* 11 (1976):15-31.

456. _____. "Is There an African Philosophy?" *Second Order* 3, NO.2 (1974):3-21.

457. _____. "Philosophy of African History." *African Studies* 32 (1973):113.

458. Ruch, E.A. and Anianwu, K.C. *African Philosophy: an Introduction To the Main Philosophical Trends in Contemporary Africa.* Rome: Catholic Book Agency, 1981.

459. Ruytinx, Jaques. *La Morale Bantoue et le Probleme de l'Education Moral au Congo.* 2nd ed. Brussels: Editions de l'Institut de Sociologique de l'Universite Libre de Bruxelles, 1969.

*** S ***

460. Sambuli, R. "The Traditional Chagga Concept of Afterlife," Paper #201 in Byaruhanga, Vol.19.

461. Sanda, A.O. "The Scientific Or Magical Ways of Knowing: Implications For the Study of African Traditional Healers." *Second Order* 7, no.1/2 (1978):70-84.

462. Sarpong, P.K. "Aspects of Akan Ethics." *Ghaha Bulletin of Theology* 4, no.3:40-44.

463. _____. "The Search For Meaning; the Religious Impact of Technology in Africa." *Ecumenical Review* (Geneva) 24, no.3 (1972):300-309.

464. Sawyerr, Harry E. "Ancestor Or Creator God?" *Presence Africaine* 74 (1970):111-127.

465. _____. *God--Ancestor Or Creator? Aspects of Traditional Belief in Ghana, Nigeria, and Sierra-Leone.* London: Longman, 1970.

466. Sawyerr, Harry E. & Todd, S.K. "The Significance of the Numbers Three and Four Among the Mende of Sierra-Leone." *Sierra-Leone Studies* (Freetown) 26 (1979):29-36.

467. Schall, J.V. "Defining What Is African - Problems in African Political Philosophy." *Worldview* 18, no.9 (1975): 6-8.

468. _____. "Problem With Problems in African Political philosophy - a Reply." *Worldview* 18, no.12 (1975):2.

469. Senghor, Leopold S. "L'esthetique negro-africaine." *Diogene* 16 (1956).

470. _____. *Liberte 2: Notion et Voie Africaine du Socialisme.* Paris: Editions du Seuil, 1971.

471. _____. "The Negritude; a Twentieth Century Humanism." *Adam* (London) 376/378 (1973):5-11.

472. _____. "Porquoi Une Ideologie Negre-Africaine?" *Presence Africaine* 82 (1972):11-38.

473. _____. "What Is Negritude?" *Negro Digest* 7 (1962):3-6.

474. Shelton, Austin J. "Causality in African Thought; Igbo and others." *Practical Anthropology* (Terrytown, N.Y.) 15, no.4 (1968):157-169.

475. Shorter, A. "African Religions and Philosophy." *African Affairs* 69, no.227 (1970):391.

476. _____. "Animal Marauders and Family Morality in Arica." *Africa* 42 (1972):1.

477. Sigmund, P.E., ed. *The Ideologies of the Developing Nations.* Revised Edition. New York: Praeger Publishing Co., 1967.

478. Singleton, Michael. "A Comment on F.M. Rodegem's Essay on Rundi Weltanschauung." *Ultimate Reality and Meaning* 4 (1981):310-311.

479. Smet. A. *Lecture et Explication Philosophiques de Textes Africains.* Lumbumbashi, Zaire: Universite Nationale du Zaire, Faculte des Lettres, Departement de Philosophie, 1972-1973.

480. _____. *Philosophie Africaine. Textes Choisis.* Kinshasa: Presses Universitaires du Zaire, 1974.

481. Smith, E.W. et. al., eds. *African Ideas of God.* 2nd Ed. London: Edinburgh House Press, 1966.

482. Smith, Pierre. "Principes de la personne et categories sociales." In Centre National (1973):467-490.

483.   Sodipo, J.O. "The Concept of Chance in Yoruba Tradi-
       tional thought." In Oruka (forthcoming).

484.   _____. "Notes on the Concept of Cause and Change in
       Yoruba Traditional Thought." *Second Order* 2 no.2
       (1973):12-20.

485.   _____. "Philosophy in Africa Today." *Thought and Prac-
       tice* 2, no.2 (1975):115-124.

486.   Sofola, J.O. *African Culture and the African Personality:
       What Makes an African Person African?* Ibaden, Nigeria:
       African Resources Publishing Co., 1973.

487.   Songolo, Aliko. " *Muntu* Reconsidered: from Tempels and
       Kagame to Janheinz Jahn." *Ufahamu* (Los Angales) 10
       no.3 (1981):92-100.

488.   Spitzer, L. "Interpreting African Intellectual History; a
       Critical Review of the Past Decade, 1960-1970." *African
       Studies Review* (E. Lansing, Mich.) 15, no.1
       (1972):113-118.

489.   Stefaniszyn, Bronislaw. "The Ambo and their Ideas on
       Ultimate Reality and Meaning." *Ultimate Reality and Mean-
       ing* 4 (1981):272-278.

       Strauss, Claude Levi. See Levi-Strauss, C.

       Sutherland-Rattray, R. See Rattray, R.

490.   Swiderski, S. "Remarques sur la philosophie religieus des
       sectes syncretiques au Gabon." *Canadian Journal of Afri-
       can Studies.* 8, no.1 (1974):43-53.

491.   Symoussa, Oumar. "Considerations sur les principes const-
       itutifs de la personnalite chez les negro- africains."
       Bulletin de l'Institut Fondamental d'Afrique Noire Series B,
       33, no.1 (1971):14-62.

                        *** T ***

492.   Tarratt, J. "Time in Traditional African Thought." *Jour-
       nal of Religion* (London) 7, no.2 (1977):117-126.

493.   Tasie, Gom. "African Religions and Philosophy." *Journal
       of Modern African Studies* 12, no.2 (1974):326.

494.　＿＿. "Concepts of God in Africa." *Journal of Modern African Studies* 12, no.2 (1974):326.

495.　Taylor, John V. *The Primal Vision.* Philadelphia: Fortress Press, 1963.

496.　Tempels, Placid. *Bantu Philosophy.* Paris: Presence Africaine, 1959.

497.　＿＿. *Le Concept Fondamental de l'Ontologie Bantu.* Translated by A.J. Smet. Kinshasa: University of Zaire Press, 1977.

498.　Terris, M. "An Ancient Basis For African Philosophy or an Old Myth in New Dress? a Reply To Edward P. Philip." *Second Order* 5, no.2 (1976):27-36.

499.　Theuws, Theodore. "Philosophie bantoue et philosophie occidentale." *Civilisations* 1, no.3 (1951):54-63.

500.　Thomas, L.L. *Black Eschatology: Death and Existence in Traditional African Thought.* Rockville, Md.: Black Orpheus Press, 1973.

501.　Thomas, L.V. "Animisme, religion caduque," *Bull. Ifan.* Series B, 1-2 (1965).

502.　＿＿. "Breve esquisse sur la pensee cosmologique du Diola." In Fortes & Dieterlen (1965):366-382.

503.　＿＿. "Les constances de la culture cegre: reflexions a propos du livre de Janheinz Jahn -- *Muntu.*" *Bull. Ifan* B.T. 26, no.1/2 (1964):258-271.

504.　＿＿. "La mort et la sagesse africaine (esquisse d'une anthropologie philosophique)." *Psychopathologie Africaine* 111, no.1 (1967):13-80.

505.　＿＿. "La pensee de l'homme noir d'Afrique orientale et Australe." *Notes Africaines* 118 (1962):42-48.

506.　＿＿. "Philosophie de la religion negro-africaine tradition-nelle." *Afrique Documents* (Dakar) 79 (1965):51-73.

507.　＿＿. "Le pluralisme coherent de la notion de personne en Afrique noire traditionnelle." In Centre National (1973):387-420.

508.   _____. "Remarques sur quelques attitudes negro-Africaines devant la mort." *Rev. Fse. de Sociologie* 4 (1963):395-410.

509.   _____. "Un systeme philosophique senegalais; la cosmologie des Diola." *Presence Africaine* 32/33 (1960):64-76.

510.   Thomas, Northcote W. "The Week in West Africa." *Journal of the Royal Anthropological Institute of Great Britain and Ireland* 54 (1924).

511.   Thompson, Kenneth W., ed. *The Moral Imperatives in Human Rights.* Washington D.C.: University Press of America, 1980.

512.   Tonkin, E. "Lega Culture - Art, Initiation and Moral Philosophy among a Central African People." *Canadian Journal of African Studies* 9, no.2 (1975): 366-368.

513.   Towa, Marcien. "Consciencisme." *Presence Africaine* 85 (1973):148-177.

514.   _____. *Essai sur la Problematique Philosophique dans l'Afrique Actuelle.* Point de Vue no.8. 2nd Edition. Yaounde: Editions Cle, 1979.

515.   _____. *L'Idee d'une Philosophie Negro-Africane.* Point de Vue no. 18. Yaounde: Editions Cle, 1979.

516.   _____. *Philosophy in Contemporary Africa.* Rockville, Md.: Black Orpheus Press, 1972.

517.   Towet, Taita. "Le role d'un philosophe africain." *Presence Africaine* 27/28 (1959):108-128.

518.   Tshibangu, Thareisse. "Problematique d'une pensee religieuse africaine." *Cahiers des Religions Africaines* (Louvain, Kinshasha) 2 (1968):11-21.

519.   Tshibangu-wa-mulumba. "Metaphysique-cette philosophie qui nous vient d'ailleurs." *Cahiers Philosophiques Africaines* 3/4 (1973):41-50.

520.   Turnbull, Colin. *Forest People.* New York: Doubleday, 1962.

521.   _____. *The Lonely African.* New York: Doubleday, 1963.

522. Turner, H.W. "A Topology For African Religious Movements." *Journal of Religion in Africa* (Leiden) 1, no.1 (1967):1-34.

523. Tutu, D. "The Ancester Cult and Its Influence on Ethical Issues." *Ministry* (Marija) 9, no.3 (1969):99-104.

524. Twesigyi, Emmanuel. "Traditional Religion: Death Among the Bakiga of Uganda." Paper #19 in Byaruhanga, Vol.2.

*** U - V ***

525. Udechukwu, Obiora. "Concept Into Form: Religion and Aesthetics in African Art." In Kalu (1978):86-94.

526. Udosen, William. "The Impact of Change on the Aesthetic Values of the Ibibio." *Second Order* 4, no.1 (1975):66-73.

527. Van Caenegnem, R. *La Notion de Dieu chez les Baluba du Kasai.* Brussels, 1956.

528. Vantoan, Tran. "A Propos de la question des languages dans la philosophie africaine." *Cahiers Philosophiques Africaines* 1 (1972):172-180.

529. Verger, Pierre. "La notion de personne et lignee familiale chez les Yoruba." In Centre National (1973):33-43.

530. Veto, Miklos. "Unite et dualite de la conception du mal chez les bantou orientaux." *Cahiers d'Etudes Africaines* 8 (1962).

531. Vibert, Paul. *La Philosophie de la Colonization; les Questions Brulantes, Exemples d'Wier et d'AuJourd'hui.* Paris: E. Cornely, 1906.

532. Vilasco, G. "La philosophie negro-africaine face aux ideologies." *Annals of the University of Abidjan,* Series D, 12 (1979):127-145.

*** W - Z ***

533. Wallace, Anthony F.C., ed. *Fifth International Congress of Anthropology and and Ethnological Sciences, Selected Papers.* Philadelphia: University of Pennsylvania Press, 1960.

534. Wamba-dia-Wamba, E. "La philosophie en Afrique ou les defis de l'africain philosophie." *Canadian Journal of African Studies* 13, no.1/2 (1979):223-244.

535. Wanger, W. "The Zulu Notion of God According To the Traditional Zulu God-names." *Anthropos* 18/19 (1923-1924):656-687.

536. Warren, Dennis M. "Disease, Medicine and Religion Among the Techiman-Bono of Ghana: a Study in Culture Change." Ph.D. Dissertation University of Indiana, 1974.

537. Weiskel, T.C. "Nature, Culture and Ecology in Traditional African Thought Systems." *Cultures* 1, no.2 (1973):123-144.

538. Wellington, John H. *South West Africa and its Human Issues.* Oxford: Clarendon Press, 1967.

539. Welton, Michael R. "Themes in African Traditional Belief and Ritual." *Practical Anthropology* (Terrytown, N.Y.) 18, no.1 (1971):1-18.

540. Willoughby, W.C. "Some Conclusions Concerning the Bantu Conception of the Soul." *Africa* 1, no.3 (1928):338-347.

541. Wilson, G. "An African Morality." *Africa* 9, no.1 (1936):75-99.

      Wiredu, J.E. See Wiredu, Kwasi

542. Wiredu, Kwasi "How Not To Compare African With Western Thought." In Wright (1984).

543. _____. "On an African Orientation in Philosophy." *Second Order* 1, no.2 (1972):3-13.

544. _____, ed. *The Place and Role of the Humanities in Africa Today.* Proceedings of the International Council For Philosophy and Humanistic Studies, Legon, Ghana, April 22-24, 1974.

545. _____. *Philosophy and an African Culture.* N.Y.: Cambridge University Press, 1980.

546. _____. "Points de vue." *Consequence* 1 (1974):56-83.

547. _____. "What Can Philosophy Do For Africa?" In Wiredu (forthcoming).

548. Wright, Richard A., ed. *African Philosophy: an Introduction* 3rd Edition. Washington, D.C.:   University Press of America, 1984.

549. Wright, Richard A. "Investigating African Philosophy." In Wright (1984).

550. Yai, Olabiyi. "Theory and Practice in African Philosophy: the Poverty of Speculative Philosophy." *Second Order* 6, no.2 (1977):3-21.

551. Zahan, Dominique. *Reincarnation et Vie Mystique en Afrique Noire.* Paris: P.U.F., 1965.

552. ____. *Religion, Spiritualite et Pensee Africaine.* Paris: Payot, 1970.

553. Zuure, B. *Croyances et Pratiques des Barundi.* Brussels, 1926.

554. ____. "Imana, le Dieu des Barundi." *Anthropos* 21 (1926):733-776.

BIBLIOGRAPHY INDEX

This is a subject index for all items in the bibliography, with subjects determined by the major emphases in the item being considered. Names of individuals and titles of works are included here only if they are the subject of consideration in the indexed work. References to African groups or nations are by name as subject, e.g., 'Ashanti', and by specific subject, e.g., 'Art, Ashanti'. To read all items on one group, such as the Ashanti, only the heading 'Ashanti' need be consulted; to read only on the Ashanti views of causality, for instance, reference is to 'Causality', where 'Ashanti' will be found as a sub-heading. Philosophy is treated as a subject, with all references not otherwise indicated being understood as covering African philosophy. Specific topics within the discipline of philosophy, such as Ethics or Epistemology, will be found in separate subject headings. For other bibliographies see 'Bibliography' as a subject.